CONSULTING ESSENTIALS

CONSULTING ESSENTIALS

THE ART AND SCIENCE OF PEOPLE, FACTS, AND FRAMEWORKS

JEFF KAVANAUGH

LIONCREST
PUBLISHING

CONSULTING ESSENTIALS

The Art and Science of People, Facts, and Frameworks

ISBN 978-1-5445-1025-5 *Paperback*
        978-1-5445-1026-2 *Ebook*

For my parents, Irma and Lee Kavanaugh

Mom, who inspired a lifelong love of learning, and
Dad, who instilled an ethic of work and persistence.
I love you both and appreciate all you have done.

CONTENTS

Support your local teacher.

Ten percent of all the author royalties from this book will be donated to educational not-for-profits, including DonorsChoose.org.

FOREWORD

BY TONY GERTH

I've known Jeff for well over ten years. I was one of the initial partners at Infosys Consulting in 2004 and Jeff was one of our early senior hires. It was clear when I met Jeff for the first time that he had a lot of energy, experience, and enthusiasm for the consulting profession. It was no surprise to me—or others—when he became a partner and a leader in the firm. In addition to being a great consultant, Jeff is a great developer of talent and this book is a clear result of that passion for developing people.

Jeff and I have a lot in common. I'm a native Hoosier as well. I was raised in a small, rural town, went to college in Indiana, and went to work in a manufacturing company after my undergraduate studies. After a time, the work seemed dull and I stepped into the world of management consulting by joining Deloitte, a world-class firm. I rapidly made partner there and it was a formative time in my professional career, as was my time with Infosys Consulting. Overall, I spent fifteen years as a consultant before transitioning to an academic career with the Kelley School of Business and earning a doctoral degree in management.

Why is this relevant to Jeff's book? First, like Jeff, my skills in problem solving and communication were forged in the crucible of management consulting.

I know firsthand how valuable and impactful these skills are for both consultants and businesspeople in general. These skills are not generally taught in business programs—UT-Dallas and the Kelley School being notable exceptions—but rather during the new hire training of top consulting firms. Marvin Bower, a great early leader of McKinsey & Co., demonstrated that firms don't need a retired CEO to advise executives, but that young, intelligent people are effective if well-trained. Such knowledge is contained in this book.

As Jeff would say, "so what?" The "so what" in all of this is that these skills are critical to being a successful business professional. The world is forever getting more complex and digital technology continues to accelerate that complexity. In that context, the first chapter on learnability sets the stage for the rest of the book. It's a cliché to state we should be lifelong learners, but it's also a reality. In an age of accelerating change, we need to continually learn new skills. The later chapter on Agile also addresses this dynamic.

Critical thinking is the basis of the problem solving that we do every day. We are constantly inundated with information that we are forced to triage, prioritize, and incorporate into our decision-making, both professional and personal. It is said that a person today processes more information in a day than a person in the sixteenth century did in a lifetime. But how do we know we're solving the right problems? In a recent article in the *MIT Sloan Management Review*, the authors make the case that, "there are few management skills more powerful than the discipline of articulating the problem you seek to solve before jumping into action."[1] I've seen project teams waste a lot of time in analyzing the wrong problem!

The focus on "soft skills" is important. I can teach an eighteen-year-old without any business education to model with a spreadsheet or statistical software. What is missing is context, critical thinking, and effective communication. However, most business education at the undergraduate and graduate level focuses on technical skills, be they programming, spreadsheet modeling, financial analysis, market research, or operations improvement. That is fine to a point,

---

[1] Astor, T., Kieffer, D., and Repenning, N., "The Most Underrated Skill in Management," *MIT Sloan Management Review*, 58(3), 2017: 39.

since we all start careers as functional contributors. But to be a leader, it's the soft skills that matter. In an environment where the world is becoming more dependent on technology in various forms, the soft skills tend to be pushed into the background. That's unfortunate and this book steps up to the challenge of bringing them more into balance.

This book provides a broad tool kit for the consultant or businessperson who wants to keep pace in a rapidly changing environment, become a more rigorous problem solver and develop a more effective communication. In other words, it's for anyone who wants to be a more well-rounded and successful professional.

TONY GERTH, D.B.A.

CLINICAL ASSOCIATE PROFESSOR
OF INFORMATION SYSTEMS

KELLY SCHOOL OF BUSINESS, INDIANA UNIVERSITY

BLOOMINGTON, INDIANA, DECEMBER 2017

INTRODUCTION

"You enter the forest at the darkest point, where there is no path. Where there is a way or path, it is someone else's path. If you follow someone else's way, you are not going to realize your potential."

—JOSEPH CAMPBELL, *THE HERO'S JOURNEY*

This book isn't a standard guide to consulting. It can't be, because I'm not a standard consultant. I grew up on a farm in Indiana, like my dad before me. He was the second of ten children, told by his parents that he wasn't smart enough to go to college. He refused to buy that, worked a factory job to save enough for school, and became a teacher and coach, all while staying close to his farming roots. My mother came from humble beginnings herself; she was the daughter of a housekeeper, who went to college only through the GI Bill, after her father was killed in World War II. They were traditional people in non-traditional circumstances, who seemed to do things their own way, even if it was the hard way. Looking back, I believe some of those qualities made their way to me.

I may have grown up in a sports-crazed family, but work always came first. Between tending a three-acre family garden, keeping the overall farm in shape, and being lent out to work on other farms, I seldom knew "free time" during daylight hours. At times, it seemed to my siblings and me that my dad wanted us to be busy as much as he wanted us to be productive. It was a case of, "Idle mind, Devil's workshop" perhaps, but it certainly reduced the motivation to work smart, knowing that some other task would simply take the place of any I completed. I wanted to break that mold. I worked hard, but I also wanted to make things easier, and to enjoy that rare elixir of time to myself. My father couldn't understand it at the time, but I knew that I wanted to help companies become more productive, even if I had no idea how.

I never had the standard consulting background. I graduated from our farming high school—with a senior class of forty-seven students—and then from a small nearby engineering college called Rose-Hulman Institute of Technology. Rose-Hulman was a top-ranked engineering college, with 100 percent placement for engineers, but did not have a business school. Even after an engineering degree and well into my first corporate job, the world of consulting was alien to me.

Until I was two years out of college, taking my first master's class, I didn't even realize that business consulting firms existed. It seemed to me that they were part of another world, far away from my day-to-day life and skills. I soon became very curious, and started to piece together an understanding of what consulting was, and how to get closer to it.

I figured things out as I went. This meant working a lot of nights and weekends, doing my own research, then applying what I was learning to my projects along the way. It was stressful, because in the early days I did not have a foundation of consulting tools and training to draw from. As a result, I can identify with the 99 percent of the population who didn't go to the elite business schools, or benefit from consulting firm training and client engagements straight after graduation.

After getting my engineering degree, I went to work at Texas Instruments in Dallas. Initially, I was in a technical role, working closely with senior engineers, many of whom held multiple patents. It was an exciting time, working on a space-based missile defense system, with lots of innovation. After a couple years enjoying rocket science, I rotated to a more mature and mundane radar system program, where I was focused on managing assembly line operations. Although it was a promotion, I quickly became bored. So, I started arriving at work early every morning and experimenting with process improvements on the assembly line. I was on the factory floor at 6:00 a.m., getting my innovation fix before going back to my day job to manage operations. The latter was important work, but it did not have the same kind of analysis-driven, project-based thinking that characterized my earlier assignment and kept me excited.

That was when I realized that the operational aspect of business wasn't for me, and that I was primarily interested in making businesses better. In a way, it was my introduction to consulting. This led me to graduate school, where I complemented my engineering education with useful skills such as accounting, finance, and marketing. I also began to meet people with consulting backgrounds. I was intrigued.

In a subsequent role, I was lucky enough to meet a former consulting partner from Peat Marwick, now known as KPMG. It was an eye-opening experience. He described the responsibilities of a consulting partner, and I thought, "That's for me." That was when I started to understand the workings of a modern consulting firm. It was an experience that sparked my hunger to learn more. From that point, whenever I met anyone with a consulting background, I got as much information from them as possible. I asked lots of questions. What was their expertise? What were their methodologies? How did they sell and execute projects?

Instead of taking a traditional route into consulting, with formal training at an established strategy firm, I constructed my understanding of the consulting world piece by piece. I constantly questioned the information I was given and built on my knowledge base. In some cases, it was highly productive and the knowledge was useful. Sometimes—for example, when a methodology fell apart under rigorous testing—I realized that things I had been told simply weren't right. This journey helped me build a tool kit of what to do and what to avoid. In many ways, the processes I used were similar to Agile, years before Agile became mainstream.

Recession hit, and the defense industry became stagnant. I could probably have stayed on the same career path at Texas Instruments for the next thirty years, but without the opportunity to develop and explore in the way I wished. Despite my unconventional background, accounting and consulting firm Grant Thornton took a chance on me. In that role, I first learned a lot of the skills that are detailed in this book. Over the years, I worked with consultants or alumni of consulting giants such as McKinsey, Boston Consulting Group, and Bain. Each new project was another data point, gradually developing into my own integrated framework of tools and techniques.

There's a long-standing cynical joke that consulting is taking somebody's watch and telling them what time it is. Some people may think that's the essence of consulting: interview people, create reports, and document what's already known. It's not. Good business consulting is about addressing important but ambiguous issues, and deconstructing them in a way that makes it possible to find root causes and address them effectively. Good consultants help their clients make multimillion, sometimes even billion-dollar decisions. A good consultant is a trusted advisor, who helps clients solve problems and makes a real impact on their business. In the trusted advisor role, consultants have an obligation to disagree with clients when the facts and our beliefs warrant it.

There may be times when a consultant affirms a client's initial ideas. When making such high-stakes decisions, even confirming an initial approach is a valuable contribution. Backing up intuitions or ideas with solid, fact-based reasoning can allow clients to take major decisions with greater confidence, along with helping them create a feasible plan to implement that decision.

To the casual observer, it may not always be apparent what consultants bring to a situation. It may appear that we trade in "just words." Yet, consultants undertake tasks such as canvassing diverse opinions and taking the political temperature of an organization. They delve into the challenges of implementing a given course of action, developing understanding and buy-in. At the highest levels, much of consulting is dedicated to "soft" skills. It would be a mistake to underestimate the value of those skills. Initiatives tend to be more successful when hard analysis is paired with insightful understanding of the people involved and methods of implementing change.

Some may balk at the idea of consultants, especially junior ones, coming into businesses and working with people who may have fifteen years of experience in their fields. On the other hand, how many of those years have been spent doing similar things, in similar ways? A year of consulting experience can be so content laden and outcome focused that it may be worth two or more years of experience in industry. As a manufacturing engineer early in my career, I mostly solved known—or at least defined—problems, grinding through formulas and answering narrowly defined questions. What sets consulting apart, and makes it such an exciting field, is that consultants constantly define and redefine the scope of challenges, and how to overcome them. Even in contexts where a technical solution appears to be straightforward, non-obvious dependencies and the challenges of working with multiple stakeholders always add complexity.

In 2013, the *Economist* surveyed senior executives to discover whether they found consulting valuable.[2] Almost uniformly, they confirmed that they did. The people at the top of global organizations are subject to enormous pressure to justify their investments. If they were unable to justify the outlay on consultancy, they wouldn't approve it. As anyone who works in business knows, it can be hard enough to secure

2   "To the Brainy, the Spoils," *The Economist*, May 11, 2013.

financing for essential improvements. If consulting services didn't provide value, it would be nearly impossible to find the money for them.

At the other extreme, some people believe that consulting is mysterious. Consultants may seem to have almost an uncanny ability to quickly understand and remedy the problems in an organization. When done well, that can certainly appear to be the case. This book is about demystifying the skills that go into good consulting, so that it seems less like magic and more like a learnable, repeatable collection of capabilities.

The qualities that make a good consultant are talents we can all cultivate. Perhaps the most important is intellectual curiosity and the desire to learn, closely followed by the persistence to continually test and refine hypotheses and methods. In a field evolving as rapidly as consulting, it's essential to be humble enough to incorporate feedback from colleagues, clients, or simply from trying things that don't work.

Beyond these basics, there are other abilities, such as the capacity to synthesize information from disparate sources into a distinct perspective and the resilience to accept failures without becoming discouraged. It's worth mentioning, too, that just as the tools described in this book are applicable across numerous industries, so are the character traits that lead to success. We'll use the words "consulting" and "consultant" to describe the environment and the target audience for this book, but most of the content and insights contained here apply to any professional. In every industry, a problem-solving, project-based approach is increasingly common, making these skills more relevant and valued than ever.

Routine jobs are increasingly difficult to find, and even where they exist, they may not hold your interest for long. Beyond the ever-growing prospect of automation, companies require creativity and originality, directed toward a specific objective. Professionals are more accountable than we used to be. Consulting makes this connection more clearly and directly than most industries, because clients hire consultants to achieve a specific result, but the trend toward demanding results is universal.

Everyone has deadlines. Everyone works under pressure. Everyone is expected to learn. The difference is that, in consulting organizations, the clock tends to tick faster and louder. The deadlines are nearer. The learning is accelerated. In addition, the criteria by which consultants are judged are especially rigorous, meaning that consultants are expected to create more output, deliver more value, and communicate more effectively.

In many ways, I think my background gives me an advantage over people who have taken a classic management consulting career path. It makes me a better teacher. The University of Texas at Dallas asked me to develop a course for their graduate business school to teach these skills to their students, who were technically strong but had lacked sufficient critical and creative thinking foundations—in other words, consulting skills. I decided to teach the course as well as create it. Like me, these students haven't had a textbook consulting skills' education. They want to do well in their professions, and they're excited to learn.

There's no value in me telling them to go back and live their lives differently, or learn other skills in the past. They are where they are. Whatever path they've taken until now, it's my job to support them to take their next steps. Perhaps you're like them. Perhaps you want to learn the skills that make consultants successful, but you don't have an Ivy League MBA. The good news is that anyone can learn. Even if you *do* have an MBA from an elite school or a strategy firm pedigree, chances are there is still something in this book for you.

The skills I seek to teach my students are applicable in many walks of life: for example, critical thinking, with its horizontal and vertical logic, and deductive and inductive reasoning. These are foundations for all professions. I also attempt to instill qualities such as empathy, which is an essential skill for people who need to keep their customer or user in mind, even while working in high-pressure situations.

I'm not trying to turn every one of my students into a management consultant. I'm interested in teaching them skills that they can apply to many difficult scenarios, yet are often treated as overly complex and out of reach. There's no need for them to feel that way. These skills can be learned by almost anyone, and they have broad applicability.

I learned through examples and exposure to methodologies, then practicing and iterating repeatedly and evaluating feedback from the outcomes of my own experience. Much of this was before the internet was mature, when access to information was slower. Yet, that also had some benefits. It required me to think through everything I did, contextualizing knowledge and applying it, instead of assuming an answer was always available at the click of a keystroke.

It's my hope that with this book I can accelerate that process for you. If you're a consultant, you should find that it is a valuable handbook. If you're in industry, you can learn and apply these skills to your job as well. They're applicable to far broader contexts than simply consulting. Perhaps you're a student, eager to take the first step on the career ladder. In that case, hopefully you'll find that the perspective offered here provides you with a condensed version of my journey, in a way you can absorb and integrate.

There are a lot of bright consultants in the world. The unique perspective I can offer is that I haven't simply learned consulting. I've proactively pieced together a tool kit over the course of decades, questioning every step. I want to do more than present you with the skills. I want to teach you how to use them.

Management consultants receive a lot of instructional content during their MBA programs and throughout their consulting careers. They may have little cause to question information from their formal training and their firm methodologies. Without that established base from which to work, I was forced to test each new tool and technique I learned. Everything in this book has been field-tested on actual projects. At times, I've worked on double-blind assignments versus industry-leading PhD experts, with clients comparing my output with theirs, to determine the most effective solution.

This is not to criticize those who have taken a different path. Far from it. If you already have a solid consulting skills foundation and relevant experience, you may have compressed your learning into a much shorter timeframe than my own. However, for those without the benefits of a top-level consulting education and experience with a major firm, I think the approach outlined in these pages can be more relevant and more accessible. Throughout this book, you'll find stories from my own experience as a consultant, coupled with frameworks and tools that you can apply immediately.

You'll also find some philosophical elements. You may be a

young person with few commitments outside of work. You may have a family and feel constrained by your obligations. Whatever your situation, be assured that consulting—or any job—will consume all the time and energy you're willing to give it. In that sense, work is like a black hole. There's always more to do. Every piece of you that you allow to be pulled into your work will be consumed. The question is, where will you set the boundaries?

Whether you call that work/life balance, quality time, or retaining your sanity, you'll need to make some decisions about how you organize your time and how you protect the aspects of your life that matter to you outside of work. It's always possible to go faster and farther professionally, but at what cost? Sometimes it's important to tap the brakes and focus on other things, even if only for a brief period.

I don't claim to have this totally figured out. I'm only human, and I'm frequently readjusting my own parameters. What I can say is that there is no silver bullet, no single best answer. There are self-help books on every subject imaginable. One may promise to teach you how to be a wonderful parent. Another may offer you the secrets to financial success. A third may provide you with invaluable tips for your working life, while a fourth will lead you down a path of yoga and meditation.

Those are four competing priorities, and you may find that

it's deeply challenging to integrate all those aspects of your humanity. You're a multi-dimensional person. While this book focuses primarily on the skills that will help you to excel in a work context, it's worth remembering that there are always choices to make. We live in the real world. There may be times when the most valuable next step for you is to temporarily step away from the world of employment, or simply to remember what it's like to have a life outside of work. The material in this book is about working smarter, not always harder, and that applies to the big picture of your life as much as it does to your consulting abilities.

This book is divided into three sections. The first covers the concept of *learnability*. Before you can absorb the skills and tools detailed in the following parts of the book, you'll need to understand *how* to learn. This is crucial, which is why it is a distinct section. We'll discuss the process of learning, what it takes to learn, and how to learn more quickly.

The second focuses on *foundational competencies*, which are the most important aspects of professional services, and are important for any industry. These skills are also enduring. They were valuable years ago and they will continue to be valuable decades from now. This section includes chapters on critical and creative thinking, oral communication, written communication, frameworks and estimation, productivity, and leadership.

Everyone, at every level, should possess foundational competencies. They enable people to think, interact, and be effective in the workplace. A study conducted by *USA Today* revealed that many people complete their formal education unprepared for the workplace.[3] Intrigued by this insight, I also conducted a survey on workforce preparedness, surveying over ten thousand employers, students, and university career center leaders. The key finding was that employers were much less confident of student career readiness than the students themselves. The primary aim of this book is to help aspiring consultants and professionals become more prepared to enter their chosen fields, and existing ones to be more effective and reach their true potential.

The third and final section tackles *evolutionary competencies*: tools and trends that have emerged more recently and which are having a powerful impact on consulting and industry as this book goes to press. As of 2017, their enduring relevance and extent of their impact is still to be determined. This part of the book includes discussions of design thinking, project-based and agile thinking, data visualization, automation, and artificial intelligence.

Think of these tools arranged in the form of a pyramid, with learnability at the base. The capacity to learn informs the foundational competencies, which feed into the evolution-

---

3   Jon Swartz, "Businesses Say They Just Can't Find the Right Tech Workers," *USA Today*, March 28, 2017.

ary competencies. Improving the capability to learn will accelerate and amplify the other skills.

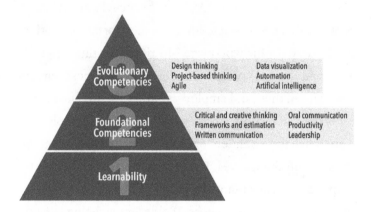

It's not my objective to make you an expert in each area. Indeed, there's sometimes more value in developing a foundational knowledge across a broad range of subjects than there is in becoming an expert in a single specialization. At the same time, the market values deep subject matter expertise. The optimal approach is a combination of both, and I hope to provide a foundation that will complement the depth you already have or are in the process of attaining. Time is of the essence here. If it takes you ten years to become an expert in a new skill, that's slow—too slow, in the digital economy. Beyond the risk of skills obsolescence, there is also a huge amount of opportunity cost—time that could have been devoted to learning other skills, developing new relationships, and adding new experiences.

The crucial question is, "when does the law of diminishing

returns kick in?" Imagine that in a single year you could learn 90 percent of what commonly takes ten years. That would be a highly productive use of your time. Further imagine that in only a month you could learn 50 percent of what you need to be considered competent in the field, and perhaps you could even pick up 30 percent of that information in a mere week. Rather than be skeptical or point out the benefits of long experience and repetition, think instead about what it would take to attain these levels of competence. You would understand the big picture, the guiding principles, the most common frameworks, important vocabulary terms, and even some golden examples of world-class performance in a given area.

This is the basic premise of consulting, to give yourself a basic education in a new skill in the shortest time possible, trusting that you'll be able to fill in any important gaps as you proceed, through study and under the tutelage of an expert, akin to the classic apprenticeship model. Then, you can go deeper, faster, and iterate to develop real depth. This approach can allow you to understand the core concepts in multiple fields, quickly, instead of forcing you to choose only one, which will likely evolve anyway. This ability to learn quickly used to be a skill that was nice to have, one that could slingshot a person past others in career development. However, with the rapid pace of change and disruption, this approach needs to be adopted by anyone wanting to stay relevant and be flexible.

Another major difference between methods of education is the distinction between *just-in-time* learning and *just-in-case* learning. To illustrate the difference between them, let's consider an example. I hold an MBA. I've considered investing several years into studying for a PhD. However, I decided not to, at least to this point in my life. Why? Because up to now, I have decided that what I could learn during a PhD program—along with future opportunities in academia—is outweighed by the opportunity cost to attain it. No doubt I'd learn a lot of interesting information, much of which might become useful over time. However, the several years required for a PhD, and the loss of income during that period, means my time may be better invested in shorter bursts of project work and applied research.

I can use that time to educate myself in subjects that are relevant to my current business responsibilities, and then *use* that information to become a better consultant. This is not to diminish the potential benefits of a doctoral degree, however. A PhD could help someone—including me at some point—move into a formal role in academia, or it could offer enduring credentials and aid advancement in fields such as psychology.

Just-in-time learning is particularly valuable because you can apply it today. You can decide what to read tonight based on what you need to know now, or will need to know soon. You should have an idea of areas your company or the market is prioritizing now and will prioritize in the near future, so you can focus your research and learning on those areas. As Thomas Friedman said in his famous 2005 book of the same name, the world is indeed "flat." Technology and connectivity is changing the way we do business and relate to one another. This is making it harder and harder to differentiate yourself from others.

Understanding the material in this book will help you to do that. Information is available to everyone. In the twenty-first century, the way to stand out is to learn more quickly than others, then to apply that learning and make a tangible impact.

The competition for slots in top graduate schools and positions in blue-chip companies is greater than ever. At the same time, more and more work can be outsourced to people in other countries at much lower wages, or—alternatively— automated away. I work with people located across India and China, as well as across Europe and indeed all over the globe. They are highly intelligent, ambitious, and have access to technology that allows them to compete globally. Starting in the 2016 edition of its World Development Indicators, the World Bank made a big choice: it no longer distinguishes between "developed" countries and "developing" ones in the presentation of its data. The advantages of the so-called "developed economies" are disappearing before our very eyes.

If you are willing to put in the effort, this can be an exciting and empowering prospect, no matter where you live. We all have the freedom and the technology to learn from one another and find new markets for our products and services. On the other hand, no one can rest on their laurels or assume a legacy advantage will continue. Those who learn in a linear, incremental fashion can still experience success. However, those who learn in a non-linear, agile fashion, will outstrip those linear thinkers at some point, learning more, generating more opportunities, and earning more.

Just as the world is getting flatter, so are companies. Hierarchies are becoming less defined, with fewer discrete levels. The responsibilities of individuals are becoming broader, while the role of middle management is shifting significantly. There is less need for them to act as intermediaries or aggregators of information. It's possible for a company CEO to write a blog or create a video and communicate directly with everyone in their company.

How can we measure skills such as critical thinking and leadership? There are some metrics, notably observed behaviors, but these skills also manifest their value in other areas, ultimately driving better decisions and improved results. Human beings aren't robots, although it won't be long until they replace us in some areas. We need a sense of well-being, or a sense of purpose, to stay motivated. Achieving our targets is only meaningful to us if we have a *reason* to achieve those targets, and we can relate to the goal and the process.

Human beings are extremely resilient, but we're not very good at behaving like automatons.

Attempting to grind through our days without a sense of meaning isn't sustainable. It can lead to a deterioration in health and happiness, a sense that something is missing from our lives. For example, I enjoy consulting because I find helping clients meaningful. There were certainly roles early in my career that had an operational focus. This was important to my company's success, but it simply wasn't as exciting to me. On the other hand, some people are drawn to the process and cadence of operations—it's a question of individual preference. The desire to make work meaningful has always existed, but previous generations subordinated it to short-term financial performance and operational efficiency. To the Millennial generation and beyond, the necessity of meaning and purpose is paramount. They and many others refuse to tolerate work that doesn't bring them fulfillment. This has put employers on notice to provide a better experience. Nonetheless, you shouldn't rely on your employer to do the work of creating meaning for you. It's a task that starts with you as an individual.

While not every part of every job is meaningful, we can take steps to maximize the parts that are. Soft metrics aren't enough here. After all, people who feel good but navel-gaze and produce little aren't valuable to their clients, their companies, or themselves. It's important that we create measurable value. That's how we justify receiving paychecks or client fees, and making our way through professional life. The important word here is *value*. It comes from generating benefits, in excess of costs. The internet provides us with all the information we could possibly consume. It's never been easier to generate output. The question is how all this data and analysis will improve results.

Will it help a client make a better decision? Will it save money or time? Will it make customers more likely to buy our products and services? Only an intelligent combination of analysis, decisions, and execution will achieve that. Good consultants drive results because they are constantly looking at situations through the lens of value. They seek the greatest value for a given investment.

I recently experienced an example of this phenomenon, while submitting a proposal to help an industrial client develop their Agile software development capabilities. We initially advised them to invest a significant amount, to achieve the optimal impact across their many global locations. They responded that due to budget constraints they needed something much less expensive, with significantly less scope—and lower fees—than originally proposed. We took a hard look and reduced the services and the proposed fees somewhat, but stopped at the point below which we believed the initiative would not be successful. If we'd removed any more, it would have been detrimental, and we were prepared to walk away. The client agreed on the value, and in the end the Agile program was a convincing success. It's essential that project activities are organized to create value, not simply to complete work. Many people stay busy and create output, but value is created when work is aligned to an overarching objective, and when the impact of its delivery exceeds the cost of investment. This impact also provides meaning to those who create it.

One of the most fascinating challenges of consulting is effective communication across disciplines, because people communicate in ways that reflect their individual skills and experiences. Accountants may speak in financial terms, while IT professionals may prefer technical language full of data and programming terms. People in other disciplines will use their own descriptive language and jargon. As a consultant, you need to be able to communicate with clients across their functional areas, and at all levels in the organization, tailoring your message to their individual and distinct priorities.

If you can only speak one "language," you'll only be able to communicate with people who think like you or share similar backgrounds. The success of your communications will be gauged not only by the quality of your speaking or writing, but by how well it's received by those you intend to reach. Often, that means modifying what you produce for their benefit, not yours. Good communicators understand that, even if they have their own agenda, they need to understand the viewpoints of the people they want to influence.

The tools in this book are intended for your use. I recommend that everyone read the first chapter, because it underlies all the others. After that, feel free to skip to the chapters that are most interesting to you. If one of the chapters is relevant to a project you're working on currently, read that chapter and experiment with the tools it contains. If you want a complete overview, work your way through the chapters in order. This book is intended to be a practical aid, not merely a decorative bookend. Use the principles discussed above to maximize the value you get from it.

As Ralph Waldo Emerson once said, "The mind, once stretched by a new idea, never returns to its original dimensions." Consider this a voyage of discovery and mind expansion.

Bon voyage!

PART ONE

LEARNABILITY

CHAPTER ONE

THE PROCESS OF LEARNING

"The number one thing we look for is general cognitive ability, and it's not IQ. It's learning ability."

—LAZLO BOCK, SENIOR VICE PRESIDENT OF PEOPLE OPERATIONS, GOOGLE

Learnability is the desire and ability to quickly grow and adapt one's skill set, in order to stay relevant and succeed. It can also be viewed as the capacity to consistently learn at an accelerated pace. Too many people hide behind the false notion that some individuals are born smart and others are not. Often people develop these beliefs when they are children, so they find it hard to let them go, but in practice, they are a way for people to avoid confronting their own limitations and asking themselves how they might learn more quickly and effectively. Learnability is more about the process of learning than the ability to memorize rote material for a test. Even if people learn slowly at first, they are making progress, and will get better with practice. Everyone can increase their learnability.

The starting point is to create a safe environment and make learning tangible. Before you can learn, you need to understand *what* you're trying to learn. What are you trying to accomplish? What are your goals? What questions are you trying to answer? How do those questions relate to the task in front of you? Use them to plan a series of actions, deconstructing your learning into manageable chunks.

It's vital that you give yourself permission to learn and permission to fail when experimenting. Remember when you were a child and life was all about action, not playing it safe? This beginner's mindset allows you to step away from fear and instead open yourself to what may be possible. In every situation, there are objective facts, and there are interpretations. An experience is how you interpret the facts, what you make of them. An extreme example of this is Viktor Frankl, who succeeded in being grateful for the horrific experience of being interned in a concentration camp. Ultimately, he felt that he learned an enormous amount about what it is to be human from those years.

Fear often stems from a sense of unfamiliarity. We fear what we don't know. One of the best methods of tackling fear, therefore, is to investigate the unknown and make it known. As the legendary sales trainer Tom Hopkins famously said, "Do what you fear most, and you control fear." Sometimes we experience the unknown outside a safe, comfortable environment and do not have the luxury of time to investigate. In those circumstances, reckoning with it takes real courage.

Most of us will never need to exercise Frankl's level of discipline, but the principle is the same. How can you remove the barriers that prevent you from learning and from seeing your experiences in a positive light? Controlled conditions, in which you can explore your capabilities and relish failure as part of the learning process, can play a key role here. The next time you encounter a setback, remember this example and determine what positive outcomes you can take from the experience.

There is no single quality that guarantees a person will be able to learn, but there are several clues. One of the biggest is intellectual curiosity. In my job with Infosys, it's one of the key things we look for in potential hires. Another is persistence, and a third is confidence. As it turns out, Millennials excel in these qualities. They've grown up knowing that information is only a search engine away, and they have an expectation that anything is possible.

Previous generations were more willing to accept data and

technology limitations, but Millennials are impatient to plow through them. In this case, I think impatience is a good thing. It drives the creativity that inspires individuals to conduct research, talk to people in the field, or do whatever else it takes to acquire the information they need. The people who quickly convert ambiguous situations to clear recommendations stand out from their peers, because they demonstrate that they can learn and learn fast.

In a constantly evolving workplace, the capacity to learn is possibly the single greatest asset a person can have. It enables every other skill, and it allows people to reshape their careers and their lives. We all need to be able to reinvent ourselves. Careers no longer travel along a smooth and carefully planned trajectory. They take unexpected twists and turns. Being able to learn is essential to adapt and succeed.

My father was a cross between legendary US General George Patton and famed Indiana University basketball coach Bobby Knight. He was a hardcore sportsman with a drill sergeant mentality. When I was growing up, he wanted me to stay busy, so whenever he went away, he left me with an itinerary designed to fill the entire day. Of course, I wanted to complete the tasks he left me within as little time as possible, so that I had some time to myself. There is no productivity technique ever created to match that of a farm youngster trying to get a little time to themselves.

In my view, the point was to get work done as quickly as possible, and enjoy the extra time. My father, while he accomplished a lot, also valued hard work for its own sake. As mentioned earlier, he grew up on a farm in Depression-era Indiana, and hard work was a core element of his value system. His mother stayed at home with the children, while his father worked in the coal mines in Pennsylvania and the older kids ran the farm. From an early age, he took care of both the house and the garden, while his eldest brother looked after the barn animals. This was in a time with no social safety nets. They took care of themselves, or they starved.

He passed that attitude on to me and to my brothers, in part because he thought we represented him to the world. The way we competed at school and on the sports field was, he felt, a reflection of his abilities as a parent. It was a pressure-filled environment, but he promised me that anything else I wanted to achieve in life would be easy in comparison. Turns out he was right.

My father was not a man to take risks beyond established methods. He viewed my experiments with productivity and process improvements a little suspiciously. He saw my efforts to learn, change, and grow, as risks. Small risks, admittedly, but risks nonetheless. He was from the "if it ain't broke, don't fix it" school of thought, and he doubted the utility of making changes. After seeing my improvements, he sometimes joked that when I was older it would be my job to find ways to do things more efficiently. Little did he know that would turn out to be the case. Innovation was an important part of his world, but only to solve problems, not for improvement and new ventures. Leaving Indiana and starting work at Texas Instruments far away in Dallas was an unusual move for someone growing up in that environment. For me, however, it was an opportunity to take a chance and experiment, even if the eventual outcome was unknown to me.

That hunger for experimentation carried through into my role with TI, even when my job didn't require that kind of innovation. The production line manager role mentioned earlier was not easy, but after a month the learning quickly tapered off and the job became monotonous. Rather than resign myself to simply fine tuning a mature operation, I found within it a vehicle for learning—understanding the assembly line, the people, and figuring out how to improve it in ways that mattered. This is where I learned about product quality, line speed, factory layout, and several other areas of industrial design and manufacturing. After that experience, I knew I wanted to move into a field that offered me the opportunity to keep learning, experimenting, and growing.

With a background in engineering, I wasn't sure where that desire would lead me. I was inclined to take risks and experiment to improve things, but I lacked a robust tool kit that could take me there. Remember, this was prior to the internet, so it was much more difficult to understand what was out there, and to access information.

An early inspiration was listening to tape recordings by the great Earl Nightingale, in which he described the exponential qualities of the mind. The body has limits, but the mind is essentially limitless. Another concept of his, which I still cherish today, is the value of adopting an attitude of *grateful service*. When we stop feeling that people owe us anything and instead appreciate what we have and what we can offer to others, our power to create change increases radically. We start to find meaning in the journey, instead of simply craving the destination or looking for shortcuts.

What really got me going in consulting was joining Grant Thornton as a leader in their Dallas office. To learn, I needed to venture beyond my comfort zone. It was a real stretch, more challenging than I envisioned, and it was initially a mixed experience. With few pre-conceived notions, I did many things that more experienced consultants may not have done. Sometimes they worked out well, and sometimes they didn't. However, each situation was an opportunity to learn.

Much of my early work at Grant Thornton involved creating frameworks that others could follow. I discovered that teaching is also an effective way to learn. To teach anything, we need to know it well enough to explain it to others, and to help them internalize it. On one occasion, a leading men's apparel client requested someone to lead their order management initiative. I knew I could manage the project, but I was not experienced in apparel, so I completed a crash course on the industry after locating a textbook written by the leading professor on the subject. Again, this was pre-internet, and certainly pre-Amazon, so finding exactly what I needed, fast, was a tall order.

I had the other areas the client requested covered, but lacked the industry experience they desired. I located the best reference books, identified the top hundred and twenty questions to ask (I'm serious), and found answers to each of those questions within the first two weeks on the project. My approach was thorough and detailed, and attributable to a determination to quickly find accurate answers to the client's questions. The client was so impressed that they thanked our managing partner for assigning such an "expert" to the project.

This is not to imply that subject matter expertise is not valuable. It is. This example simply shows what is possible with a focus on learning the right information, at the right time, and rapidly reinforcing that learning with many small but relevant data points. I already knew industrial manufacturing well, and used the new information to contextualize that knowledge to the specifics of a different industry, in this case, soft goods apparel.

This technique has served me well in many other situations.

When learning something, quickly get a big-picture understanding, then go as deep as possible into the specific area needed in the time available. Think of the process like a "T." The broad understanding is the top of the T, while the focus area is the vertical line of the T. Over time, the broad "top of the T" will become a strong asset, metaphorically thicker, and it will be easier to go deep in specific areas needed for a given assignment or role. Once you've developed the capability to do this, you can go into any situation with the confidence that you can learn quickly.

Several years ago, I worked with a senior-level consultant, Sam, who had been a high performer but whose career motivation was beginning to drift. He lacked an area of focus and an anchor client, plus he wanted to get off the road to spend more time with his young family. An opportunity arose for Sam to take on a project with a large local client. The project itself was small, but it provided him with a chance to dive deep into a specialized functional area and establish a beachhead from which to grow the client account.

For five or six months, he engaged in great detail with the client, becoming known as an expert in his niche and developing strong relationships at that client. Even though he was a senior consulting professional, he delivered like an individual contributor, doing the detail work himself and delivering each part of the engagement. The process of refining his functional and account focus made him a better consultant, improving the quality of his work and catalyzing a promotion to partner. This is an example of the value that hyper-focus can bring. In the age of the instant-gratification internet, it's easy to find information, but there's no substitute for exploring specific topics in-depth. The two approaches outlined above are not mutually exclusive. They are both good approaches to learning, and the key is to know when to apply each of them.

Early in my career, I was fortunate enough to work with some highly skilled and experienced consultants, both in my firm and as part of client teams. I asked them a lot of questions. As we worked together on engagements, I noticed their techniques to utilize frameworks, make calculations, or organize data. The more I learned, the more curious I became. I wanted to learn from others as much as they were willing to share. These experiences reinforced my confidence in the things I was doing well and helped me improve in other areas.

It's not easy for young consultants to validate their ideas and intuitions about what works. In many cases, that knowledge is not readily available; it's being used by experienced professionals who are charging hundreds of dollars per hour for their expertise. Some of this can be learned in college, but there's a big difference between the people who are *teaching* consulting skills and those who are *doing* it. Hopefully, you'll find that this book answers your questions about consulting methodology, based on what has been tried and tested in the crucible of the real world. It may validate your ideas, and sometimes it may challenge them. Regardless, this book should save you time, because it's a synthesized version of much of what I've learned over the course of a long career.

You may believe that you need to be the smartest person in the room to be a good consultant. It's not the case. If you're in a consulting or other professional environment, you'll be around very intelligent people, many of whom may not apply their ideas or see the application through to completion. Having ideas is fantastic, but results are generated in the execution. Being an inventor sounds exciting. Innovation, however, happens when intelligence is converted into action. If you consistently exercise curiosity and combine it with persistence, you'll make steady progress, outstripping those who are brilliant but lack the fortitude to follow up on their insights.

Journaling is a habit that can help you keep track of your development and uncover new insights. You can do this high-tech, using a digital tablet and an app, or you can go old school, with a notebook and a pencil. Don't think that your journal needs to be packed with nuggets of genius and look like a finished document. In fact, only wanting to write fully formed content, with "perfect" wording, holds people back—including me, for years. Write down loose thoughts that occur to you, whatever their form or fashion, whenever they occur, or simply track the cadence of your life in a slightly more structured fashion. The act of creating a bridge between your thoughts and your laptop, or sheet of paper, is itself an act of learning. As you write, you will capture and refine your ideas and they will take on new meaning.

Your desire to learn is more important than your background. You may not have attended the greatest schools, but you can still develop the skills you need to succeed and enjoy the journey. Don't let your beliefs about what a successful person looks or acts like prevent you from achieving success in your chosen field. One reason I wrote this book is to reduce the perceived gap between those with the "correct" background and those without it. I want to level the playing field.

What does that mean? Let's take an example. Perhaps you're a highly intelligent person with strong ideas. Yet you've never learned how to communicate with people at the executive level. Perhaps you've never learned to develop an argument using fact-based analysis. How will you attract the support of senior management and generate the opportunity to test your ideas? Improving your communication skills will rapidly amplify the impact of your other abilities, enabling people to trust you and make high-stakes decisions based on the information you provide.

Attitudes to work and learning have changed a lot since I started my career. In the early days, there was far more of an institutional feel to work environments. People were hesitant to rock the boat or challenge the status quo. That has evolved to a less formal, less certain atmosphere. People know that changes will happen, and that they need to learn new things on a regular basis to keep up. Learning has always been important, but its value has now permeated every aspect of our working lives. In the twentieth century, it was assumed, or at least hoped, that people went to college or learned a trade, then took a job for life, only switching companies when forced to do so.

The speed and uncertainty of change means that the concept of a job for life is virtually obsolete. For millennia, humans lived in small, tightly knit bands with little mobility. Even a century ago, most people settled in the places where they grew up, close to people they knew well. This relative sameness, combined with slow-moving trends, created a sense of certainty—or at least a linear view of change.

Whether those days were truly a golden era or we're viewing them through rose-colored glasses, there's no returning to them. Cycles are shortening, and the speed of change continues to accelerate. Complex physical products that went through innovation life cycles once every decade in the twentieth century are evolving every few years. Software products change even more frequently, with new versions arriving mere months or weeks apart, and smaller features updated as often as daily.

This trend makes it more important than ever to learn

quickly. If you want to compare two consultants with similar skills, how can you differentiate them? One metric is how quickly people learn new information and can put it to productive use. As information becomes ubiquitous, the speed at which we can process it and generate insights grows more important.

The World Economic Forum (WEF) is the ultimate government and business think tank, and a great place to understand the trends that are shaping the world of work. Starting in 2016, WEF thought leaders became more focused on the Fourth Industrial Revolution and its implications. As a summary—albeit an oversimplification—the First Industrial Revolution was a transition from hand production to machines, the second was rapid industrialization marked by manufacturing interchangeable parts, and the third was the advancement from analog and mechanical to the digital technology available today.

The Fourth Industrial Revolution is truly digital, characterized by a range of new technologies that fuse the physical, digital, and biological worlds, impact all disciplines, economies, and industries, and even challenge ideas about what it means to be human. The resulting shifts and disruptions mean that we live in a time of great promise, yet also great peril. We have the potential to connect billions more people to digital networks, dramatically improve efficiency, and even manage assets in ways that can help the natural environment.

What does this mean for individuals? It means that although digital technology enables us to learn rapidly, it also challenges our certainties about working life and society overall. For those willing to face this proactively, it presents a huge opportunity. The world is becoming increasingly non-linear, amplifying the impact of good ideas, and propelling those who can adapt to this exponential model.

Linear thinking follows known cycles or step-by-step progression. It is incremental. Humans are wired for linear thinking: work a little harder, make a little more money, and live a marginally improved life. We imagine the future similarly to the present, with some incremental improvements. That approach worked well for thousands of years, but the digital revolution has changed the calculus. Linear growth results from repeatedly adding a constant, whereas exponential growth is the repeated multiplication of a constant, or even growing, factor. This is why linear growth produces a stable straight line over time, but exponential growth eventually skyrockets.

We often miss exponential trends in their early stages because the initial pace of exponential growth is deceptive—it begins slowly and is hard to differentiate from linear growth. Hence, predictions based on the expectation of an exponential pace can seem improbable. By the time the linear thinker realizes that they're falling behind, it's too late to catch up.

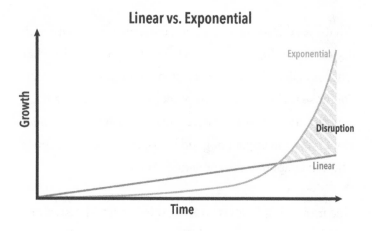

Linear vs. Exponential

Sound far-fetched? Ask yourself if Barnes & Noble felt threatened when Amazon was in its infancy. Moving beyond books, compare brick-and-mortar retailers with the likes of Amazon. These companies grew steadily for decades. Yet, they have struggled to compete with the new model pioneered by Amazon. By the time they became aware of the danger—and took action—it was too late. Airbnb is doing something similar in the hotel industry, while Uber is changing the face of the taxi industry. By the time their linear competitors understood how powerful they were becoming, these former industry leaders had to play catch up to simply survive.

The rate of change continues to accelerate. According to think tank American Enterprise Institute, 88 percent of the Fortune 500 companies in 1955 no longer existed by 2015. The average corporate lifespan used to be fifty years, and now it is less than twelve. With advances in technologies such as artificial intelligence, robotics, 3-D printing, and synthetic biology, the potential for exponential growth continues to expand. This affects all of us.

When new ideas emerge, they reach the market faster than ever before, driving rapid growth. Companies like Facebook and Google initially looked cool but insignificant compared to "real" established companies. They made for great media stories, but the companies themselves didn't command noticeable market share for some time. To casual observers, it appeared that their sudden breakout took place overnight. What wasn't so apparent, however, was that their growth took place on an exponential curve. The velocity and acceleration were always there, but at a scale no one noticed in the early days. By the time their rapid growth reached an observable level, their competitors had a much more difficult task to catch up with them.

Add to that the reluctance of market leaders to cannibalize their own revenue, and it gave these digital upstarts even more of a competitive head start. The traditional industrial mindset of the incumbents emphasized optimization on a linear scale. That model emphasized lengthy planning, thorough product development, and carefully launching to the market—the "get it right the first time" principle. While quality is important, in the digital age, customer-centricity and speed rule. Moving quickly, experimenting, and adjusting once in the market are the new norms.

For some, the faster rate of change is very unsettling. They're comfortable in their current lives and they don't want to make changes. However, the world is not asking your permission. If you can summon the courage to acknowledge reality, you will be able to make the most of the potential presented by exponential change. Instead of living in anxiety that machines will make your skill set redundant, you'll be able to seize opportunities as they arise. These opportunities come in the form of what exponential thinker Peter Diamandis calls "unexpected convergent consequences." What he means by this is that when we combine multiple exponential trends, the resulting potential for change is colossal.

How can we take advantage of exponential thinking? First, understand that if the world is changing faster than ever, we need to evolve—learn—more quickly. Each of us is aware of *what* we learn, but few of us are conscious about *how* we learn. We follow the processes laid out for us throughout school and college, gradually acquiring our body of knowledge. Yet we don't make the conscious decision to learn more effectively, or even consider how we might do so. We don't ask ourselves how we can learn faster, or increase the relevance of what we learn. Don't get me wrong, even a slow steady pace of continuous learning is a good thing, and historically that has been enough. Going forward, however, people will need to supplement this with periodic focused bursts as new opportunities and challenges arise.

Prior to the internet, it was commonly believed that information was power, and people tended to hoard that information to gain an advantage. Now we each have access to vast reservoirs of information. The question is how we use that information to develop insights and make improvements. For many of us, intelligent automation will eliminate the mundane aspects of our jobs, leaving us with more time to develop those insights, through analysis and decision-making. If you want to learn, it's essential to maintain a beginner's mindset. The more experienced you are, the harder it is to muster the humility required to accept that you will still make mistakes, and even look a little silly on occasion. However, unless you're prepared to admit to what you don't know, how can you learn?

Perhaps you're working on a presentation. What should be your theme? Do you want lots of graphs and charts, or a few bold slides? Can you make physical prototypes to illustrate your point? Will you make more impact through a big conference room or more intimate setting? Maintaining a beginner's mindset allows you to ask these questions without assuming you already know the answers, even if you have given presentations many times before. This allows you to take a fresh look, avoid bias, and reduces the pressure to be perfect right out of the gate.

Perfectionism is the enemy of the beginner's mindset. If you're convinced that you need to be perfect from the start, you won't share low-fidelity prototypes and early-stage ideas.

Ironically, this means that when you *do* share your ideas, you'll be deeply invested in them. This will make it harder for you to accept feedback and more likely that you'll defend them instead of being open to improvement.

When you adopt a beginner's mindset, you don't need to be the best at everything you do, every time you do it. This will free you to experiment and explore, learning about a new industry, company, or software tool. This isn't to say that we should ignore the technical aspects of learning. Ironically, the more technically complex a subject becomes, the more important it is to reintroduce a human aspect, otherwise people find it difficult to understand and relate.

Before I visited China, I could read about Shanghai and watch video footage of the city. However, until I saw wave after wave after wave of office towers with my own eyes and walked in the midst of millions of tech-savvy consumers, I didn't have a full sense of the city's electric and unique atmosphere. A similar thing occurs when starting a new project. You can read documents and study financials, but to truly understand a company, you need to meet the right people, spend time in the relevant locations, and experience it for yourself.

What are the metrics of professional success? You may focus on making more money or getting promoted. These are lagging indicators of success, but how can you attain those goals?

To get more, you need to do or be more. Rather than look at the output, think about the input and the levers involved. The foundational question is this: How can you *serve* more people? How can you multiply your impact to reach more people, or those you already serve with more value? Can you do it in less time? It is common to imagine that it takes people ten to fifteen years of working in the same field to become experts. How much of that time, however, is spent learning something new and truly incremental? After the third experience of a process or functional area, how much more learning remains? How many situational variants are left to explore? This is not to minimize the complexity in enterprise processes or functional areas, but to challenge you to find common characteristics more quickly.

The challenge for consultants, or anyone wishing to learn quickly, is to remove the waste and the redundant repetition, yet still develop expertise—or at least competence—in a given area. Perhaps competence is enough in some fields. In my personal life, I'd like to be an expert at fixing things around the house, but I don't need to be. As long as I'm competent, I can handle most situations. For anything that requires true expertise, I can call in a professional. The same holds true for professional skills. For example, it would be nice for everyone to be a data scientist, but it is not a practical objective for most of us. However, to be effective, every professional should have some base knowledge of data and analytics.

You get to decide the level of depth in which you explore each discipline. You may need to go through a few full cycles of similar projects before you have a solid understanding, but if competency is all you need, you probably don't need the level of refinement that comes with several years of experience. You can also relate what you've learned in one field to another, similar field. If you've worked in product development, for example, you can relate that to supply chain, because you will understand which components go into the creation of the product and the intersection of product launch with physical distribution. As you move from one area to another, you may realize that you understand 20 to 40 percent of a new specialty very quickly, and you can fill in remaining gaps once you have an overall framework to organize your thinking.

Treat every scenario as a learning opportunity. Approach your role actively, dig into the subjects you're learning and ask questions based on your genuine curiosity. Maybe you're learning about human resources, but you can investigate the underlying financials at the same time. Why not do a little more research, so that you understand the state of the industry? What do leading thinkers on the subject say about the topic? By deciding to learn, you can enrich whatever situation you encounter.

Exactly how fast *is* accelerated learning? In *The Matrix*, there's a scene in which Neo, played by Keanu Reeves, learns judo and kung fu in a moment, because he has an experience of an incredible amount of cognitive and emotional experiences "uploaded" to his brain instantaneously. You won't be able to replicate that kind of pace, but what does accelerated learning look like for you? How much can you reduce the time needed to discover what you need to know? For example, can you talk to a true expert in the field and learn the four or five elements that make the biggest difference? That may be more productive than simply reading about it. While there is no substitute for personal experience, there is also no faster way to gain wisdom than to learn vicariously from the distilled wisdom of a master practitioner.

There are some skills which can be approached at a general level, while others require specialization. People reinvent themselves several times over the course of a career. This continuous need to learn can be frustrating or empowering, depending on your viewpoint. You may find yourself thinking that you knew a lot about a subject five years ago, and that you've been left behind. However, if you have a solid foundation from your previous experience, you will be able to refresh that knowledge quickly.

There are skills that do require specialization. Unless you are interested in becoming a true expert, you probably don't want to invest significant time to learn about them. An example is technical skills in SAP software, one of the world's largest enterprise software companies. It's a juggernaut, and for over twenty years its ecosystem has allowed practitioners to have attractive careers. To succeed in this discipline requires deep skills and regular certification and training. For technologists with the inclination to specialize, working with SAT has been a lucrative field that has allowed them to enjoy a comfortable career, knowing that their skills are in demand, and are likely to be for some time to come.

There may not be many opportunities to specialize so clearly over such a long period, but there are lots of niches where you can work effectively. In fact, an effective career strategy is to find the intersection of two or three areas, and become the expert in that niche. Combining an industry, process area, and perhaps a language can be effective. I remember Frank Fitzpatrick, a professor from my business school days who decided, early in his career, to carve out a niche for himself. In the late 1960s, he took stock of the number of people in the United States who were MBAs, licensed attorneys, and certified public accountants (CPAs). He discovered that there were only thirty-five people in the entire United States who carried all three designations.

He aggressively pursued this trifecta, becoming uniquely qualified for advanced business opportunities early in his career. He crafted a career in which he worked with luminaries in real estate and media, along with becoming a top accountant for the Penthouse empire. He was also an early investor in Berskhire Hathaway, buying in at $39 per share.

As of this writing, shares in Berkshire Hathaway are worth nearly $300,000 each (he recommended them to me at $5,000 per share, but the price was "too high" for me at the time). His unique mix of skills helped him qualify for and then act upon such opportunities. You may not be able to put together quite such a unique and valuable portfolio, but you can certainly plan ahead and decide what skills you want to learn. What one skill can you add to become special, more valuable, and more fulfilled as you develop or refine your career?

Imagine a bell curve. At the far right are the top 10 percent of students in your high school. If you are reading this book, you're probably part of that top 10 percent. Now, explode that 10 percent into another full bell curve, and you have your college peers. Those high school high performers now form the collegiate bell curve. Ask yourself, what does it take to remain in the top 10 percent? Now, explode the rightmost portion of that bell curve once again. The far right of this third bell curve is your new peer group, which could be a top professional services firm. Most professionals in a good firm were likely in the top 10 percent in college. Even to be mediocre at this level, you need to be very good. The analogy holds true whether you use the top 50 percent or the top 1 percent—the point is that the further you advance, the more skills it takes to remain even "average" in a new peer group.

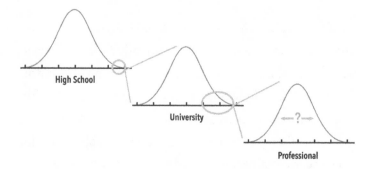

High School

University

Professional ←—?—→

Transitioning from one level to another, like any change in context, can be tricky. You could allow yourself to become complacent because you were in the higher quartiles in high school and even in college. On the other hand, you could become disheartened, because you're now surrounded by people who are *also* very smart. Working for a top firm in any industry, especially in consulting, is like going from college to the professional ranks in sports. It's harder to compete. At the same time, it's an honor to be playing at that level, and it is a crucible that refines your skills like no other.

It may sound obvious, but goals are an essential element for progress. Whether you're looking to get a job, earn a promotion, or secure other advancement, goals get and keep you on track. They also help you prioritize your time, which ultimately is your most precious resource. Be purposeful about how you consume it. I'm a big believer in the adage that work expands to fill the time available. Give yourself short time windows in which to accomplish tasks, so that you're working with at least a little time pressure.

When I was a sophomore in high school, I was a mediocre athlete. I had the skills, but I matured late, got in my own way psychologically, and tried too hard. My basketball coach Joe Todrank gave me a book called *Psycho-Cybernetics*, by Dr. Maxwell Maltz. Essentially a form of meditation, the technique involved deep breathing, slowly moving focus from the top of the head through the body to the soles of the feet, while imagining stress leaving the body. It was a process of methodically relaxing the body.

After becoming relaxed, I then visualized scenes of shooting baskets, defending effectively, and coming through in clutch moments. The key was to do this vividly, so that I could hear the crowd, experience the emotions, and feel the sweat. After practicing the technique for some time, my confidence—and my performances—dramatically improved. I went from mediocre to all-conference in three sports, and became a staunch believer in Dr. Maltz's approach. You can do something similar. When you're about to face a high-pressure situation, focus on your breath, methodically relax your body, and visualize the intended experience as clearly as possible. See yourself succeeding, whatever that means in your situation. Today this approach could be called flow or mindfulness. While it is best to incorporate this or a similar technique into your regular routine, even small focused doses can make an impact, such as when preparing for an important meeting or event.

One area where people waste a lot of time is email. While

it started out as a wonderful productivity tool, it has pro-liferated into endless requests for time and attention. You probably receive more emails than you can effectively respond to, even if you are only copied on many of these messages as a courtesy. If you're in a client-focused business, how can you spend more time focused on value-added activities, and less on non-essential emails? As you progress in your career, it does not take long before you find that there are many more demands on your time than you can possibly meet. What do you do?

One approach is to set a target and decide that you won't go to sleep until you've completed all your tasks—in other words, cleared your email inbox. I've done that before, working until 6:00 a.m. and then going straight to the shower to get ready for a new day. There are times when this might be the right approach, such as when you have a big deadline to hit and it is all core work. Imagine a surgeon with a patient on the operating table. They can't go to sleep and come back when they've had a good night's rest, because their patient will be dead. They need to complete the operation before they can relax.

Long term, however, this isn't a sustainable approach. You need sleep. After a couple of days without it, your perfor-mance will be so impaired that any gain from burning the midnight oil will be lost due to the plunge in productivity. Worse, going without enough sleep isn't any fun. Arianna

Huffington of *Huffington Post* fame has become a spokesperson for sleep, and has provided plenty of compelling evidence on this topic. Thankfully, in recent times it has become less of a badge of honor to skimp on sleep. That makes it even more important to find ways to better manage your schedule. One simple option is to experiment with email filters so that you receive the correspondence that's most important to you, and you can batch the rest and deal with it on your own terms. Some outliers will slip through, but you can greatly reduce the time you spend on unproductive distractions.

Another perspective on this is the concept of a *manager's* schedule versus a *maker's* schedule. The manager's schedule involves a lot of processing and communication—and lots of meetings! As a manager, you are focused on people, appointments, and relationships. The maker's schedule applies when your role is primarily to create, and this takes large blocks of uninterrupted time—the kind of time business professionals don't usually have. Many of my challenges have come from trying to manage the conflicts that arise when attempting to set aside time for a maker's schedule, with a trail of emails and unkept, implied commitments lurking in the inbox.

The world of the professional is typically ruled by the manager's schedule, as we try to make those endless meetings more productive. However, consultants and other project-based professionals must also include elements of the maker's schedule, even if those blocks of time are infrequent. To justify charging for your time, you need to create output that your client—or leader, if internal—finds valuable. You can't get away from the manager's schedule entirely, however, because if you ignore the needs of others, you'll find yourself in trouble. Again, the key here is to be proactive and set your schedule accordingly. Seek balance if you can, but know your priorities, or your inbox will set them for you. Be mindful to allocate adequate time to work on a maker's schedule, while also accepting the necessity of administrative time. Like a good skier, be aggressive but keep the edge, and don't lose control. If nothing else, you will experience the joy of making something, which is truly creative thinking in action.

Mindfulness has reached buzzword status, so it is important to look at what it really means on a practical basis. There are two elements to mindfulness. The first is to be deliberate, to plan and visualize, so that you can respond effectively and on your own terms. The second is to be fully present in any given situation, so that you can bring all your skills to bear as you craft the most appropriate response. This single-threaded mindset seems antiquated in a multitasking world. The trouble with multitasking is the dilutive effect of context switching, along with the prevention of the deeper thinking which leads to breakthroughs and optimal solutions.

Formal mindfulness practice, whatever that means for you, can help you develop this skill, so that you can harness more of your mental horsepower to increase performance. At the same time, things frequently won't go according to plan. That's life. In those cases, the key will be how well you adapt to changing circumstances. How present will you be? How well will you adapt to whatever comes your way? Like a doctor in an emergency room, you'll be faced with competing priorities and difficult decisions, and you'll need to address them with calm, clarity, and confidence. The life of a professional isn't predictable. Mindfulness is important because it allows you to handle that unpredictability.

Give yourself permission to experiment. You will risk failure, but you'll also learn. Be willing to forgive yourself when things don't work out quite as anticipated, because they're learning experiences. Entrepreneurs and startups set the benchmark here. They have a level of comfort with failure that leaders in larger, more established companies find difficult to comprehend. They're willing to try something for a few weeks, then modify it or give up on it entirely if it's not working. For people who work in established industries, this is often eye-opening. When I conduct innovation workshops and bring in startup leaders, our large company clients are amazed by the speed at which startups experiment and change.

It's not easy to experiment. There are corporate cultures in which employees appear waiting to take advantage of others' "failures," and it may not feel safe to take a risk. Nonetheless, company leaders desperately want people who are willing to take chances. The more effectively we can create an environment in which people feel safe to experiment, the more chance we have of discovering fresh new ideas and solutions. No environment is a guarantee of safety, however. It's up to you to identify ways in which you can do things differently.

Ultimately, learning is a choice. When you take responsibility for your career trajectory, you'll discover the power to develop and assert your own brand. When you know that you can learn, and learn quickly, you'll be confident when entering new situations. In the next section of this book, we discuss the specific competencies that will allow you to do that.

PART TWO

||||||||||||||||||

FOUNDATIONAL COMPETENCIES

CHAPTER TWO

CRITICAL AND CREATIVE THINKING

"Give children problems to solve, not answers to remember."

—ROGER LEWIN, PROLIFIC SCIENCE WRITER

Critical thinking is an intellectually disciplined process of analysis, interpretation, evaluation, and self-direction. These skills may sound dry, but in reality, they're fascinating. Critical thinking is based on universal intellectual values that transcend individual subject matter areas. In other words, critical thinking is a foundation that applies to and enhances all subject matter skills. Once you understand these skills, you can go through history and see that every great orator, thinker, or statesman wielded these timeless tools with confidence and precision.

Critical thinking is sometimes perceived negatively. Why, people wonder, should we not think positively? The distinction, however, is not about emotions, or about being complimentary as opposed to critical. Critical thinking is a way to use your brain to its full potential, and increase the quality, not just the quantity, of thought.

Many people believe that critical thinking is not relevant to business. Once a staple of liberal arts curricula, critical thinking has come under attack as it competes with STEM subjects for space on the curriculum. This pressure has trickled down from college to high school. After all, there is only so much time in the school day—and everyone needs to learn to code, right? The problem with a specialist approach is that learning a skill without knowing how to understand and solve the real problem behind it reduces that skill to a commodity, rendering us too inflexible to adapt with the times.

Many of the candidates I interview are mediocre critical thinkers. Critical thinking isn't a technical topic, and it doesn't seem to have a direct application to core business functions, so it falls by the wayside. This is a huge loss, both for individuals and for companies. Critical thinking addresses what to do, and why, before attempting to understand how. Adding this element of problem framing and problem solving increases the value for any business output, especially in non-commodity functions.

Imagine spending $1,000 on a new bicycle. You go into the

bike shop, put down the money, and wait for the assistant to bring your bike out from the back of the shop. When they return, they hand you a bag full of bike parts and tell you that you need to build the bike yourself. How would you react? You would not be happy at all. This is similar to what happens in a lot of businesses. Analysts give their leaders a lot of data, but they may not help those leaders make *sense* of that data, or explain what actions they should take in response to it. In essence, the analyst dumps a pile of data on the virtual table and says, "I'm done, now you can make sense of this." That's where critical thinking comes in. It's a set of tools that enable individuals to organize information, evaluate that information carefully, and use it to meet agreed-upon objectives. Critical thinking creates clarity.

DAVID'S STORY

Several years ago, I worked with a colleague named David. He was a highly intelligent, analytical consultant. After he joined our firm as an MBA campus hire, we staffed him at a major high-tech client in Silicon Valley, working in their distribution channel organization.

This was a small engagement to increase revenue through their distributor network. David's responsibility was to analyze point-of-sale data across these distributors. Initially his data gathering and calculations were solid, but his conclusions lacked insight and were not compelling. He did not present recommendations clearly or persuasively, making them difficult for the client to understand and implement.

The client did not doubt his analytical abilities, but they initially lacked confidence in him overall because he did not communicate in clear, actionable terms. While his calculations were good, his thinking and presentation didn't lead to logical conclusions. His presentations were like a road that ended in the middle of nowhere. Worse, because he did not articulate business value or root cause explanations, the recipient did not know how to prioritize the recommendations or how much they would cost to implement.

For a multibillion-dollar manufacturer like our client, many variables affect the choice of data to include in an analysis. Applying the same supply chain cost calculations to data center hardware as to home office routers would have led to misstatement and inaccurate results. David could compute formulas, but he failed to set up models appropriate to the operating model characteristics or product line characteristics.

Seeing David's early struggles, I asked the client for some additional time to work with him. I sat with him and showed him how to organize his activity and establish clear logic in his work. I asked him to concentrate on the "what" and "why" of analysis, not merely the "how." Within a few weeks, David's work improved dramatically. By the conclusion of his eight-week engagement, he could clearly articulate why the topic mattered, explain the overarching problem, and communicate the data-driven, non-obvious implications of his analysis. Then his recommendations were compelling, had real impact, and they were adopted. The improvements he made in his critical thinking abilities established his reputation with the client and with me, buying him time to develop and mature in other areas—as one would expect of any young professional joining a new firm.

David's improvement came after we looked at how he could apply the four major areas of critical thinking: analysis, interpretation, evaluation, and self-direction. Like most freshly minted business school graduates, he was comfortable with the mechanics of analysis. What he lacked was the capability to interpret data effectively and evaluate his results. This required him to ask new questions. How do I know what I know? What does the data mean? How sensitive are each of these outputs to the inclusion or exclusion of outliers? Keep in mind that when you see an appealing graphic in an article or news program, it took a lot of work and several iterations to reach that level of relevance and insight.

THE UNLIMITED POTENTIAL OF THINKING

You are probably familiar with the story of Colonel Sanders, the iconic face of Kentucky Fried Chicken. He lived out of the back of a station wagon at the age of sixty and was rejected hundreds of times before he finally found a recipe that he could sell. It's a well-known story of persistence and American entrepreneurship. However, you may not have considered the parallels between the persistence of Colonel Sanders and critical thinking in a business context. It takes a great deal of self-direction and analysis to continually ask "so what?" and refine your approach until you get it right. Insight is much more than simply producing a data dump. It's about interpreting and evaluating a result to generate insightful outputs. That requires intellectual curiosity and aggressive experimentation.

The brain is like a muscle. It can be trained. Unlike other muscles, however, the brain's capacities are non-linear. A couple hundred years ago, most people worked on farms or trades connected to the land. It was possible to get stronger and more efficient, but only to a certain extent. Despite the advances of early industrialization, the same principle continued to apply. The fastest worker in Henry Ford's automobile factory could stamp out a few more components than the next fastest worker, but there were still limits as to what could be achieved. No matter how strong and fast you are, in the linear world the law of diminishing returns kicks in sooner rather than later.

With the brain however, the potential is nearly infinite, at least for our purposes. With practice, it's possible to radically reshape the brain's capabilities. This is known as plasticity, the ability of the brain to change in response to our experiences. Neuroscience has shown that to generate new neural pathways, training should be varied. Doing the same things over and over again has less psychological, and less physiological, impact.

This principle frequently plays itself out in industry. You may gain experience in a specific industry and function, with an initial experience of excitement and learning. After doing the same thing for a long time, however, it becomes repetitive— not easy, but not enriched with true learning. It's not your company's fault—they need to manage this procurement function, or that operational area. Even in situations like this, you can overcome inertia and get inside and beyond your function to learn how it works, why it works, and how it can be improved. For your sanity and your job security, you can enrich the mundane aspects of nearly any job to provide a growth experience, and to generate new neural pathways in the process.

Whatever the job or project requirement, there is a distinction between what you *need* to do, and what you *can* to do to grow. In a consulting context, I refer to this as "thinking beyond the statement of work (SOW)." What does this mean? The SOW—literally, a statement of your work requirements— represents your minimum responsibility. It's what you're hired to do, either as an employee or a consultant on engagement. It is more than a job description, and if you don't have a SOW of some kind, create one. Make sure that you at least fulfill your SOW, as it is a basic requirement of success.

Nonetheless, you can always build on this foundation, doing more than the minimum. You can gather more information, conduct more analyses, develop more insight, and recommend more options. That will certainly be more valuable for your client or manager, and it will also help you to grow as an individual. Importantly, it also reaffirms the empowering principle that you are responsible for your development, and you don't need permission to grow as a professional. Whether as part of formal training or for on-the-job enrichment, you can grow as much as your passion and energy allow. And this growth is ultimately the only thing you can count on as a personal competitive advantage.

Why is all this important? Because the world of work has changed due to the digital revolution. Digital technology has created tremendous mental leverage, whose potential far outstrips that of the physical. Professional skills are amplified both by the impact of content and the digital medium, which can scale rapidly and is less constrained by the friction of the physical world. When an individual is trying to accomplish more physical work, they must lift more, move more, and encounter diminishing returns. In the realm of the mind, there is almost no limit.

This is not only good for media or podcast hosts who reach

millions of listeners. It is relevant for you. Good ideas, properly articulated and communicated, can rapidly strengthen your brand across your company or industry. Whether through blog posts or simply making things happen in the trenches, the potential leverage from your work is much more than you realize, no matter your level in the organization.

This is what makes the digital world of software such a game-changer. Years ago, I worked with several AT&T manufacturing plants. The one in Shreveport, Louisiana employed 3,500 people and made most of the pay phones in the United States. It was an enormous facility, so large that it felt impossible to walk from one end to the other. The big, boxy product they produced was the linchpin of the mobile world for decades. People on the go used payphones and planned their travel around knowing where they could find a payphone. At their peak in the mid-1990s, there were 2.6 million public pay phones in the United States. However, they weren't portable, so anyone looking to make a call in public was forced to hunt for a payphone.

Now consider the mobile device that's almost certainly sitting in your pocket or on the table next to you. Not only is it a fraction of the size of a payphone, its capabilities are thousands of times greater. It is essentially a supercomputer in your pocket. The early "mobile" phone (payphone) went digital, and dematerialized while improving performance exponentially.

The music industry has changed in a similar fashion. Fifty years ago, music was consumed through vinyl. The cassette, eight-track, and then compact disc changed that, and the industry has since gone through yet another revolution. At the press of a few clicks, we can download or stream almost any track we desire. Moreover, the same music can be played by thousands or millions of people simultaneously, with no need for a physical object. Tell that to someone living a hundred years ago, and they would think it magic.

On a smaller scale, you could write a good blog today and wake up tomorrow to find that it has been read by thousands of people. Now that we're in the digital age, the potential leverage of thinking well is far greater than it has ever been. Ten thousand years ago, you might have been a better thinker than me, but if I could run faster, climb more quickly, and throw a spear more accurately than you, you were at a disadvantage. Now, the rules of the game have changed. If you're a better thinker than me, you can leverage that to a huge advantage. The combination of non-linear thinking and digital amplification is incredibly potent. The flip side is that if your thinking and communication are below average, you may be left behind faster than ever.

With the new digital calculus, do we throw away all the old rules? Huge volumes of data, instantaneous communications, and exponential processing power are overwhelming to contemplate. Yet, ironically, the digital age is reaffirming the importance of the age-old concept of critical thinking. Critical thinking comes from the Greek word *kritikos*, meaning to judge. At its heart, critical thinking is about developing insightful analysis, making sound judgments, and acting on those judgments in a self-directed manner. If you work in a professional field, you already know that a lot of your job is about making good judgments.

This seems simple, but it's less common than you may think. As mentioned in the introduction, I conducted a wide-ranging study involving over ten thousand employees, business school students, and university career services leaders, in conjunction with the University of Texas at Dallas. The study found that the vast majority of employers across the United States consider critical thinking to be a primary skill, yet two-thirds of employers believe that students leaving universities aren't adept enough in this crucial skill to thrive in the workplace.

This is not to throw stones at institutes of higher education. The requirements for business education are shifting so rapidly that it's difficult for them to keep up. Universities have long been bastions of higher thinking and evolved their curriculums deliberately to avoid whipsawing students as fads change. In the digital economy, however, employers are raising the bar, because they need more from their new hires. You are responsible for your own education. If you are still a student, make sure you get the best of what your school offers and complement it through independent study. If you're already in the workforce, take full advantage of company programs and develop necessary skills independently.

Critical thinking can help you argue more effectively at work. I'm not talking about arguments over whether your favorite sports team will win the playoffs. This is about arguing in a critical thinking context. More Perry Mason, less Jerry Springer. In other words, this is not the kind of argument that involves two people shouting at each other. In this context, an argument is a claim or statement supported by evidence. Critical thinking is about building a case, not winning a shouting match.

This kind of argument can be about which investment option to fund, how to launch a marketing campaign, who to hire for a vacant position, or how to identify the root cause of a problem. The more important the problem or opportunity, the more vital it is that the conclusion is backed by sound critical thinking. If you think back over your life, I'm sure you can think of many small decisions, and possibly some large ones, that were made based on incorrect assumptions or poor reasoning, or without proper evidence.

FACT, OPINION, AND BELIEF

A good way to view critical thinking is to look for the distinction between fact, opinion, and belief. No doubt you know what a *fact* is. It's a descriptive statement that's verifiably true. The ambient temperature is a fact. The time is a fact. Facts are essential building blocks of any analysis.

The next building block is *opinion*, or its more elegant cousin, inference. An opinion is a judgment based on facts, an honest attempt to draw a reasonable conclusion from factual evidence. We can state opinions about anything, with or without information to back them up. An opinion's value is often proportional to the reputation of the person issuing it. Inference goes beyond a statement of fact to interpret, draw logical conclusions from given data, and project implications from the facts. It contains a viewpoint, but there is more to it. If there are recent torrential rains, I may infer that a nearby field, which is close to a river that regularly floods, is underwater.

The third building block is *belief*. Unlike an opinion, a belief is a conviction based on cultural or personal faith, morality, or values. Beliefs cannot be disproved or even contested in a rational or logical manner. However, they are powerful forces in the minds of the people you are trying to convince, so understand them and the burden of proof necessary to overcome them where they are not based on evidence. Importantly, our own beliefs can diminish sound critical thinking when we allow preconceived notions to get in the way of fact-based analysis. In fact, the word *prejudice* originates from when we *pre-judge* a situation, often to the detriment of others.

We build compelling arguments when we correctly use facts, opinions, and inferences. Keep in mind the old saying that you are entitled to your own opinions, but not your own facts. The pitfall comes when we fail to base our opinions and beliefs closely enough on facts, or when we try to draw inferences and conclusions without reference to facts. When that happens, we risk communicating inaccurately and not making our case. There's nothing wrong with making mistakes. We all make them, and they are great learning opportunities. The problem occurs when they occur because we do not test our ideas and claims against available facts.

To improve your critical thinking, notice when you're using facts or opinions, when your inferences are driven by unexamined belief, and when conclusions are made to accommodate the prevailing sentiment. Once you have the facts, you can build on them and understand them in original ways. Peter Thiel, an exceptionally successful venture capitalist and one of the first investors in PayPal, likes to ask the question, "What is something you know to be true, that no one agrees with you about?" The answers to that question have allowed him to see the world differently, evaluate potential colleagues, and recognize investment opportunities that others do not see. He couldn't do that without being able to identify facts, and having the discipline to act on them. It's unlikely that he'd have been so successful if he made suppositions simply based on what he felt, or unquestioned conventional wisdom.

There is a fundamental question in critical thinking: *How do I know what I think I know, and what evidence do I have to support it?* Building on this foundational question, there are practical ways you can improve your own critical thinking. The next time you're faced with a task that requires analysis, ask yourself the following questions:

- What do I already know?
- What have I assumed?
- What questions can I ask?
- What does this data mean?
- What evidence do I have?
- What are my criteria?

Get into the habit of asking these questions whenever you evaluate data. Keep a journal of your conclusions and note your thoughts, both prior to the exercise and afterwards. Identify the places where your initial ideas have proven correct, along with the places where evidence has disproved your original theory.

After you've done this in several situations, you should start to notice patterns in your thinking. You may find yourself resisting the urge to leap to judgment. If so, you'll be well on the way to developing sound critical thinking. The difference between average and excellent critical thinkers is that they base their arguments on a rock-solid factual foundation.

As you increase your level of responsibility, this approach

will be more and more important. When you stand in front of executives and ask for millions of dollars in funding, you had better be prepared. Your argument must be based upon strong data, not hearsay, rumor, or opinion. The more you practice exercises such as this one, the more quickly you will be able to identify the strengths and weaknesses in any argument. In later chapters, we add additional thinking tools, and also cover the attributes of a strong presentation. For now, it's important to realize how to identify and use facts as the foundation of your thinking.

Too often, knowledge workers rely solely on the tremendous power of their spreadsheets and the volumes of data they run through them. Without effective critical thinking, these tools only allow people to make poor decisions faster, albeit with better graphics. To improve your critical thinking, try an exercise called "Red Team, Green Team." It drives better results through using a combination of negative and positive bias to draw out more comprehensive thinking.

RED TEAM, GREEN TEAM

When your work group has an important decision to make, divide into two teams who will review the situation from opposing viewpoints. The Red Team is charged with the responsibility of putting forward every reason why it's not a good idea to move forward, or how the current approach is flawed. In the case of a big deal, the Red Team focuses on reasons why the deal may fail, and then develops an understanding of what is needed to overcome these issues.

The Green Team takes the opposite approach. They put forward an argument for all the reasons why the proposed project or course of action may succeed, and what needs to happen to take advantage of all the positive potential. Why does this approach work so well? It brings out extreme perspectives on either side. If only one team were evaluating a scenario, they might feel a responsibility to be balanced in their assessments. Red Team, Green Team invites every ounce of positive and negative bias into the open, where it can be effectively considered and evaluated. Note that while "art of the possible" brainstorming is encouraged early in the process, both teams need to converge on plausible outcomes that can be implemented.

This approach also has the advantage of bringing extreme users into the picture. Historically, companies tested their products or concepts for the average user. Visionary product designers, however, seek information about the outliers, the people who use a product much more or much less than the average. What is it about the product that makes it so appealing to those people? Why do non-users avoid it? How could we encourage more people to adopt it like an extreme user?

Even when you're analyzing a situation on your own, you can practice the Red Team, Green Team approach. Simply split the negative and the positive viewpoints into separate cases. Start by examining all the reasons why a proposed course of action could fail. Then consider all the reasons why it could succeed. When you're finished, compare the two sets of evidence. Notice how reasonable it is to use the same facts and yet reach very different conclusions. With both sides of the story, you can consolidate the information and develop a more thorough and compelling approach to making the project or opportunity successful.

Some friends of mine used a similar exercise in law school. On a regular basis, they argued both sides of a case. It's instructive to realize how opinions and beliefs can creep in and allow people to use the same data to reach different, sometimes diametrically opposed conclusions. This is why it is important to base analysis on facts, so there is a solid foundation for recommendations and decision-making.

INDUCTIVE AND DEDUCTIVE REASONING

Although there are several types of reasoning, we'll cover two major types relevant for business: deductive and inductive. Deductive reasoning is familiar to every lover of detective stories. It's what Sherlock Holmes does to crack cases wide open. It requires the creation of a logical chain from premise to conclusion, and it works well in situations where facts are available in abundance or known with certainty. For a chemist observing reactions between two chemicals, or an engineer who knows the characteristics of the surfaces involved, it works well.

Inductive reasoning involves making inferences, often from a small number of observations or data points. When more inputs arrive, they either confirm or refute the original hypothesis. Inductive reasoning works well in situations where data is limited or ambiguous, making it a useful tool for business. A common pitfall I see in business is the use of deductive reasoning in situations where there is no logical chain of events that can be followed with clarity. You've probably heard the phrase, "a chain is only as strong as its weakest link." In deductive reasoning, that's very much the case.

Imagine a presentation as a chain of reasoning. As it begins, you establish your assumptions. Based on those assumptions, you make a case. By the time the presentation concludes, you're asking your audience to take action. Now imagine that one of your original assumptions is flawed. As your presentation progresses, each step may increase the risk that your audience does not buy into your story and accept your recommendation. Each misstep along the path of deductive reasoning could break the chain, losing the confidence of your audience. If your assumptions are wrong and they still believe you, the consequences could even be worse. They may accept your recommendations and make a costly mistake.

In the same scenario, inductive reasoning requires less certainty but more realism. By stating your conclusion early, then providing a few supporting examples and supporting them with evidence, you increase your credibility, while simultaneously allowing yourself more leeway to make mistakes. Making each slide or report section self-contained, it is like creating multiple watertight bulkheads on a ship. Even if one recommendation turns out to be wrong, or one inference doesn't hold up to scrutiny, you won't sink your entire case. Deductive reasoning gets good press because it appears to show how people think, and it can deliver solid conclusions. Inductive reasoning, however, is a better way to construct and communicate a report with findings and recommendations. This is an important point: *deductive reasoning is how people think, but inductive reasoning is how we should communicate that thinking to others.* More on this later.

An example of this distinction might be the purchase of a new software program. With deductive reasoning, you can analyze the multiple vendors involved to determine which scores most highly across several categories. Deductive reasoning will help work through individual analyses and even consolidate the findings into recommendations. However, there is undoubtedly time pressure and limited funding, and speed will be important, so thorough analysis of every possible permutation will not be possible. Quickly identifying what is most important will enable you to go into depth where it matters.

Each software vendor will have advantages and disadvantages. If a detailed, sequential approach is used to create the report, many readers will not make it all the way through the document. Inductive reasoning can communicate the recommendation quickly—that is the goal, after all—and then support it to the extent needed. Additionally, deductive reasoning implies precise answers, but using it in situations where precise answers aren't possible distorts the recommendations and can damage credibility. Inductive reasoning makes it easier to allow for conclusions that acknowledge uncertainty.

Making a persuasive argument is more than using logic. Yes, *logic* is used to develop an argument, making carefully reasoned claims and relying upon evidence. However, *rhetoric* is the use of language and images to persuade. It includes logical reasoning, but it goes beyond logic by incorporating emotion and empathy for others. Rhetoric aids in establishing trust and credibility with an audience.

There are three aspects of rhetoric: logos, pathos, and ethos. *Logos* is the appeal to reason. *Pathos* appeals to feeling or emotion. *Ethos* is based on credibility or trustworthiness. There are entire schools of thought based on these three pillars of persuasion, but for our purposes you can consider this loose analogy: logos as mind, pathos as body, and ethos as soul. This is not some archaic Latin vocabulary quiz about dusty, millennia-old ideas. These elements are the essence of any argument, sales pitch, or proposal made today. And the better you are at engaging with them, the more your ideas will see the light of day and the greater success you will enjoy in your personal and professional life.

How does this work in the real world? In some cases, it may mean infusing communications with messages about social or environmental responsibility. Many people are cynical about businesses, assuming profit is their only motive. When they see evidence that your business has deeper motivations than this quarter's earnings, your messages reach them in a different way. Perhaps your company donates a percentage of its profits to a social cause. When recruiting on campus or giving an introductory presentation about my firm, I highlight the work of our foundation, especially the initiatives which take advantage of a relevant capability, such as analytics or artificial intelligence.

Engaging emotions (pathos) can be as straightforward as creating a personal connection with the people to whom you're presenting. In recent years, the concept of personas has become a staple of business vocabulary. Products are no longer shipped to a vague entity known as "the market" or an average user. They're aimed specifically at Andrea, the stay-at-home mom, or Richard, the manufacturing manager. These personas put a name and a face to potential customers, making them real. True personas include demographics, wants and needs, and behaviors.

Here's an example. Maybe you have an idea that will save your organization money. That's great, but how will it affect people on a personal level? Will it help a worker go home at 6:00 p.m., instead of at 8:00 p.m.? Will it allow one person to do the work of two? If so, that's a tangible benefit. But that is not enough. Workers will appreciate it only if they can see themselves in the solution, and relate the facts to their wants, needs, and behaviors.

In the automotive industry, the current transformation trend is autonomous or self-driving vehicles. CEOs could say they are pursuing autonomous driving to maximize their profits. This is a real goal, but it's hard for the average person to relate to. Volvo Cars, one of our automotive clients, chose to articulate their mission in the following terms: "By 2020, no one will be killed or seriously injured in a new Volvo car or SUV." That is a vision that both individuals and society at large can get behind. Although this target has clear business benefits, the human impact makes it easy for employees, customers, and other road users to relate to and appreciate.

What is credibility (ethos)? It is about trust, and how you create it. This does not mean you must behave like a lawyer in a three-piece suit, speaking in somber tones. You generate trust through what you say, what you do, and your consistency. This is why reputation is so important when working with the same people over time. You want to generate trust? Do what you say you will do, when you say you will do it, consistently. That alone will separate you from the pack. Become very good at something. Show evidence, and demonstrate that you are not trying to mislead your audience. People will associate your depth and expertise in one area with whatever else you have to say.

Some leadership gurus claim that *gravitas* is not relevant anymore, that it refers to an outdated masculine command-and-control approach to communication. This misses the point. *Gravitas*, or presence, allows empowerment, humility, creativity, and other inspirational attributes of modern leadership and persuasion to shine through. The creative spirit is great, but no one buys crazy. Weave a level of credibility while keeping your authentic style, and people will want to believe you.

Sound reasoning is important for critical thinking. Just as important, however, is the avoidance of faulty reasoning. Imagine a scenario in which a presenter claims that, "successful marketing campaigns drive revenue increases, our revenue increased, therefore our campaign drove an increase in revenue." Is it accurate to say that this specific marketing campaign drove the increase in revenue? Not definitively. It may have done so, but there may have also been other reasons for the increase. Perhaps the product is new. Perhaps prices have increased, with no corresponding drop in sales volume.

Faulty reasoning is perhaps most obvious in the political

arena. Politicians are usually keen to attribute improvements in the economy to their policies, while deflecting blame for any negative news. We all do this to some extent, whether explaining why our sports team won or lost, or why we or someone else got a promotion. As a critical thinker in an analytical environment, it's important to go beyond coincidence, seek correlation, and confirm causation only when objectively verified. While it's tempting to provide only the data that confirms an analyst's hunch or the prevailing sentiment of executives, a responsible analyst takes the time to root out bias in their work, and only claim what the facts and data allow.

The *comma effect* is a simple yet deceptively effective tool to increase insight when communicating, especially through reports or presentations. A report always has some purpose, whether it is a lowly status update or a strategic briefing document. Typically, a graphic in a slide describes a series of facts and summarizes them in some way: sales are up, defects are down, or similar. This conveys a message about what happened.

However, it is more interesting to highlight two contrasting points simultaneously. Create a compound sentence divided by a comma, which acts as the pivot point linking the contrasting statements. As an example, "Although sales increased last quarter, cost overruns actually decreased profits." The comma effect introduces contrast into a sentence, converting two interesting facts into a genuine insight. Practice the comma effect frequently, and see how you can combine related phrases to create more insightful statements. Over time, this will become second nature, and you will be able to integrate the comma effect into both conversation and informal writing.

CREATIVE THINKING

Creative thinking is a way of looking at problems or situations from a fresh perspective. Often, it suggests unorthodox solutions, some of which may initially appear unsettling. In a business world of data analysis and report writing, creative thinking is a distinct skill that is more important than ever. People who think creatively bring new things into existence. Creative thinking is a remarkable skill, and it is at the root of new insights and new products. No product was ever launched, no movie ever made, without some level of creative thinking.

Whatever roles we play in life, there's always room to think more creatively. We can inject creativity into our presentations, conduct more effective team events, or learn to program more compelling software code. Even if you feel your job doesn't allow you the freedom to be creative, you can still learn new skills on your own time, nights or weekends. This is a heartening and empowering message. Whatever your situation in life, you have more power than you think.

Don't be constrained by a belief that a job or the economy is somehow stacked against you, or that you lack the resources needed to be successful.

It may seem counterintuitive, but creativity often increases in a constrained environment. We may think that we need more time, or resources, to be creative. In fact, working within constraints brings out creativity, because it challenges people to come up with innovative responses within those constraints.

Paradoxically, the fewer tools and resources we have, the more creative we tend to be. If you're a college student, or you don't have a huge budget to work with, that should give you hope. You can be more creative than a large, well-resourced company. Then, when you *do* gain access to more resources, you'll be able to use them more intelligently than someone who has always had them but never maximized their potential.

WHAT IS CREATIVE THINKING?

Creative thinking is a way of looking at problems from a fresh perspective, which suggests a new, potentially unorthodox, or unexpected solution. It's grounded in the consideration of alternatives. Until we can see alternatives, we can't think creatively. At the heart of creative thinking is imagination; the capacity to understand different ways of seeing, doing, and feeling. The goals of the creative thinker include developing insights, gaining a fresh perspective, and inspiring flexibility of thought and action.

An essential characteristic of creative thinking is an openness to new ideas: the most original thinkers always believe that there is more than one way of doing things, and that there's value in testing out the various available options. Creation implies building something where nothing existed before, and it is a more challenging yet rewarding activity than consumption. In a world of readily available information, it's easy to consume. Creativity, however, asks something more of us. It asks that we engage actively and create something, be that a physical product, a piece of software, or simply a novel idea.

Historically, creativity has been associated far more with art than with business. When most people think of a creative person, they imagine a lone inventor or artist experiencing a moment of inspiration. In most cases, that's not an accurate picture. Thomas Edison may have invented the light bulb, but it took him thousands of iterations. During that time, he was also running a large lab, full of assistants and other workers. Edison received feedback as he developed prototypes of the light bulb, and he continued to improve it until it reached a point of feasibility. Then he took it further still until he made it economically viable. In most cases, creativity is a result of a willingness to experiment and improve, and the intellectual curiosity and persistence to do so.

Following the second Industrial Revolution in the early twentieth century, management became viewed as a science, an equation to be optimized, based on analysis and logic. Henry Ford of Model T assembly line fame was probably its most famous proponent, although other industry leaders like Alfred Sloan at General Motors took a similar approach. By the 1980s, Bob Galvin of Motorola and later Jack Welch at General Electric (GE) achieved great success using the Six Sigma framework of continuous improvement. This was also during a time when Western companies feared the relentless march of Japan Inc. and its kaizen approach of continuous incremental improvement. Again, management was perceived as a science to be optimized. Creativity was not on the executive agenda.

The general perception was that creativity was for writers, painters, and musicians. Real businesspeople relied on analysis. In the 1990s, however, that belief started to shift. Incremental improvement can approach diminishing returns, and then creativity is needed to generate further gains. The emergence and massive success of Apple and other Silicon Valley companies may be the most obvious examples of creativity manifested, but there are many others only a Google search away. Writing this book in 2017, it is clear that creativity has taken its place in the business world as a vital tool for generating improvements. The need for creative thinking has expanded beyond the arts and into everyday business, aided by the ever-increasing necessity of cultivating a distinct brand.

This is true for both individuals and organizations. In a world where everyone has access to information, and where incremental improvements are approaching their limits, creativity has become a distinguishing factor. Developing a product that stands out from competitors demands a high degree of creativity. This is not to say that analysis is easy. It's difficult. The problem is that good quantitative analysis alone is not a differentiating factor when everyone has access to analytical skills, and people in low-cost economies are able and willing to do the same work at far lower rates than those in so-called advanced economies. Creativity becomes a differentiator. And for workers and companies in other economies, creativity can improve their competitive position as well, as their own cost advantage decreases.

Creative thinking often works in conjunction with critical thinking. The archetypes of the artist and the analyst suggest that the two are separate skills, but the consultant of the future needs to see them as complementary. As creativity becomes more embedded in the business world, the half-life of ideas is shrinking. A hundred years ago, the pace of innovation was slower and new innovations could last a decade or more before they were superseded. Even looking back to the late twentieth century, new products or ideas could be expected to lead the market for at least a few years. In 2017, companies such as Amazon make changes to their commerce site—their "product"—every few seconds. Many of these are minor, but the rate of change is so fast that it's virtually constant. No industry can assume that a successful product will still be in demand in its current form in five years. The ability to think creatively is the difference between seeing these realities with fear and viewing them with excitement. It allows people to think of new ideas, take novel approaches, and proactively adapt to change.

While the influx of creative thinking in business is welcome, it shouldn't be forgotten that creativity must be applied to specific objectives. Google is an archetypal example of a company that makes full use of creativity, innovating constantly. Yet, they are also hyper-focused on turning that creativity into results.

Professionals may think of decision-making as a single event that occurs at a point in time. In fact, it is a constant practice, and creativity contributes to improved decision-making. In business circles, it is common to take an advocacy approach to decision-making, in which one person pushes an agenda and a solution that benefits their self-interest. However, it is more effective to utilize a process of creative, unbiased inquiry. This allows people to consider a variety of options and determine a better solution.

Fostering an environment in which creative inquiry can flourish requires that people are committed to embrace diverse perspectives, and through a process of discussion, progressively converge on those that are most suitable. Once feasible alternatives have been considered, the final decision should be sound and more likely to be adopted.

CREATIVE THINKING TECHNIQUES

In this section, we will explore some specific creative thinking techniques and their applications, for use in both a business context and in daily life, and will also cover other aspects of creativity. The first of these is the SCAMPER method.

GENERATING IDEAS USING SCAMPER

SCAMPER is an acronym for an approach to generate ideas. Each of the letters stands for a way to spark creative thought. The examples given are for products. They also apply to processes—simply swap "process" for "product" as necessary.

- S = Substitute. What materials or resources can you substitute or swap to improve the product? How can you substitute your current approach for a different one?
- C = Combine. How can you combine this product with another, to make something new? What information or content can you add?
- A = Adapt. How can you adapt a product to a new environment? How could you readjust this product to serve another customer, at a different level of performance, or another geography?
- M = Modify. How can you take a feature of an idea and

modify or magnify it so that it becomes more important? What could you emphasize or highlight to create more value?

- P = Purpose. How can you identify other possible scenarios and situations where this topic can be used? Who else could use this product? Can you use this product somewhere else, perhaps in another industry?
- E = Eliminate. What can you remove from the idea and still retain value? How could you make it smaller, faster, lighter, or more fun?
- R = Rearrange. How can you change the product through rearranging or reversal, and make it more appealing? How can you evolve a new concept from the original concept?

PARALLEL THINKING AND THE SIX THINKING HATS

Dr. Edward de Bono is widely considered the father of modern creative thinking. He pioneered numerous practical thinking tools, used worldwide in schools and businesses. One of the most famous is the Six Thinking Hats. De Bono understood that arguments can easily become biased or adversarial. This can lead to an ego-driven approach, where the goal is simply to win the argument, not to reach the best solution. To counter this tendency, in the 1980s he codified the Six Thinking Hats technique, which invites people to explore multiple perspectives of a question or problem.

Even in situations where teams share common goals, diverse

thinking styles often hamper the creative process. In effect, the thinking styles intersect or block each other. De Bono developed the concept of parallel thinking, where each team member uses the same thinking style for a period of time, then rotates through a series of thinking styles to capture diverse styles, but doing so in parallel to avoid creative conflict.

The technique helps individuals and groups adopt a variety of perspectives, broadening their thinking and potentially encouraging fresh solutions. Each hat is assigned a different color and refers to a different thinking approach. An individual or a group "wears" each hat in turn, fully exploring the mode of thinking it represents. Then they switch to the next. In a group, each person wears the same hat at the same time, to encourage collaboration and minimize conflict. The six hats are as follows:

The **white hat** is the information hat. It requires the wearer to seek out hard, factual information related to the project or question at hand. Look at the information that you have, analyze past trends, and see what you can learn from it. Look for gaps in your knowledge, and try to either fill them or take account of them. The white hat is objective and implies no judgment of the value of the information.

The **red hat** invites the wearer to focus on their intuition, gut reaction, and emotion. Think how others could react emotionally. Although emotions and intuition aren't easily explainable, feelings play an important role in thinking and decision-making. Seek to understand the responses of people who do not fully know your reasoning.

The **black hat** is for judgment, to look at a decision's potential negative outcomes. It's an opportunity to be critical or skeptical without inhibition, a useful technique to avoid mistakes and guard against excess optimism. This is important because it highlights the weak points in a plan. It allows you to eliminate them, alter them, or prepare contingency plans to counter them.

The **yellow hat** is devoted to benefits. It helps wearers to think positively about potential outcomes, seek the merits of an idea, and reach an optimistic assessment of how it can work. This hat helps maintain momentum and a positive spirit in the face of a challenging situation.

The **green hat** represents creativity. It explores possibilities, alternatives, and new ideas. This hat can be intimidating, because many people tell themselves that they're not creative. Like a muscle, creativity can be developed and strengthened with practice. The green hat gives people a safe space in which to think creatively.

The **blue hat** is the organizing hat. It controls the process of using the other hats and clarifies the objectives. It can also be used to explore the process of implementing an idea. How will it be done? In what sequence will actions need to be taken?

The six hats divide neatly into pairs. The white hat is about information, while the red hat is about emotions. The black hat is negative, while the yellow hat is positive. The green hat encourages creativity, while the blue hat focuses on process. It's worth noting that the black hat and the yellow hat are broadly equivalent to the red team and the green team in the Red Team, Green Team exercise.

This technique sounds simple, but does it really work? Yes, it does. It has been around for decades, but I have used it in several recent situations to generate additional ideas and reach resolutions quickly. I like it, because it is fast and it is possible to use subsets of the method to fit situational needs. From proposal development to project planning, giving each hat its own time and place allows ideas to be quickly shared and heard by the working team.

Is the Six Thinking Hats approach just for business? No. It was used to help millions of people after the 2004 tsunami in Sri Lanka. Relief planners in Sri Lanka after the tsunami used the Six Hats approach to plan and implement reconstruction efforts more effectively. The method was used to generate a shared sense of the major issues in the reconstruction process. It took only twelve hours to get the plan ready and two days to hammer out a detailed and sustainable solution.

The next time your team is faced with a problem you're not sure how to solve, try addressing it from the perspective of the Six Thinking Hats. This can also be done as an individual. Practice this approach on a regular basis, noting the insights you generate as a result. It will help you see situations from multiple perspectives and develop your creative thinking capabilities.

LATERAL THINKING

Lateral thinking is another concept introduced by Dr. de Bono to help overcome our natural proclivity to get locked into preconceived patterns and access creativity on demand. Lateral thinking solves problems through an indirect and creative approach, using reasoning that is not immediately obvious. Critical thinking is primarily concerned with judging the true value of an idea. Lateral thinking helps us move from a known idea to the creation of new ideas.

Lateral thinking is comprised of several thinking tools or habits. Taken together, they form an overall approach. These tools are intended to challenge current thinking, routine patterns, and the status quo. One aspect of lateral thinking is **idea generation**. This is about defining new ideas. Imagine, for example, that you need to create a training program for your department. What training courses do you need? What would they look like? How would they be administered?

There are several types of idea generation tools: **random entry, provocation, challenge, focus, harvesting,** and **treatment.** **Random entry** utilizes unexpected input that takes the mind in new directions, often leading to surprising connections, sometimes between seemingly unrelated pieces of information. **Provocation** is the use of an apparently impossible statement that is used to stimulate new ideas. For example, "A river-located factory must take its water input from downstream of its output." While this seemed impossible when it was first postulated, it eventually became law and helped reduce river pollution.

Challenge is a method of questioning why things are the way they are. It is not about criticizing, it is about understanding and deconstructing the rationale behind decisions and processes. If they are solid, challenging them will confirm their solidity. If not, it will reveal opportunities for improvement. This approach is fundamental to being a professional. Consultants have an obligation to understand the positions of clients and, if necessary, to disagree with them. By way of comparison, think about visiting a doctor. You would not want your doctor to simply agree with your self-diagnosis. You would want them to offer you the benefit of their expertise and their own diagnosis.

Another tool is **focus**. Focus is the application of increased intensity. When we focus, we consciously direct our attention to small matters, avoiding the pitfalls of trying to solve an entire problem at once. If idea generation is about taking an overview and gaining a broad understanding of what is required, focus is about zeroing in on a specific aspect of a problem.

Harvesting tools are intended to ensure that more value is received from idea-generating output. How can we get the greatest return from ideas already generated? For example, perhaps we can sell the same product in new markets, or sell different products to the same customer. **Treatment** tools promote consideration of real-world constraints, resources, and support, adding feasibility to idea generation.

Lateral thinking may sound simple, but it has never been more relevant. In a world of rapid technological innovation, coupled with the convergence of different industries, random input allows us to cast a net a little more widely, and focus helps us access the recesses of our minds, revealing ideas that might otherwise have remained hidden. Provocation and challenge force us to look at situations in fresh ways, confronting our habitual beliefs and assumptions. Harvesting gets more value from the ideas we do have, and treatment makes sure our ideas respect the constraints that will enable adoption.

CONCEPTUAL THINKING

Creative thinking is often conceptual thinking. Conceptual thinking links ideas and allows us to see their similarities. Automobiles, buses, and bicycles, for example, are very different vehicles, but they're all linked by the concept of personal transportation. This is important because, once we identify a concept, we can identify alternative ways of working with that concept. Random input can help us to do this.

Most of us, for example, don't buy cars because we want to own a hunk of metal. We buy them for transport, for status, for comfort, or for other reasons. Similarly, we don't visit coffee shops purely because we want coffee. We can get that more cheaply at home or in the office. We visit for the atmosphere, to meet friends, to use the free Wi-Fi, or for other reasons.

Conceptual thinking allows us to identify the essence or essential component of an idea; the part of it that people value, sometimes called the value proposition. This is a vital skill for professionals and consultants, because it helps us to understand what people are willing to pay for. There are several aspects of an idea, but the essence is the most important.

COGNITIVE HUMILITY

Another aspect of creative thinking is cognitive humility, the understanding that none of us has all the answers and we always have more to learn. It's important to understand this before we make decisions, otherwise those decisions may be based on faulty or partial information. Cognitive humility doesn't necessarily lead to certainty. In some circumstances, understanding leads us to recognize uncertainty and proceed anyway. Failing to recognize uncertainty may place us in a risky position.

Never underestimate the value of failure. It can be a positive force that ultimately liberates future success. We tend to study our failures more than our successes, so they naturally create more learning opportunities. Failure also reinforces humility. I'm not talking here about the "I am so humble to be honored as employee of the year" version of humility, but about genuine humility, based on a desire to learn. We tend to grow in humility after failure, opening us more to feedback. Success can become a trap of its own. We enjoy the experience of success, and that makes us averse to taking risks. We don't want to deviate from the blueprint that has worked for us. Failure and adversity break down those barriers, opening us to new approaches.

Creativity thrives on the possibility of constraint. When we work within scheduling, financial, or other limits, we naturally ask ourselves how we can innovate to make the most of what is available to us. Failure can help us to recognize, accept, and respect our constraints, and to adapt accordingly.

Some phenomena are best understood in pairs, with the relationship between those pairs offering an insight into each individual phenomenon. Light, for example, can only be understood in contrast to darkness. In business, the notion of pairs has often translated into a choice between opposites. In the past, if a company believed that cost and quality had an inverse relationship, they could either seek to drive up quality or to drive down cost, holding the other constant. They could have assumed either that customers were willing to pay for higher quality, or that customers would tolerate lower quality due to low cost.

This dichotomy no longer holds true. In a world immersed in consumer technology, we've come to expect high quality at little or no cost. Companies that provide both high quality *and* low cost are outcompeting those that position themselves at either end of the spectrum.

When we focus on only one aspect of a duality, we tend to limit the potential for creative thinking. Another example is the duality between humanity and technology. We tend to think of them separately, but in fact technology can amplify our humanity, and vice versa. It's becoming increasingly important for companies to ensure their offerings incorporate this human-technology duality, and appeal to our emotions as well as our brains.

One of the most famous examples of transcending duality comes from the original *Star Wars* trilogy. When Luke Skywalker discovers that Darth Vader is his father, he is faced with two options. The first is to join the Dark Side. The second is to be destroyed by it. This turns out to be a false ultimatum. Eventually Luke manages to confront and overcome the darkness within himself, redeeming his father. The robot hand he wears as a replacement for his own symbolizes this duality of human and machine.

IMAGINATION

What is imagination? Long recognized as an important feature of our personal lives, it is equally important in our business lives. Albert Einstein famously said that "imagination is more important than knowledge." In a world where information is becoming ubiquitous, those words ring truer than ever.

Imagination is an engine that drives creative thinking. We are all born with imagination in abundance, yet it is a capability that we too often ignore as we get older and allow to atrophy. Why is that? Most of us go through years of formal schooling, during which we are taught that analysis and data are more important than imagination. In the United States, we work with highly developed technologies, but we're seldom taught to apply imagination to our work. Technological change has made basic technological literacy a necessity to function, but it can't replace imagination. Even artificial intelligence, at least for the foreseeable future, requires creativity to set up and frame its powerful capabilities. We need imagination to bring fresh perspectives to the problems we face.

How can we increase our imagination? There are several techniques readily available to everyone.

Notice deeply. This is a practice of using careful observation to experience the world around us. It opens us up to layers of meaning that might otherwise be ignored. When augmented by note taking, our minds make connections that are not obvious at first glance.

Embody. As adults, we are used to experiencing products, objects, and ideas intellectually. Over time we lose our original childlike sense of wonder and emotion. When we embody, we experience things through senses and emotions, through physical and psychological engagement.

Question. When we question, we begin to explore our world. To spark the imagination, try asking questions like "what if?" or "how might we?"

Make connections. We can connect what we see to our knowledge and previous experiences, identify relationships between details, link them together, and group them into patterns.

Empathy. Empathy helps us to understand the experiences of others, both intellectually and emotionally. When we empathize with others, we can respect the diversity of their perspectives.

Embrace ambiguity. Many workplace issues can be interpreted in more than one way. There is often no single, certain solution, at least not initially. When we embrace ambiguity, we can be patient with uncertainty and work through it.

Create meaning. We all need to feel that information *means* something. When we give meaning to content, we make it easier to relate to, understand, and act upon.

Take action. To implement new ideas and behaviors, it's important to do more than talk about them. We need to take action that stretches our capabilities, without overwhelming ourselves. Somewhere between too easy and too difficult is a sweet spot where we can learn, develop, and grow without succumbing to boredom or stress.

Reflect and assess. Between activities, it is useful to take time to reflect and consider what we've learned. This allows us to develop as thinkers and prevents us from repeating mistakes.

OVERCOMING CREATIVE ROADBLOCKS

What are the best ways to overcome creative roadblocks? Have you ever had a brilliant idea that you were excited to explore? And have you ever experienced the frustration of hitting a roadblock after pouring hours and hours into your idea, and wondering whether all your effort will be wasted?

Every creative person knows this experience. Typically, the sequence looks like this:

- You have a moment of inspiration.

- You dedicate every spare moment to making your idea a reality.

- You keep your idea in the back of your mind, even when you're working on other projects.

- A few weeks down the track, you encounter a roadblock you can't overcome.

- Your enthusiasm gradually wanes, and your idea never comes to fruition.

It's an exhausting and frustrating process. However, it's also unnecessary. No two businesses are the same, and no two problems are identical, so the work of a consultant requires me to constantly generate and execute new ideas. To do this successfully, it's essential that I overcome creative roadblocks. This repeatable process is a simple yet effective way to do that, which you can use whenever you start to struggle.

Give your imagination space to work. A starting point to do this is to eliminate distractions. You can raise your imagination quotient simply by cultivating silence. A blinking phone or a TV blaring in the background will prevent you from reaching into the deeper recesses of your mind, whereas sitting in silence will allow space for inspiration to express itself. Failing this, soothing background music or a movie that you know extremely well can act as "white noise," creating a buffer against random noises and visual distractions.

Cal Newport, in his phenomenal book, *Deep Work*, says:

"If you keep interrupting your evening to check and respond to email, or put aside a few hours after dinner to catch up on an approaching deadline, you're robbing your directed attention centers of the uninterrupted rest they need for restoration. Even if these work dashes consume only a small amount of time, they prevent you from reaching the levels of deeper relaxation in which attention restoration can occur. Aim for times when your energy is high and you can focus for an extended period of time."

In my work with clients, I've found that "context switching" severely affects creative and productive work. Engineers who were deep in thought and suddenly received an email notification lost as much as twenty minutes before they rediscovered their flow.

Use empathy to avoid obstacles. Approach problems as though they are cases. The first step is to determine whether you're working on a puzzle or mystery. Puzzles are known problems requiring a solution, and adhere to standard equations and practices. Mysteries are ambiguous problem spaces with a general goal, novel situations where the problem itself is not known. If you jump into problem-solving mode before you have diagnosed the issue, you run the risk of finding a great answer to the wrong problem. Here's a practical approach to using empathy.

- *Who*—identify the players involved

- *What*—understand the context and situation

- *Why*—understand their motivations

Identifying the *who* is the first step, because we solve problems for people, and it is through people that the real context emerges. If other people are involved, walk in their shoes to understand what they are thinking and feeling. Assess and reflect to identify what is happening beneath the surface.

The fact that you are trying to solve a problem suggests that there is no easy answer, otherwise it would already have been solved. When clients hire me and my firm, it is because their problem is difficult, ambiguous, and fraught with organizational implications. They have a need or a broad goal, but they aren't 100 percent clear about what they want, or how to meet their needs. The *what* is about context and how stakeholders see a situation. The *why* is their wants and needs, and the impact of their biases. Empathy is critical to ensure you don't start down a path without understanding the people and factors that affect their behavior. Empathy invites familiarity, and that avoids or overcomes roadblocks.

Test your hypothesis with a 90/10 approach. Once you understand the situation and the people involved, formulate a hypothesis. This is straightforward: identify the problem, construct an educated estimate, identify major variables, ask questions, and identify patterns and connections. Testing your hypothesis is a trickier proposition. It can be tempting to expend a lot of effort to analyze a plausible yet flawed hypothesis before testing to see whether it's valid, or—even worse—to make the available data fit the intended narrative. Instead, create a hypothesis and test it using a 90/10 approach. Take an idea 10 percent of the way to completion, then test it. If it doesn't make sense, quickly dismiss it. Repeat this process until an idea seems to have promise, then invest more time in it. The 90/10 principle is a lot like the Pareto Principle, which states that 20 percent of the input is responsible for 80 percent of the results achieved. An example of this is that 80 percent of a company's sales will come from 20 percent of its salespeople. The 90/10 principle is a derivative of this concept, prioritizing earlier and more ruthlessly to identify and then develop the inputs which will generate the vast majority of results.

Be confident in your conclusion. Once you've tested your hypothesis and reached a conclusion, be willing to take a stand. You may be wrong, especially if you are early in a project, but standing behind your conclusion enables you to prove it right or wrong. People often include caveats and "weasel words," such as *arguably* and *conceivably*. This is ambiguous doublespeak that appears safe and covers the broadest set of outcomes possible. These phrases are useful and may be necessary at the end of a formal report, but they have no place in early conclusions. The clearer the conclusion, the easier it is to test, learn from, and improve.

Creative confidence, in the words of innovator Ben Grossman-Kahn, is "having the freedom and courage to fail or take creative risks and the knowledge that all of the ideas you create have value."

This confidence extends throughout the entire creative process. Generating a hypothesis requires courage and confidence. To push yourself toward the best possible conclusion, you must have confidence in your ability to draw insights. However, complement this confidence with self-awareness. Approach problems with the confidence that you will solve them, but also with the expectation that you will learn something new in the process. As Tom Kelley, IDEO founder and co-author of the book *Creative Confidence*, says, "No matter how high you rise in your career, no matter how much expertise you gain, you still need to keep your knowledge and your insights refreshed. Otherwise, you may develop a false confidence in what you already 'know' that might lead you to the wrong decision."

This process can literally save lives. Tommy Thompson was a client of mine who produced high-tech medical products for open-heart surgery and other long-term implantables. He was CEO at Quest Medical, and an energetic inventor and innovator. Tommy attempted to solve a vexing problem: how to keep the human heart healthy during open heart surgery, or a cardioplegia delivery system, as it is formally known. The existing method only allowed for a brief window of safe operation and was therefore risky. He and his product team worked diligently on this problem and developed most of the required technology. However, they hit the metaphorical brick wall with the question of how to increase the device's effective duration. He stepped back and looked more broadly for inspiration. A few days later, he was driving in a light rain. He activated the windshield wipers on the intermittent setting, and unconsciously began to visualize how it accomplished the task through timed pulses. Tommy then made the connection with his own product, raced off to the lab, and worked through the details with his team. This insight solved a critical design problem, even though the products themselves had little in common.

He implemented the equivalent intermittent pulsating mechanism into his product, allowing surgeons to keep a heart healthy much longer during an operation, with less sensitivity to fluid input. This innovation helped save many lives. Tommy had tested and tested, yet when he stepped back and enabled his imagination to work, it helped him overcome a creative roadblock.

The next time you're faced with a challenge, try this process and find out how it can work for you. Discover your *Who-What-Why*, find a quiet state, test your hypotheses, take a confident stand, and see what happens.

CREATE A PHYSICAL ENVIRONMENT THAT AIDS CREATIVE THINKING

How can we create a space that enables us to do our best creative work? Our environment has a considerable impact on our state of mind. It's important to keep in mind the purpose for the space. We want it to be functional. To demonstrate your work easily, you need your environment to be clean and your work accessible. Consider the metaphor of the carpenter's workshop. You would not expect everything in a carpentry workshop to be neat and complete. You would see prototypes, ideas, and sketches. If you want an environment in which you can do creative work, think in similar terms. Accept that you may be working on several different projects and several different ideas at any given time. Allow unfinished models and ideas to inhabit your environment and spark your creativity.

In an office, you share your space with other people. How do you make it more creative? There are a few basics, like furniture choice and strong Wi-Fi connectivity. You need individual work spaces, along with quiet places for people to reflect. Allocate an area for formal meetings. Seek decorative elements, such as posters or paintings on the wall, to inspire creativity and foster a pleasant environment. The more senses you can engage, the better. A rule that I've found to be helpful is that you'll want twice the space you think you need. Why? More space gives you more opportunity to move around. It helps you to think and work from a broader perspective. This flies in the face of traditional facilities management logic, because industrial engineering efficiency formulas show that more people per square foot is less expensive and therefore better. However, there can be common ground here, as flexibility creates options that save the overall space required.

A good space for creative work is flexible. Things change frequently, so be willing to adapt. Tables and chairs should not be anchored in one position. If they are on wheels to enable easy movement, so much the better. You can use moveable partitions as interior walls, so that the space can easily be opened up or closed off. White boards cannot only aid group discussions, they can serve as temporary walls if on wheels.

Several years ago, I changed my own studio space at home. Early in my career I used a formal desk, which was the classic rectangle, lots of drawers and anchored in place. I got rid of that and shifted to a semicircle shaped desk, wood-topped, with iron legs, a mix of classic design and modern utility. Incidentally, it was designed by futurist Faith Popcorn, whose BrainReserve research firm boasts a 95 percent hit rate on predicting consumer trends. She hit the mark with this desk, incorporating creative thinking into the age-old desk before it became a trend. At this new desk, I feel as though I'm sitting in a command center. I added casters, so I can move the desk and other pieces of furniture, giving me the capacity to swiftly reshape the room. None of these innovations were expensive, and they significantly altered my relationship with the space. And they are fun. Try this in your own space—when you free the objects, you free your mind.

Another aspect of designing a space for creativity is that the present is given priority over the absent. What does this mean? At Infosys, leaders don't have an office. They may command the most important conference rooms, but they are not there to take up space. They travel frequently and meet with clients. If they're not using an office regularly, there's little value in holding it for them. This policy enables us to make more of the space we *do* have. Look back a few decades, and you'll see that space was usually considered private by default. Individuals had their own offices with clear delineations of power. There were only a few public areas, such as water coolers and break rooms, and yet those were the places where most communication occurred.

This has changed. The best modern spaces are public by default and private by choice. This encourages a free flow of information, while still allowing people to find spaces in which to relax, think, or connect one-to-one. Some businesses have been following this approach for a long time. In Wall Street, for example, trading desks are typically situated right on the trading floor, with the senior trader in the middle. A client of mine operated a similar system. He was a senior vice president, yet his desk was in the middle of the action. Whenever something important emerged, he was immediately aware and able to contribute.

Some people are unsettled by this approach. They want their own desk. They want distance and privacy. Culturally, flattening hierarchies and making senior people accessible implicitly gives junior colleagues permission to be more vocal. This shift in office design is not universal, and every company is in a different place in the journey. I worked with an automotive client in Shanghai, with a beautiful office on an upper floor in a coveted downtown location. We had just delivered a successful innovation workshop, which included several large hand-drawn posters that illustrated the client's digital roadmap. However, the participants weren't allowed to display the posters in their office, because the company facilities' team was concerned about appearing "professional." So, the office walls remained adorned with corporate pseudo-art, while the creative inspiration of their people was rolled up in the corner.

Work used to be perceived by many as drudgery. In the twenty-first century, we can redefine that. Why do you go to coffee shops? Museums? Parks? What is it about them that makes you feel comfortable and creative? There's no reason why your own work environments shouldn't share some of those creative features. By the same token, why not include touches that make you feel as though you're in a familiar space? The outdoors is a tonic for the soul, and personally meaningful art is inspirational as well. In my studio and library, I have a view of trees, plus musical instruments and prints by local artists from my favorite places around the world. You might have an easel, instrument, or something else that inspires you to reach a creative state of mind. It can be anything that is meaningful to you.

All things being equal, people will be more effective when they enjoy their work and they feel comfortable in their working environment. The more you like your working environment, the more willing you will be to invest yourself into it, and to inspire others to do the same.

CRITICAL AND CREATIVE THINKING IN SERVICE OF COMMUNICATION

Critical and creative thinking are foundational skills in business. Even after you have learned these basics, it's a good idea to revisit them periodically. With the rapid pace of change, it is easy to forget these foundational elements.

Most people never really learn these skills, and those who do seldom take conscious steps to keep them strong. If you cultivate and refresh them, you will have an advantage over those who do not. In addition, excelling at critical thinking and creative thinking will allow you to express more of your humanity, relating to people and information in a more meaningful and insightful way. In a technological world, critical and creative thinking have a key role to allow us to sustain and develop our humanity.

Critical and creative thinking may be important skills on their own, but they become even more valuable when they're used in the service of communication. The following chapter focuses on oral communication, while Chapter Four covers written communication.

CHAPTER THREE

ORAL COMMUNICATION

"First learn the meaning of what you say, and then speak."

—EPICTETUS, GREEK PHILOSOPHER

In 1995, I was working with Haggar Clothing Company, a leading apparel company based in Dallas. At 9:00 p.m. on the evening of Friday, May 5—yes, *Cinco de Mayo*—their main distribution building was hit by a major storm, resulting in flooding and collapse. The disaster killed two employees and ruined a hundred thousand pieces of clothing inventory. I was lucky to escape, leaving the building only thirty minutes prior to the roof's collapse.

While the event was both a tragedy on a human level and a massive setback to the company, I was amazed by the speed and focus with which company leaders rallied. They communicated clearly and compassionately with employees, partners, and the market. They emphasized the importance of the human element, using a variety of forums: in-person meetings, all-hands calls, and press conferences. Their communication tone was authentic, and they succeeded in retaining the support of their employees and the respect of the community. This allowed Haggar Clothing to get back on its feet and swiftly return to prior performance levels.

The content of the messages was only part of the company's communications. The combination of facts, empathy, and a willingness to listen to employees created an overall message that genuinely met the needs of the people whose lives were affected by the storm. While the company acknowledged the business impact, they did not dwell on or over-emphasize this element. I was proud to serve them and felt part of something larger than simply a clothing brand.

In this case, a deeply negative situation brought out the best in the company leaders. It would be a mistake to assume that communication is only important in crises. We each communicate daily with colleagues, partners, and clients. The way we do this shapes our relationships and our career success. Rarely is our communication as high-stakes as in the above example, but it always matters.

In the famous words of John Donne, "no man is an island." We are all connected. This is even more true today than it was when he penned that phrase in the seventeenth century.

Everything we do is with, through, or for others. No matter how intelligent we are or how hard we work, our potential for success is proportional to our ability to communicate.

What are the fundamental components of communication? In a business context, the primary objective is to convey information or to persuade. Therefore, effective communication should be focused on the audience, not the speaker. Communicating effectively is not simply a matter of mastering specific techniques. It is about maximizing the recipient's understanding. To communicate effectively, be audience-centric.

One way of visualizing this is to think about a pipe of comprehension. Imagine that there's a pipe between you and the person with whom you're communicating. If you're communicating with multiple people, imagine multiple pipes, each tailored to the unique preferences of each individual. Your job as a communicator is to open those pipes as wide as possible, enabling your audience to receive the full content of your message as quickly and clearly as possible. What does this mean? Primarily, it means that your communications must be designed for the benefit of your receivers, not your own.

This basic premise is the fundamental guideline for everything a good communicator does. This doesn't mean that you abdicate self-interest entirely. You may be employed in a sales or negotiations role, but you still need to address communications from the perspective of your audience. What do *they* need?

COMMUNICATION IS A LEARNABLE SKILL

Many people believe that good communication is a gift, given only to the charismatic. It's not: it is a skill that can be developed and learned. This essential insight is good news. People with highly extroverted personalities may be good at getting up on stage and speaking their minds, but that doesn't make them good communicators. A more introverted person who delivers a thoughtful, considered communication aimed at delivering real value may influence an audience far more than a brash, overconfident person who doesn't take the time to understand the needs of their audience.

Good communicators are prepared. They put in the time to understand the people they want to reach, then address their specific needs. If you're not naturally comfortable in the spotlight, don't be discouraged. It doesn't take a naturally charismatic person to do this. You may not be eager to speak, but if you genuinely have something to say, that shouldn't prevent you from becoming an effective oral communicator.

The word "communication" is based on the Latin word *communicare*, meaning to share. Good communication is a form of sharing. When you're thinking of another person, you might give them a gift to show consideration for their needs. At its best, oral communication can be like a gift to the receiver, conveyed either in person or through digital means. Each channel has its own challenges and advantages. On an audio conference, for example, speakers can't see each other's faces, but on the other hand participants can refer to prepared documents without worrying about losing eye contact.

As an engineer, I'm familiar with the concept of the signal and the noise. In oral communication, the message you wish to transmit is the signal. Everything else is the noise. This noise may be natural. It could be poor lighting or acoustics, crackly telephone reception, or side conversations taking place during a presentation. The greater the noise, the lower the chances of an audience receiving and interpreting a message as you intended it. The goal of good communication is to maximize the signal-to-noise ratio.

COMMUNICATION CHANNELS

Let's break down the six channels we use to communicate and discuss how they're used. They are: **verbal, vocalics, chronemics, kinesics, proxemics**, and **haptics**. These terms might sound confusing at first, but each one relates to a commonly understood concept and allows us to focus on a specific attribute of communication.

Verbal communication is the most familiar, relating to the actual words we use to communicate. Words are important, especially in situations where other elements of communication are limited, but they are far from the whole story. Keep in mind the complexity that different languages create, especially if one speaker is using a second language, in which they are less precise with their wording.

Vocalics, also known as paralanguage, is an important form of non-verbal communication. When you give a presentation, the audience will ask themselves whether they can trust you and believe what you're saying. They'll assess how well you hold their attention, possibly in the face of distractions. This is where the pitch of your voice plays an important role. Varying your tone is important, because a monotone becomes boring quickly. The more engaged your recipient, the wider the pipe of comprehension between you and them.

Chronemics refers to the role of time in communication. The pace and cadence of your voice convey important information. The ability to pause, for example, can greatly increase understanding and retention of key points. A pause allows the audience to think about what they've just heard and to formulate ideas about what comes next, renewing and reinvigorating their attention. We all understand the value of a "pregnant pause"—literally a pause that promises the birth of a valuable concept or idea.

Time flows differently for speakers and recipients. What may feel like a long time to a speaker may be only an instant to a recipient. For this reason, many speakers underestimate the value of pauses. In addition to giving speakers an opportunity to organize their thoughts, pauses convey confidence and elevate the *gravitas* and eloquence of a speaker.

Kinesics is physical activity. During in-person discussions, bodily movement can significantly contribute to or detract from the message impact. Gestures such as moving the arms or pointing can emphasize an important point. On the other hand, nervous or uncontrolled movements can indicate that the speaker lacks confidence in their message, confusing or distracting their audience.

Proxemics, from the word "proximity," is another non-verbal channel. Like kinesics, it's a physical way of supporting the verbal content of a message, in this case with the use of space. You've probably seen presenters who wander haphazardly across the stage when speaking, perhaps even withdrawing somewhat when making key points. To an audience, this approach indicates a lack of confidence and perhaps authenticity.

By contrast, picture a speaker who makes a small yet decisive forward step when making a key point. Also, imagine a speaker giving a presentation mostly from behind a podium, but stepping forward at crucial points and to respond to questions. These small moves add impact to the message in ways that words simply cannot.

Finally, **haptics** is the role of touch in communication. In a business context, it's important to exercise care when using haptics, especially when working across cultures and with unfamiliar people. Nonetheless, there are situations in which touch is important. Shaking hands may be the most obvious example, but there are others. Presenting others with business cards or documents may require contact. Physical props, such as a prototype or model to be passed around a meeting, can also engage participants' sense of touch.

Cultural differences also play a role here. In Japan, it's traditional to present business cards formally, with both hands holding the card and a slight bow. In other cultures, this might appear contrived. While haptics may appear to be minor, they can be powerful and it would be a mistake to dismiss them. Dr. Albert Mehrabian, a former professor of psychology at the University of California, Los Angeles, conducted a famous study in which he found that only 7 percent of a message was conveyed through words. In his study, 38 percent of a message was attributed to vocalics or tone, while the remaining 55 percent came from physical factors such as body language and touch. While this study was situation-specific (women, in informal settings) and sometimes misquoted, the point is that non-verbal factors, including touch, have a significant impact on oral communication effectiveness.

SPECIFIC COMMUNICATION TOOLS AND PITFALLS

We've discussed some of the principles of good oral communication. Now let's explore some specific approaches that can improve your oral communication skills and some problems that you will likely face along the way. The first is to prepare for uncertainty.

In a technological world, we have come to rely heavily on our tools. When they fail, all hell can break loose. You may have a collaboration document to share in a meeting, but what if the collaboration software fails and you need to email it at short notice? In a major presentation, what happens if the projector stops working? Are you prepared? Make sure that you can convey your points verbally, even if you're unable to share a polished document. Written communication is important, but person-to-person interaction is where connection ultimately occurs.

People are also unpredictable and represent another important reason to prepare for uncertainty. For an hour-long meeting, should you create an hour's worth of content? Yes and no. Yes, in that you should be able to address the topic in-depth. However, you need to anticipate the possibility that an important participant will show up late or leave early, so allow time to address the questions you hope your presentation will generate. The goal is to communicate effectively, not to speak for sixty minutes. Know your objective, and be flexible to make your presentation a productive experience for your audience. When you prepare for uncertainty and deliver with empathy, dialed into your audience, you may be surprised to find that only a fraction of the allotted time is needed to accomplish your objective.

Excessive use of jargon is a common mistake made by junior professionals—and some not-so-junior ones as well. We typically hire consultants with high grade point averages, notable extracurricular activities and relevant internships. They're eager to show what they know and to impress their senior colleagues and clients. This leads to them falling into the trap of using jargon excessively. The words might be trendy, but they may sound out of context and come across as hollow. This does not help listeners understand their message and fails to establish their reputation as communicators. If you've ever seen the *Charlie Brown* cartoons, you are familiar with the teacher whose voice blares out across the classroom, uttering incomprehensible words ("mwa-mwa-mwa"). The compulsive user of jargon risks being perceived in a similar fashion.

Many people use jargon as if to demonstrate they are part of an exclusive club. At best, it is a hollow attempt to project expertise. A cynical interpretation of this approach is that it's a way to shield practitioners from competition, perpetuating a sense of mystique around their area of expertise and safeguarding their job security. Those who have the courage to resist the use of jargon stand out from the pack. Tempting though it can be to use jargon, it is better for professionals to communicate through words which convey content, as clearly and simply as possible. Jargon might work for some occupations, but not for business professionals.

It may not be obvious, but the effectiveness of a business professional is proportional to the communication and adoption of their ideas by others. This contrasts with professions such as medicine and law, along with technical trades such as plumbing. In these fields, when skills are revealed to the public, their value is reduced—if you knew how to diagnose the illness, or to fix the leaky faucet, you might do so yourself. In business, the ability to communicate effectively is part of the value delivered by a professional, so better communication equals better results.

One way to measure this is to think of a professional as someone who understands their material so well that they can explain a complex topic in simple words. Imagine discussing one of your projects with your grandmother or school-aged nephew. Could you explain it to them? This is also known as the Feynman Technique, named for iconic physicist Richard Feynman. You project expertise more effectively when you can speak plainly about an abstract topic, describing context and relevance and avoiding an overreliance on buzzwords. This is not to say you should avoid industry-specific words where they are needed, only that you should avoid forcing them into the conversation in a misplaced effort to sound knowledgeable or experienced.

A corollary of jargon is the acronym, an abbreviation composed of the initial letters of other words and pronounced as a word. These are particularly prevalent in government, military, and scientific settings. Sometimes acronyms are useful. Would you rather say, "sound navigation radar" or SONAR? "Automated teller machine" or "ATM"? The problem arises when acronyms constrain comprehension, excluding those who don't understand them.

On these occasions, acronyms obscure meaning, requiring audiences to exert additional cognitive energy to decode them. They may be unwilling to do this and tune out, causing the pipe of comprehension to shrink, leading to unproductive communication. For example, say "business process re-engineering" instead of "BPR." If nothing else, the phrase invites increased engagement, allowing more time for listeners to absorb and understand your meaning.

There are dozens of buzzwords that are common in professional circles, yet usually are best avoided. Here's a selection:

seamless integration throw under the bus ducks in a row
incentivize net-net PUSH THE ENVELOPE seismic shift
turnkey as per forward initiative impactful on the same page
pursuant to UNDER THE RADAR at the end of the day
going forward kick the can down the road operationalize
putting lipstick on a pig strategic alliance utilization, utilize
BACK OF THE ENVELOPE bandwidth go rogue let's do lunch
optimize recontextualize strategic dynamism value-added
BRING OUR A GAME client-centered guesstimate
let's take this offline level the playing field out of pocket repurpose
verbage COME-TO-JESUS harvesting efficiencies leverage, vb.
paradigm shift rightsized synergy where the rubber meets the road
core competency HIT THE GROUND RUNNING liaise parameters
sacred cow think outside the box win-win CYA impact (verb)
MISSION-CRITICAL scalable throw it against the wall and see if it sticks
results-driven socialize best of breed

How many of these words do you use on a regular basis? How
can you make your speech clearer and plainer?

Here's an example of a paragraph that's riddled with buzzwords, to give you a clear sense of how confusing they can be:

> *Bring to the table win-win survival strategies to ensure pro-*
> *active domination. Leverage agile frameworks to provide a*
> *robust synopsis for high-level overviews. Iterative approaches*
> *to corporate strategy, foster collaborative thinking to fur-*
> *ther the overall value proposition. At the end of the day,*
> *going forward, a new normal that has evolved from Gen-*
> *eration X is on the runway heading toward a streamlined*

cloud solution. Override the digital divide with additional click-throughs from DevOps. Organically grow the holistic world view of disruptive innovation via workplace diversity and empowerment.

Here is the same message, stripped of buzzwords and simplified:

Create a strategy to succeed before we fall behind. Use flexible approaches that can be communicated clearly and concisely. The younger workforce will embrace new technologies, and this will help overcome problems experienced in our software development operations. This combination of fresh thinking and experience will help our company thrive in an environment of rapid change.

This example is an exaggeration, but makes the point. Simple, specific words communicate more effectively than large ones with ambiguous and convoluted meanings. It's easy to believe that long, complicated words make you sound smart, but do they make it easy for your audience to understand your meaning? Using short, readily understood words does this more effectively, because they require little to no effort to decode on the part of your audience. This also means that when you *do* use longer words, they resonate more strongly and are remembered.

Former British prime minister Winston Churchill was a

highly skilled orator who understood this principle exceptionally well. He chose his words carefully, wanting to convey specific messages from the literal words and what they conveyed, even using word length as a tool. When he needed to reach many people with a communication, he preferred words with only one or two syllables.

Churchill is famous for his speeches during World War II, and these talks inspired his compatriots to extraordinary acts of bravery. His use of short words, coupled with other rhetorical skills such as repetition, conveyed the gravity of the situation he was describing while also creating a sense of possibility and potential. His word choices were also enhanced by other aspects of his oral communication. His use of pauses, for example, held audiences' attention and communicated a level of certainty and confidence that radiated throughout the nation, and indeed the world.

This approach enabled Churchill to speak to broad segments of the population, including Britons from all walks of life and citizens of allied countries for whom English may not have been a first language. His famous speech, in which he says that Britons, "shall fight on the beaches, we shall fight on the landing grounds, we shall fight in the fields and in the streets, we shall fight in the hills; we shall never surrender," contains hardly a word of more than two syllables.

Instead of hiding behind buzzwords and jargon, be bold.

There's no need to be afraid of saying what you mean. Weasel words may appear safe, but they communicate little or nothing. It's better to take a stand, discover that you're wrong, and change approach, than to avoid making a definitive statement.

Admittedly, this can be a challenge in the corporate world. Firms may say that they want individuality and uniqueness, but they push consistency and standards. Templates are good to enable productivity and scale, but they don't encourage originality in communication. They make good aids, but they can also rob messages of spark and excitement. The template overwhelms, the message becomes forgettable, and the messenger fades into the background.

To counter this tendency, try a hybrid approach. Use templates as a starting point, but keep the experience of your audience and your objectives at the top of your mind. Understand your audience, define the problem statements, and make your message compelling and uniquely your own.

A HUMAN, SPEAKING TO HUMANS

Another way to overcome the pitfalls of standardization and sameness is through intentional imperfection. This may sound counterintuitive, so allow me to explain. Imperfection is not about injecting typographical errors and factual inconsistencies into your work. It is about avoiding sterility and striving for connection instead of perfection. Most people can create a professional-looking presentation. If you want your message to be memorable, you also need to showcase your humanity.

For example, consider the difference between reading from a prepared script and working from a set of talking points. The former option may limit mistakes, but it also runs the risk of coming across as dry and disengaged. Taking the latter option shows that you trust your understanding of the material and that you care about the experience of your audience. It also helps you to interpret the mood of the room, adjust your delivery, and respond to feedback or questions.

Being human means being authentic. I've already said this, and I repeat it throughout the book. Don't be a robot. Communicate what truly matters to you, and allow your fear to be replaced with a genuine desire to tell your story. There was a time when checking your personality and humanity at the door was acceptable and even preferred in the workplace. No longer. Clients and colleagues expect the same kind of experience in their business communications as in their personal ones. A sterile and uninspiring message will not convert listeners to your ideas, even if it is factually correct.

As professionals, it is important that we take our roles seriously, but not ourselves. Inject some levity or contrast to the message, lest it become dark or monotonous. If you are naturally funny, that's great, and you can use humor as a competitive weapon. My daughter Terri Lynn is extremely intelligent and she can take mundane topics and liven them up effortlessly with humor. On the other hand, you do not need to be a stand-up comedian. You can still enrich and invigorate your message simply by bringing your personality and a lively sense of engagement.

With proper preparation and rehearsal, you will gain confidence and start to own your material. When you're confident, you will find that there's more opportunity for anecdotes and small jokes to emerge. One way to do this is to relate current events to the topic at hand. Perhaps you can pick up on a foible of your company, or a well-known annoyance such as a poor corporate computer system.

Personally, I have no comic abilities, yet I have learned to do this to an extent. One of your secret weapons here is to use self-deprecation. In a politically correct world, there may not be many things you can make fun of, but yourself is one of them. Again, this is not easy in a world that wants perfection, but it's important to practice vulnerability. It took me a long time to reach this point, and professionals who embrace this early in their career have a distinct advantage. The only true north is to be authentic and empathetic, and use those qualities as guides in your communications.

Email is an exceptionally useful communication medium, but

it can also be a way of avoiding human connection. Instead of always relying on email, pick up the phone on higher-value communications and speak to the person you want to reach. You will both get more from the conversation. In a world where email is the norm, engaging with people one-to-one will help you stand out.

A word on texting. It has become to email what email was to earlier communication—even shorter, and even faster. On the one hand, this is awesome and highly productive, and works perfectly for low-impact acknowledgments like, "be there in five." On the other hand, a handful of words or an emoji cannot be relied upon to fully convey a message. Texting represents the lowest amount of effort possible to communicate with another person, the least you can invest into a discussion. Is this what you intend to convey, that you are doing as little as possible to communicate with your colleague? Being a little less productive, and a little more expressive, can be more rewarding and accomplish your goal more effectively, which should ultimately be the definition of productivity anyway.

We frequently communicate to persuade. In a sales situation, you may be tempted to aggressively push your position, product or service, but a different approach can help you to stand out, especially in the world of consulting. You sell most effectively through credibility, which is why it's important to build a fact-based case for your position. Highlight both pros and cons, the negative or contrary aspects of a situation. You will appear more balanced than you would if you simply presented the positives. If there's an unspoken negative element, the audience is probably aware of it anyway. Bring it out into the open and mitigate it to the extent possible. This allows you to proactively explain how you will overcome negative elements, in your own words. Don't allow them to go unaddressed, or your audience will fill in the blanks, in a less favorable way.

This will boost your credibility, because it conveys that you're aware of the negative and that you're willing to actively engage with it. Allow your audience to go through a cycle of evaluation and draw their own conclusions, instead of forcing your point of view on them. As a corollary, don't be afraid to call out your own mistakes. If you stumble over a word or notice a typo on your slide, mention it yourself. Don't try to cover it up, but don't let it get in the way of your story either.

Here's an example of the principles discussed above, pulled together in an unexpected way that worked brilliantly. Many years ago, while a consulting manager at Grant Thornton, I worked with a consulting partner who had a very dynamic personality. His name was Colin, and he was the spitting image of actor Chris Farley. He acted like him, too. Colin was adamant that as consultants, our job was not merely to deliver facts but to entertain while providing value. As I said, some people are more extroverted than others.

Initially I thought he was exaggerating when he said this. A couple months later, however, we were meeting with the chief financial officer (CFO) of a major medical device manufacturer. This was at a time when standards such as ISO 9000 and the CE mark were becoming widespread, and we were working with the company to develop a roadmap to attain these standards. We were with the client ready to sign a contract for a major program, when Colin disagreed with the CFO on a minor point.

The CFO made his point again, more emphatically, at which point Colin became more vocal in his disagreement. Back and forth the conversation went, becoming increasingly heated, until I saw the entire program unravelling before my very eyes. Colin recognized the predicament and decided to take action. He got out of his chair, stood in front of the client, and said, "You know, sometimes I'm involved in situations like this with different points of view. There's only one way to resolve the matter." At which point he jumped toward the client with his arms out and said, "Let's wrestle!"

This was so unexpected, and connected so well, that the client was grinning from ear to ear. The situation was defused and we completed the deal. Is this the best approach for you to take? Maybe not. The point, however, is that human connection turned what was a tense scenario into a moment of laughter, changing the atmosphere in the room and allowing us to complete a mutually beneficial agreement.

When you present orally, work to capture and sustain the attention of your audience. You have about thirty seconds to make a first impression, and you'll need to reinforce a good first impression several times over the course of a presentation. Milo Frank was a nationally acclaimed authority on communication skills and a senior executive at CBS and MGM Studios. He maintained that people need to make points in thirty seconds or less, starting with a hook to grab attention, then state the subject, and move to an ask. Frank believed that even long speeches could be considered a series of thirty-second messages.

One way to keep people interested is to use unexpected words that cause them to unconsciously lean forward and take note. In many ways, these words are the opposite of the buzzwords discussed earlier. Often borrowed from other professions or genres, they may appear out-of-context, but their novelty is what captures attention. For example: brilliant, rebel, acidic, naked, magic, incinerate, weird. These words aren't typically associated with business, which is precisely why they can intrigue an audience. A museum curates a collection, so why can't a business curate an inventory of digital assets? The key point here is that the words are vivid. They paint pictures for listeners and help them remain engaged, similar to Pulitzer Prize-winning author David McCullough, who says that he "paints with words." The list of words that can be used in this way is almost endless, and you may feel comfortable with some but not with others. For example, borrow from your hobbies and interests, as long as the audience can also relate. It's up to you which you choose, as long as you keep it crisp, vivid, and memorable.

Think of your presentation as a story and seek to reach people through emotions, experiences, and anecdotes, using facts and statistics to support the story you're telling. Be aware that too many facts and figures without a recognizable narrative will lead to boredom. Facts and figures are wonderful supporting actors, but they're poor in leading roles. A few well-placed statistics can significantly boost your credibility and the persuasiveness of your story. One of the hallmarks of effective consulting communication is the presentation of a clear story, supported by facts each step of the way.

Remember that important business communications involve making decisions. Should we launch a product, spin off a division, or fund a campaign? Details provide the audience with confidence to reach a conclusion and move forward with a course of action that may require a certain amount of risk. Far too many business communications are bland and fail to effectively encourage action. This is hardly surprising, as many of us are over-scheduled and over-committed. We rush to put something out and sacrifice depth and detail to meet deadlines. We may face a choice between creating a large quantity of mediocre material and a smaller quantity of excellent content. There's no easy way to draw the line. It's a matter of deciding where to invest your time and assessing those situations when good is good enough.

Do the basics well. It's easy to overlook these, but they represent simple wins that you can build upon. Prepare answers to the questions you expect people to ask. Cover the obvious points. Make sure that you address simple things such as financial questions—revenue, expenses, and margins—in each likely scenario. At the same time, prepare for the worst-case scenarios. As mentioned earlier, what happens if you find yourself in a room without a projector? Do you have printouts you can use in a pinch? What happens if your laptop dies on you? What happens if Skype isn't working? Picture the worst thing that could happen and prepare for it.

Finally, embrace your nerves. If you're excited and nervous, that means you value the presentation and it is worth doing well. The important thing is to channel that nervous energy through practice and rehearsal, and to use it to convey your enthusiasm to the audience.

ACTIVE LISTENING

When we think of oral communication, we naturally think of speaking. Many of us neglect the role of listening, although active listening is a vital part of good communication. Specifically, active listening is listening with all the senses, to fully concentrate, understand, respond, and then remember the message being delivered.

Imagine giving a presentation and looking around at the audience in search of engagement, and seeing instead distracted looks and smartphones in action. How would you feel? Not good. When we are in the audience, we can also do our part and support the speaker. If communication is a gift, active listening can be considered the art of receiving that gift.

Why does this matter? Beyond a hoped-for future quid pro quo, it begins as a simple matter of respect. Poor listeners are often perceived as rude, which can damage their reputations. Poor listening is also associated with limited social skills and a lack of emotional sensitivity. More importantly, poor listeners miss out on important knowledge. Contrary to popular belief, multitasking doesn't make us more productive. Instead, it harms our capacity to comprehend valuable information.

A 2009 Stanford study found that people who are regularly bombarded with several streams of electronic information do not pay attention, control their memory, or switch from one job to another as well as those who prefer to complete one task at a time.[4] In the words of the lead researcher, Professor Clifford Nass, "They're suckers for irrelevancy.

---

4   Adam Gorlick, "Media Multitaskers Pay Mental Price, Stanford Study Shows," *Stanford News*, August 24, 2009.

Everything distracts them." My own research supports this as well. An analysis I conducted for a high-tech client in 2008 showed that engineers who multitasked—"context-switching" in our terminology—lost up to twenty minutes of productivity before they were dialed-in once more. Cognitive theorist Alan Welford understood this long before the advent of smartphones. In his 1967 "cognitive bottleneck theory," he stated that the human mind can only process a limited amount of information at once before learning capacity starts to suffer. Active listening helps you to understand, absorb, and retain more of what you need to know.

Journalist Nicholas Carr explores the effect that the internet is having on our brains in his 2010 book, *The Shallows*. "Our ability to learn can be severely compromised when our brains become overloaded with diverse stimuli online," he wrote. "More information can mean less knowledge." Carr also states that digital overload makes it harder "to distinguish relevant information from irrelevant information, signal from noise." This is all the more reason for us to improve our ability to focus, and active listening is a fundamental way to do so.

Another way to think about active listening is how well you as a speaker incorporate the experience of your audience into your presentation. For example, perhaps your hometown sports team has recently won a championship. At the other end of the spectrum, perhaps there has been a recent

IMPROVING YOUR ACTIVE LISTENING SKILLS

The question is: how can you improve your active listening skills? In 2011, Christopher Gearthart and Graham Bodie refined and adapted Drollinger's Active-Empathetic Listening Scale (AELS) for use in a social context, developing a scale on which they measured the ability to listen actively. The AELS is comprised of eleven items, in three categories: Sensing, Processing, and Responding. Here are the eleven AELS questions they used to determine a person's active listening competency.

Sensing

- How sensitive is the listener to what others are saying?

- How aware is the listener of what others are implying, but not saying?

- How well does the listener understand the emotions of others?

- Does the listener observe cues beyond the verbal?

Processing

- How well does the listener assure others that they will remember what they say?

- Does the listener summarize points of agreement and disagreement?

- How effectively does the listener track the points being made (i.e., in writing)?

Responding

- How well does the listener use verbal acknowledgment to reassure others they are listening?

- Does the listener assure others that they are receptive to their ideas?

- Does the listener ask questions that show they understand the speaker's position?

- How clearly does the listener assure others they are listening through their body language?

Gearthart and Bodie graded people on a seven-point scale (1 being Never, 7 being Always) to assess their active listening abilities, but simply asking yourself these questions on a regular basis is a good way to measure and improve your active listening.

tragedy, or corporate bad news. To ignore obvious, relevant negative news may appear insensitive.

When something is on everyone's minds, mentioning it makes you easier to relate to. This process begins well before the actual communication. Who are the participants in the communication? What are their backgrounds? What's on their minds? Ideally, you already know these people. At the very least, you should have a good idea of who they are.

Tailoring your communication to your recipient is a skill that you certainly exercise every day. You address your grandmother, your boss, and your peers in different language styles and wording. If you go to church, you speak very differently there than at a sporting event. Why? Because you understand your audience and surroundings. Yet many of us, myself included at times, neglect to make this distinction when we address a group of people in a business context.

Even when giving a presentation, you can practice active listening by taking the engagement "temperature" of the room as you speak and noticing when your audience seems disengaged. If someone is wearing a frown, has their arms crossed, or has their brow furrowed, it may be a sign that they disagree or they're not following your message. This is an opportunity to ask questions or request feedback. Far from making you appear weak, this will demonstrate that you have confidence and that you care about the experience of your audience.

The size of your audience is relevant here, of course. In a room of a thousand people, taking individual questions isn't feasible in the same way as it is in a smaller meeting. Nonetheless, you can still ask for a show of hands, an excellent way to bring people's focus back to your presentation, should you feel their attention is drifting.

The main point is to remember that you and your audience are not in an adversarial relationship. You're on the same team. You want them to get as much as possible from your presentation. Understand your audience and strive to communicate—both as a speaker and as a listener—in a way that maximizes their benefit.

EXECUTIVE PRESENCE

What creates presence? Think of a doctor: they have command of their content, they operate in a familiar environment where they are completely at home, and they have a vocabulary—and even specific clothing—that conveys that they are the expert in the room. All these factors enable them to perform effectively and with presence. *Gravitas* is a word that comes up when discussing executive presence. The dictionary defines the word somberly—as "dignity, seriousness, or solemnity of manner"—but in reality, it means to be taken seriously with perceived competence. Business is a less repetitive environment than the sterile halls of the doctor's clinic with less clearly defined domains. Nonetheless, we can develop presence and stack the odds in our favor.

One person stands out for me in this regard. Stephen Chipman was a partner at Grant Thornton, although he did all the things that gave him presence long before he became partner. Stephen was usually soft-spoken, yet he conveyed messages crisply and always had all the data he needed to make a point. When it was necessary, he disciplined colleagues or delivered tough news to clients. He rarely raised his voice, but when he did, people took note. He never gossiped or spoke loosely. Unsurprisingly, he was universally respected and advanced steadily, attaining the position of CEO and leading the firm through double-digit growth. For me, he remains a role model of *gravitas* and presence.

You might conclude that Stephen's presence came from his seniority, but I'd argue the opposite, that he attained a high position *because* of his presence. You can practice and develop presence at any point in your career. Let's take campus hires as an example. Newly hired professionals tend to embody one of two communication styles. They either speak too much, attempting to dominate conversations without proper context or substance, or they speak too little, hanging back and avoiding the risk of saying the wrong thing. Neither approach is ideal. The talker tends to be viewed as arrogant or under-prepared, while the wallflower doesn't develop a personal brand or create any impact.

It's important for junior consultants to be visible to clients, or junior professionals to their senior leaders. This may be done by presenting in client meetings as soon as possible, even if they take on only a minor task, such as delivering a small portion of a presentation. Even that is enough to bring them to the attention of the broader team and leadership, and start to establish their reputation. By the same token, however, it's important that professionals are not reckless simply to get attention. Boldness is good, crazy is not.

Another common misconception about presence is that it's only for extroverts. As with public speaking, extroverts may be more comfortable getting themselves noticed, but there is a world of difference between demanding attention and exuding presence. I suggest that, especially in professional roles such as consulting, introverts and extroverts are equally equipped to bring great presence to their interactions, perhaps more so. Why? Because, while they may not be as comfortable speaking out, they bring a sense of deliberation and empathy to their interactions that can be powerful. Consider the character of Don Corleone in the classic movie, *The Godfather*. He spoke very little, yet when he *did* speak, people listened, and acted on his words.

How can you communicate with more presence? One way is to think and speak about big, inspiring ideas, and to relate even small projects to those ideas. Libby MacFarlane was a consultant on my team who led an internal initiative to remove Styrofoam cups from our offices. She could have made the case that it was a cost-saving measure, which in part it was, but she made it clear that her primary motivation was to reduce environmental impact. By relating a seemingly small change to a broader sustainability objective, she brought people on board. We all like to feel that we are part of something bigger than ourselves.

People with presence act based on integrity, even in difficult circumstances. People respect leaders who take on difficult tasks and communicate challenging messages in a professional manner. We also tend to respect those who use challenging times as an opportunity to forge the determination to create a better future. Some of the iconic business successes of our times have come in the wake of massive failures. Steve Jobs, for example, was sacked by the company he created, then returned to lead Apple to global prominence.

I have been around long enough to experience multiple economic recessions, and had the pleasure and pain of working through tough times to reestablish growth trajectories for my business unit and myself. While never pleasant at the time, each situation provided valuable learnings that ultimately helped us become better professionals and better people. Those with presence think and talk about the future, which is another form of leadership. This is about more than sharing good news. It's about having the vision to look ahead and understand what is needed to be successful.

The term *authenticity* is one I come back to again and again. How can you become more authentic? You can share what you really think and believe, bringing your genuine values to the topic under discussion. You can also be honest enough to share stories of your professional challenges and discuss how you overcame them. Another characteristic of people with presence is consistency. People notice those who show up, day after day, month after month, and aim to do the right thing.

To develop your presence, remember your roots. As described in the introduction, I grew up in the small farming community of Montgomery, Indiana. I return on a regular basis to reconnect with family and with the people who know me best. I don't think there is a better way to remain grounded. No doubt you have your own story. Maybe you have traveled extensively, or you stayed home. Family relationships can be a sanctuary or a burden to overcome. Whatever your situation, honor your background, as it has made you who you are today and will influence your path ahead.

COMMON BUSINESS COMMUNICATION SCENARIOS

In this section, we explore some of the most common circumstances in which conversations take place, addressing their similarities and differences. The first, most obvious—yet also overlooked—is the humble one-to-one conversation. Due to increased reliance on email, conversations are far less common today than only a couple decades ago. This has made them more effective, because taking the time to connect with someone face-to-face shows a level of effort and respect.

Productivity is sometimes used as a reason not to communicate in person. It is important to be productive, but it is also important to ensure that relationships are sustained. The "machine gun email" technique that's become common culture in many companies does not promote this level of communication. In those firms, communicating one-to-one may appear outdated or simply inefficient. However, one-to-one conversation is the atomic element of human communication. In fact, it may be more productive than email in decision-making situations, if it accomplishes the purpose and enriches the exchange. Nonetheless, it is vital to balance conversation time with good time and email management.

Another common business scenario is meeting facilitation and leadership. This is another area of business communication that threatens to expand beyond reasonable limits. Clients frequently tell me that they have so many meetings that they do not have time for work, an ironic and frustrating phenomenon. If you lead meetings, ask yourself whether they are truly necessary. If you lead a standing weekly meeting, can you repurpose it to cover a different topic each week, so that each iteration feels focused and useful? In a weekly leadership meeting, it may be possible to tackle sales forecasts, operations, offerings, and performance evaluations on a rotating monthly cycle.

Another common issue with meetings is that they are frequently scheduled back-to-back, with no allowances made for the time taken to travel between one location and the next. This results in people arriving late and stressed. The same is true of conference calls, which often run overtime, delaying participants for the following call. To remedy this, give your audience some space. Schedule meetings to start on time and finish five minutes early. Your participants will thank you.

Speeches are typically believed to be the exclusive domain of senior executives. However, it is a good idea to practice public speaking at every level of your career. Speaking opportunities, whether at industry events or internal corporate gatherings, can be excellent ways to gain visibility and advance your career. They also are a crucible to develop the ability to convert your abundant knowledge into crisp, interesting, and relatable statements. To give a good speech, think of conveying an overarching idea and opening with a story that relates to the theme. Where possible, it is better to draw from your own experience than borrow a common story that the audience has already heard. How many times have you heard someone use Apple or the iPhone as a symbol of digital consumer culture?

When giving a speech, include the audience, especially if you know them by name. Mention the people who invited you to speak and the people who you're addressing. Many years ago, when I was a high school senior at a leadership conference, a television news anchor gave a speech that still resonates with me. She spoke about how most graduation commencement speeches focus on achievement and vision and striving, but they are hard to relate to on a human level. She exhorted her audience to talk instead about people, because people matter the most.

As it happened, I was scheduled to give my own Barr-Reeve High School commencement address the following month. I followed her advice and concentrated the entire speech on the people. I addressed the high-achieving students, along with those whose talents weren't widely known. I mentioned the faculty, with a focus on those who went the extra mile for their students. I especially mentioned the dedication and commitment of the parents. The speech was very well-received. Ever since, I have remembered that advice whenever I've given a speech.

Another type of communication is the interview, with question-and-answer sessions. While public relations departments typically handle media requests, professionals also have opportunities to engage in this way. This could involve an appearance on a panel or an interview for an article about your area of expertise. It could also simply be an internal team meeting featuring a question-and-answer session.

The trickiest aspect of these experiences is often preparation time, or lack thereof. Sometimes you may receive questions in advance, but frequently that may not be the case. Therefore, it's important to prepare for the most likely questions and to think on your feet as necessary. Surprisingly, the perceived lack of preparation time can work in your favor, because the audience is impressed when you maintain composure and presence in the face of unexpected questions. In these scenarios, it's important to remain calm and honest and to avoid defensiveness. Again, have command of your core area and messages.

HOW TO PREPARE FOR A BIG PRESENTATION

There will be times in your career when you need to nail a presentation. These are the moments of truth, the relatively few opportunities that have a disproportional impact on your career. You may be pitching a major account, trying to win internal approval for a proposal, or interviewing for your dream job. These presentations matter, and it is important that you prepare effectively for them. Often, they are winner-take-all situations in which you either achieve your desired outcome or you don't. There are no prizes for second place.

Before you even start to create your presentation, make some decisions about your priorities. Determine how much time you want to invest in the presentation. What is it worth to you? Traditionally, presentations were death-by-PowerPoint experiences, consisting of dozens of slides. There was never enough time to get through all the slides, let alone solicit the feedback of your audience. Good presentations are different. The key element is the story. This has always been so in our personal lives, so why not bring story-telling to our business world as well? A good story makes for a good experience for both the audience and the presenter. How can you present your story in a way that your audience will receive it positively?

As a guideline, use no more than one content slide for every three minutes. This will allow enough time for you to converse with your audience and for each one to be memorable. You want each slide to tell a segment of the story. If you're making handouts, consider using 11" by 17" (A3 size) paper and creating "table mats." These tend to be more engaging than standard 8½" x 11" (A4) sheets. Another option is posters, no more than three or four to illustrate the major components of your narrative. It may be a cliché to say that a picture is worth a thousand words, but that's because—if those images are properly designed—it is true. Visuals help your audience maintain attention and identify consistent themes in your thinking.

Think of yourself as the provider of a presentation blueprint or a framework, not a prescription. Yes, you are selling an idea, but your job is to pull the audience into your story, not push them to accept your version of events. By the time you conclude, they should clearly understand your central message, and the reasons you want them to endorse it.

Oral presentations are theater. Voltaire once said, "The way to become boring is to say everything." This applies equally to your presentations. Aim for precision and crispness, instead of excessive explanation. Content is the central element, but pay attention to delivery, as it can truly set you apart. Do more than simply lecture to your audience. Offer a distinct point of view. Take a stand. Give them opportunities to interact with you and your ideas. This allows them to internalize your perspective. Also, own your lines. Know your content, and memorize the main messages and high-impact phrases. This will allow you to be audience-focused during your presentation, instead of trying to remember what you want to say.

Oral presentations are not simply opportunities for you to speak. They are shared experiences—opportunities for the people in the room to come together as a community and discuss your ideas. You can ask them whether they understand your point and, just as importantly, whether they all understand it in the same way. Every person in your audience will be asking themselves questions. What's there? What's missing? How does each part relate to the others? Give them a chance to express and resolve those questions.

Hopefully you have delivered a presentation, an event, or another activity that brought you into a state of flow. It's a wonderful feeling, a "runner's high" for the orator. To reach this state, prepare thoroughly and be ready for the challenge of delivering your work. Invest the time and do what is needed to reduce your uncertainty and nervousness, so that your spontaneity can emerge.

When you're giving a presentation, there is a reason. Someone or some group values your expertise and your point of view. It is the combination of who you are and what you are offering. Keep introductions concise, because your focus should be on the needs of your audience, not on your own. Do not fall into the trap of trying to prove that your company is great by "showing off the headquarters pictures," or in other words, boasting about your capabilities. Your capabilities may be excellent, but are they relevant to the topic at hand? Does your audience need to know about them? How do they relate to the story you want to tell?

Here's an example. When I talk about my company (Infosys), I don't start by discussing the number of employees, the many campuses, or all the patents created. I talk about our foundation that provides a million hot meals per day to children in India to keep them in school. That gets people interested. They start to consider the logistics and the supply chain that makes that possible, and of course it's something everyone can get behind. Another aspect of our work that I like to emphasize is our leadership in computer science education in the United States, which showcases our technology expertise in an uplifting way. Examples like these give people compelling narratives to which they can relate.

It's essential when you give a presentation to find ways to stand out. This is especially true if you're pitching to a prospective client. They will probably have sat through a number of paint-by-numbers talks with similar proposals. The last thing they want is to be bored again. On one occasion my team gave a large sales presentation to an iconic motorcycle manufacturer. We didn't wear suits, we didn't wear business casual, we wore jeans and T-shirts with the motorcycle company's branding. It was a simple way to connect with them and indicate that we understood their brand. This approach helped us compete with other firms, win a large piece of work, and ultimately begin a long-term relationship with them.

USING ORAL COMMUNICATION TO CONNECT

Oral communication is a pipeline that connects your ideas with your audience, enabling them to receive, interact, and generate value from them. It's an essential part of any professional's arsenal: your ability to communicate orally will play a large role in determining the impact and adoption of your ideas, and ultimately success in work and life.

CHAPTER FOUR

WRITTEN COMMUNICATION

"This report, by its very length, defends itself against the risk of being read."

—WINSTON CHURCHILL

Amit was an architect. Not the kind of architect who builds houses; a technical architect who designed complex computer software systems. His work, and the work of others like him, underpins supply chain, order management, and other enterprise systems.

When I met Amit, I was leading a large initiative for a major energy and logistics provider, helping them create a next-generation supply chain, capable of incorporating real-time updates to fuel prices and dispatch schedules. We had completed the strategy and assessment work, and it was time to bring in a technical architect to flesh out the next phase of the project. I was excited, because I am a big believer in the value of architecture and was looking forward to learning from an expert in the field.

The first time I met Amit, I explained the project scope and deliverables and asked him to explain his work and approach. His response? "It's architecture, and it's complicated. You wouldn't understand it." As you can imagine, I wasn't impressed with his social skills, but I trusted his professionalism, at least initially, and gave him a pass. After a couple of weeks, I became increasingly concerned. As part of our statement of work, we were required to complete two architecture deliverables, and as program leader, I requested deliverable updates and progress reports from him. At first, Amit brushed off my requests, but as we approached the due date, I cornered him and insisted that we review his architecture documents.

As I reviewed his work, it was apparent that he was highly intelligent and deeply knowledgeable about technology architecture. However, he was poor at structuring his thoughts and conveying them through written communication. At the time, I lacked experience in architecture, so I plowed through the document the only way I could. I asked questions until I understood what he was trying to say, while simultaneously providing him with guidelines to help him write more professionally and more effectively.

As I proceeded with this approach, Amit's swagger started to fall away. He became less and less confident, and—ironically—easier to work with. He moved from arrogance to defensiveness to humility, and finally to excitement, as his work took on a form he had never seen before. By the time we completed the review, his brilliance was written up in a way that allowed his thinking to shine through. The jargon and buzzwords were gone and crisp, plain vocabulary conveyed his message and recommendations. Sentences were tight, the punctuation and syntax created a natural reading rhythm, and the layout made the document easy to scan and comprehend.

As professionals, we earn a living based on the quality of our thinking and our ability to communicate effectively. In the analog world of yesterday, it was clear that written communication was crucial. Newspapers, books, and letters were the easiest ways to communicate messages across distances, at scale, in a way that persisted over time. The digital revolution has changed all that, right? Wrong. Even in the digital world, the written word still rules. Video may claim the attention of viewers quickly, but the written word enables the reader to absorb ideas at their own pace, in their own style, with little technological assistance.

The leverage provided by digital technology has altered the rules of communication, but in some respects that shift has *increased* the importance of the written word. It's easier than ever to create and send communications. We can send emails to hundreds or thousands of people at the click of a button. In years gone by, it took real effort to create and transmit information, and this regulated how much communication occurred. Now we have the opposite problem: there is so much communication, and it's so easy and inexpensive to send, that it is hard to separate the signal from the noise and understand the intended message.

Since the arrival of the internet, the written word lasts forever and can be accessed by nearly anyone on the planet. Isn't that worth getting right? This is especially true for professionals. If you're in the business of selling and executing ideas, written communications are the fuel with which you will power your projects and your career. In the consulting field, written communication could be the difference between commodity gigs and work worth hundreds of dollars per hour. In industry, it can be the difference between being a cog in the corporate wheel and having an impact role in a dream job. Incidentally, don't kid yourself that you aren't selling. Even the most academically minded researcher relies on the impact of their ideas and the power of their prose. From getting grants to pursuing projects, everyone sells, and they do it through words.

You may believe that content trumps context and format, but everyone you communicate with forms opinions about you based on the quality of your work, and that extends to the format. If you produce sloppy writing, they will perceive that as a reflection of your abilities. Worse, they may conclude that you simply don't care enough to produce good work.

The good news is that with a little care anyone can become a solid writer. Yes, anyone. You may feel that writing isn't natural for you or that you lack formal training. If so, you may need to work a little harder to develop your written communication style, but there is no room for excuses. Writing is a learned skill. The more you practice, the more care you take to craft your message, the more you will develop your skills.

If manners maketh the man, as the old saying claims, words maketh the professional. As a knowledge worker, writing is a significant part of your toolbox. You likely derive a significant portion of your income from writing, even if it is from writing reports, emails, and proposals. Just as oral communication is your gift to an audience, so too written communication is your gift to a reader.

WHAT IS WRITTEN COMMUNICATION?

Simply put, written communication covers any type of message that makes use of the written word. It is the most effective mode of business communication because it persists, creating a permanent record. Writing is an active process, requiring intellectual energy. Ask yourself, how can you get more from your writing with less effort? Similarly, understanding the meaning of the written word demands attention and focus. A good reader is as essential to effective written communication as a good writer.

Written communication is also a method of revelation. The more care you take in your writing, the more you reveal of your authentic self. While emails, reports, and presentations differ in appearance, they also share multiple characteristics and principles. We cover each in more depth later in the chapter, but for now let's explore some foundational considerations common across written communications.

The advent of digital technology has massively increased the potential scope of our communications, but it has also decreased our attention span. What does this mean for you as a writer? It means that you need to deliver the goods, fast. How can you do this? First, understand why you are writing. Who do you want to reach? Is your audience homogenous, or are you focusing on several different personas?

A report is a good example of written communication with multiple potential audiences. It can be read by executives, middle managers, or individual subject matter experts. To meet the needs of executives, include an introductory summary, articulating the major points in a few brief yet comprehensive paragraphs. Address strategic concerns and relate the problem to a company-wide theme. Back this up with vivid examples throughout the report.

Middle managers, on the other hand, may be interested in a more targeted scope and execution details. This applies to different functional audiences as well, like marketing, production, finance, and human resources. Develop a story—an overall narrative supported by issues and their identified root causes. This is the information that will allow them to focus on problems, solve them, and exploit opportunities. Individual contributors, meanwhile, will likely seek detail relevant to their role, backed by supporting facts and references. There is some commonality across levels, but the point is that written communications should be targeted to the distinct needs of an audience, and there are certain patterns that emerge based on role and level in the organization.

For large audiences, you can take this principle further. Instead of picturing a generic type of individual, visualize a specific person, such as a manager, a team member, or even a personal friend, who embodies the audience for the communication you're producing. Write for them and know that by doing so you are also writing for your broader audience.

Whenever you start to write, you have a choice. You can determine a very specific audience or you can generalize. Both approaches have their advantages. When your audience is specific, you can tailor your message, accepting that anyone else who reads your work will not get as much from it. When you choose a more general audience, you can reach more people, but not as precisely. Some types of communication work best when aimed at very narrow audiences, whereas others are more effective with broad audiences in mind. For example, a project status report may be highly interesting, but only to those involved on the project. They will probably expect depth, without much consideration for the bigger picture. An effective business plan also needs depth, but requires a perspective on broader topics like impact on the overall company, competition, and so on.

Editing is an under-appreciated aspect of good writing. When you present a slide or a report, every word, every pixel, should have a purpose. Each character must earn the right to appear on the page and take up precious space and reader attention. Michelangelo was famously asked how he created his magnificent sculpture of David. He responded that he simply removed everything that wasn't David and what was left was his masterpiece. Not every written communication you create needs to be a masterpiece, but the same principle applies. Remove everything that does not contribute to your message and sculpt what remains into a shape that conveys what you want to say, as eloquently and concisely as possible. There is no perfect answer, and sometimes certain words are valuable simply because they provide a more personal tone. We are not robots—at least, not yet—and we need to retain the humanity in our writing while taking care to be concise and correct.

Far too many business writers add superfluous words such as

"literally," "very," and "global" to their prose. These words are unnecessary. Keep your writing spare and allow your message to shine through. Your reader has a finite attention span: do not make them struggle to understand you. Maximize the "return on ink" ratio, or comprehension per word. Learn to summarize essential aspects of your message at the start of a document, paragraph, or section. This makes it easier for your reader to understand what you intend to say.

Remember, the objective of your writing is to make comprehension easy for your reader, not to make writing easy for you. Do unto others as you would like them to do unto you or, in this context, write for others as you wish they would write for you. Even better, write for others as they wish you would write for them.

Avoid excessive use of the passive tense, which drains energy from your prose and remove unnecessary prepositions. For example, compare these two sentences:

- "It was believed by those in attendance that the object of their analysis was not an artifact of value."
- "The attendees believed the object was not important."

Which sentence is more effective? The first is indirect and vague, with a recursive chain of prepositional phrases that puts the reader through a mental workout. The second is clear and easy to understand. Junior professionals are tempted to use jargon and buzzwords, and they may inadvertently use passive and elongated syntax, thinking that it sounds safer, more eloquent, and more professional. While this approach does not offend anyone, it does not articulate an actionable point, and is not enjoyable to read. Readers find interest in and attribute strong leadership characteristics to those who use simple, direct language.

Look out for gerunds. No, gerund isn't another word for a senior citizen. It's from Latin, and it is a form of verb that functions as a noun and expresses generalized or uncompleted action. As you would expect from a word that means "generalized or uncompleted action," these are words that weaken business writing and should be used with care. Look for words that end in "-ing" or "-ion" and you'll soon become aware of gerunds. "Reading," "writing," and "speaking" are all gerunds, whereas "read," "write," and "speak" are not. As with passive verbs and prepositional phrases, gerunds tend to weaken impact.

Sometimes gerunds are needed to make a phrase work, for example when they are used as modifiers, and can be used as subjects or objects to smooth the sentence flow for descriptors ("business writing," in this paragraph), or to avoid excessive use of the word you ("when writing," instead of "when you write"). Also, they can be handy to avoid the use of infinitives ("writing," instead of "to write"). Minimize gerund use when you describe actions, however, and it will strengthen the impact of your writing.

One of the first principles medical students absorb is, "First, do no harm." In the context of written communication, think of this as, "First, do not distract." In other words, don't create roadblocks to comprehension in your communication. Learn and use the basics of good grammar. Avoid jargon and buzzwords, just as you would in oral communication. Refrain from random acts of capitalization, such as capitalizing only some words in a header or capitalizing nouns without reason, as it sends a distracting message about what is emphasized. As an example, look at the sentence, "Business Strategy drives the Technology objectives." Confusing, right? Is business strategy a formal area, or just the topic name? Why is technology emphasized? Resist double negatives, such as "couldn't not," and inappropriate colloquialisms, such as "couldn't hardly understand."

Ultimately, your goal in written communication is to develop a state of flow for your reader, in which they are immersed in your work and easily comprehending your intended meaning. To aid this, think about your transitions. Do they flow smoothly, creating a natural harmony between points, or are they clunky, disruptive breaks? This is not to say that you should settle for monotony. Use exciting, unexpected, and intriguing words to sustain their attention. It's acceptable—indeed valuable—to allow your personality to reveal itself in writing, but avoid idiosyncrasies that will confuse or distract readers.

This is a fine balance. Your purpose in business communication is to inform, yet also to keep your reader interested. Do not allow yourself to drift into condescension or an opinionated rant, which will turn off your audience. You can be bold and persuasive without resorting to an intimidating tone. Use your diction—your choice of words—to reflect the emotional tone of your content. Vary your vocabulary and the length of your sentences to keep the tone fresh. Occasionally, insert questions to refocus the reader's attention. Does this work? You tell me. Did your attention spike when you read the previous question?

It is common in business to rely on quantitative data to make points, but anecdotal evidence also has a place. You are telling a story, so feel free to include the stories of other people where relevant. As an employee within a company, you have license to build upon any colleague's story by using the word "we." Convey the details of your document through facts. These can be scientific facts, historical facts, or simply testimonials from people who have used your product or experienced the subject matter of your writing. It is a good idea to attribute facts to their sources so that your readers understand from where you draw your evidence. It provides credit to the source and enhances your credibility.

In addition to facts, you can use metaphors and analogies as a method to draw comparisons. They offer you an opportunity to be less formal and prescriptive, instead inviting your audience to consider the implications of what you say and relate it to something tangible. Nonetheless, resist the temptation to drift into vague comparisons.

Business communication has become less formal. There was a time when business communications used the third person, but it is now acceptable to use personal pronouns such as "he," "she," "you," and "we." When you sit down to write, think about the pronouns and modifiers you use, to produce content that people will want to read and find useful.

We live in a global world, populated by global workers. For some, English is a second language. If you are a native speaker writing for people for whom English isn't a native tongue, write in a way that maximizes their comprehension. As with any communication, your aim is to connect with your audience in a way they can understand. At times, this may mean sacrificing cleverness for clarity. In written communication, factors such as body language are not relevant, but word usage, structure, and punctuation take their place. They form the "metadata" that people use to interpret texts. This includes the use of boldface and italics, as well as the physical layout of a document, which should be organized to draw the eye to the document's most important aspects.

Imagine your readers asking themselves questions about each part of your work. They want to know what it is, how it's relevant to them, and how it relates to other sections of the document. Give them that information, in that order, and you will create a natural sequence that will make sense and be easy to follow.

Where appropriate, replace words with images. To convey the concept of extremely high performance, for example, you could use an image of a military special operations team, such as Seal Team Six. To say that a company is unknowingly headed toward crisis, you could employ an image of an ocean liner approaching an iceberg.

I've seen this second example used effectively with a client in the telecommunications equipment industry. The company was highly successful and growing rapidly, yet there were software quality issues developing that were starting to cause problems. There was only a limited window of time before the company's product exposure became so large and complex that it would have been difficult to solve the problems without jeopardizing their growth trajectory and even leading to customer revolt. Everything looked good for lagging metrics like sales and profitability, but there was a metaphorical iceberg just over the horizon. Only by tackling the problem before it worsened could the company avoid potential disaster. My client Michel, the senior vice president of engineering, was trying to direct the attention of other company leaders to the magnitude and urgency of the problem. In every management presentation, he used images of an iceberg and the Titanic to tell his story. The image, as part of a larger case, was powerful enough to convince senior management to accept the problem, fund the solution, and sustain the organizational will to successfully see them through a two-year program of change.

Make sure that you keep images relevant. The era of simplistic clip art is over, meaning that your audience should be spared generic images of buildings, highway signs, or handshakes. Yet, are high-resolution stock photos any more effective? Does seeing a group of attractive, well-dressed, diverse professionals around a conference room table say anything meaningful, or is it merely a prettier form of clip art? We live in a visual world, and images have been shown to capture and retain interest in content. However, avoid the extremes of clickbait shock value and numbing blandness. Each image or chart should support and enrich the story. A few well-placed graphics turn a dull pedestrian document into a memorable professional communication.

IMPROVING YOUR WRITING SKILLS

It can be overwhelming to sit down with the intention of producing polished, insightful content in a single sitting. No author would expect to publish their first draft, yet many people have the mindset that if they cannot create a finished product in an initial pass, it means that they are not good writers. It takes multiple iterations to create something worthwhile. At the same time, there are things you can do to get to that finished product faster, with higher quality. In this section, we discuss how to develop your written communications—no matter your current level.

Content is the central part of any good written communication. No amount of polish or technique can compensate for a lack of accurate, useful content. Combining good content with good technique, however, will maximize the impact of your words.

The principle here is to amplify the signal as much as possible, while reducing the noise. One way of doing this is to simply remove words that do not relate to the primary message. Another is to use the "communication pyramid." Imagine the content as the broad base of the pyramid, taking up most of the space. The middle of the pyramid denotes spatial arrangement, organizing the content to be visually appealing and consumable. The tip of the pyramid is the takeaway statement, the insight that provides the reader the value you seek to convey. The pyramid is a useful concept that makes it easy for readers to identify the main point quickly, and is highly relevant when creating presentation slides or posters. However, it is also useful for reports and memos. You can use size, shape, color, and proximity to highlight the most important parts of the text. Other important details follow and support the main message, with supporting or more general information included less prominently.

To do this, you need to understand your message, and an

excellent way of doing that is storyboarding. For decades, storyboarding was the default method of crafting a narrative, but it faded out of fashion with the advent of PowerPoint and other methods of electronic communication. Power-Point can be used as a storyboarding tool, but too often it's so template-driven that it simply repeats a previous story instead of creating a new one. Sometimes the most effective communications aren't the most technologically advanced, and intentionally going low-tech can be a powerful weapon. The goal is a compelling story, and it pays to invest the effort required to create one.

You can storyboard presentations and reports using index cards, Post-It notes, or even full sheets of paper. Organize your content into major messages. Write down each of your major messages in complete sentences across the top of individual cards. Sketch an image that illustrates the message, and note the information that you need on the relevant slide—or report section—to support the message. Create the story as though you were talking to a friend over coffee or perhaps on a short walk. The purpose is to document a scenario robust enough to carry a story, yet brief enough to be concise. Storyboarding is about organization and flow. Details will emerge, but it is important to have a sense of the whole, the story. In the next chapter, we cover tools to provide structure to the story, such as the Pyramid Principle.

I have seen this low-tech technique pay massive dividends.

A high-tech client needed to revamp their human resources processes, specifically in talent acquisition (recruiting). After several attempts to do this without success, they turned to us. This was a client with every type of technology at their disposal, but when we got them together for workshops prior to restarting their recruitment project, we decided to go *old school*. We used posters, flash cards, handouts, and other props, which required them to be fully present in our workshops. This increased consensus and accelerated projects because they reached better decisions, and made them faster. I call this "going analog," and have used the same approach for many other clients, across several countries and continents, with memorable experiences and positive results. This is true even in contexts where English was not the primary language.

Memorable stories require meaningful content. This helps the reader solve a problem. It can provide them with an emotional connection. It can compel them to act. Always remember that even though you are writing a business communication, you're doing it for people, and people relate to stories.

THE HERO'S JOURNEY

Willa Cather famously said, "There are only two or three human stories, and they go on repeating themselves as fiercely as if they had never happened before." What are these stories? Perhaps the most iconic is the Hero's Journey, as first written by Joseph Campbell and immortalized in a seven-page memo by Christopher Vogler in 1985. From Homer's *Odyssey* and *Gilgamesh* to *Star Wars* and *Lion King*, from the foundations of our culture to recent blockbusters, these stories follow the outline of the Hero's Journey. There are twelve steps to this journey, which occur in the following order:

The ordinary world. The hero or heroine is introduced sympathetically, so the audience can identify with them. They are uneasy, uncomfortable, or simply unaware of a larger reality. Some form of polarity in their lives is pulling them in different directions, causing them stress.

The call to adventure. Some internal or external force shakes up the situation, forcing the hero to face the beginnings of change.

Refusal of the call. The hero feels fear of the unknown and tries to turn away from the adventure. Alternatively, another character in the story may play this role, expressing the uncertainty and danger that lies ahead.

Meeting the mentor. The hero encounters a seasoned traveler, who provides training, equipment, or advice to help the hero on their journey. Alternatively, the hero looks within to find a source of courage and wisdom.

Crossing the threshold. The hero commits to leaving the ordinary world and entering a new region or condition, with unfamiliar rules and values. This signifies the conclusion of the first act.

Tests, allies, and enemies. The hero is tested and develops allegiances in the new world.

Approach. The hero and their allies prepare for their major challenge.

The ordeal. The hero enters a unique space, where they confront death or face their greatest fear. From this "death" springs new life.

Reward. The hero takes possession of the treasure won through facing death. There may be celebration, along with the risk that the treasure may once again be lost.

The road back. About three quarters of the way through the story, the hero leaves the world of the adventure with the intention of returning home with their treasure. Often, there is a chase scene to signal the urgency and danger of the mission.

Resurrection. On the threshold of returning home, the hero is severely tested once more, purified by a final sacrifice, and experiences again the moment of death and rebirth, this time on a higher and more complete level. The polarities that were in conflict at the beginning of the hero's journey are finally resolved.

Return. The hero returns home, bearing some element of the treasure, with the power to transform the world as the hero has been transformed.

A wonderful story, but you may be wondering how it applies to your career in consulting or industry. The answer is that business is the story of people, and corporations have replaced the fairytale kingdoms and sci-fi planets as the entities that must be protected. Even routine business situations or interactions address some form of conflict or polarity.

When you create significant reports or deliverables, they will benefit from having a hero. The hero can be a project manager, a salesperson, a department head, a financial analyst, a client, or anyone with a problem to solve and others counting on them to do so. You—the author—may be the hero, or you may not.

This is much more than a gimmick. The human brain has been experiencing elements of the Hero's Journey since the time of the caveman. We are pre-wired to listen to, understand, and enjoy it. Utilizing the

Hero's Journey or other archetypes in written communications will help you capture and hold attention, create a state of flow, and forge an emotional connection with your audience.

THE SIX THINKING HATS REVISITED

Returning to Edward de Bono's concept of the six thinking hats, you can adapt them to aid you in your written work. The **green hat** is a way to turn loose your creative energy: brainstorm, write down ideas, create anecdotes. This is a non-linear exercise, so don't worry about structuring your thoughts into a coherent form right away.

You'll do that when you don the **blue hat,** where you structure your ideas and develop the flow of your story. Whatever you are creating, chances are that something like it has been done before. Find examples of similar work and compare the way they are structured. There's no excuse not to learn from the best minds you can find on a subject, inside your company and across the world. Once you've reviewed a few examples of similar work, you can tailor a structure for your own needs and style.

The **white hat** represents the information itself. Once you have ideas and structure, start writing. Then take another pass through the document, and another. If what you are writing is large, work in sections—an iteration for each section, then on to the next part of the document. At this stage, your job is to write, not to critique. You may set yourself a time limit for each section, to prevent yourself from overthinking.

The **yellow hat** relates to benefits. You are writing for the benefit of the reader, so consider the extent to which your words accomplish that purpose. Think about the case you want to make, and how to do it in a way that will be easily understood. Combine this with the **red hat** to think about the emotional impact of your work. You want it to be engaging and compelling, not dull and bland.

By the time you wear the **black hat**, you should have quite a lot of content. At this point, evaluate with a critical eye. Are your facts accurate? Do they support your main point? Does your writing flow? Review sources, create graphics, and check your spelling and grammar. Then do it again, and iterate again, until the work is ready. Request feedback from colleagues, and learn to become comfortable with constructive, critical feedback *early* in the process. Strive for excellence, but don't allow a quest for perfection to become a barrier to finishing the work. Encourage people to share their thoughts with you while you still have time to incorporate it into the finished product. People will be more willing to give you their honest feedback on an early draft, because they will be less concerned about upsetting you. You know it's a draft, they know it's a draft, and that carries an implicit shared understanding that feedback is welcome.

Ask your reviewers specific questions to guide their feedback. For example:

- Does the document give you all the facts you need?
- Does it support each assertion with a fact or explanation?
- Does it follow structure and syntax guidelines?
- How easy is it to follow the narrative?
- Does it finish strongly with a motivating call to action?

DENOTATION AND CONNOTATION

Denotation and connotation refer to the distinction between dictionary definitions and cultural perceptions. A dog, for example, is defined in the dictionary as a four-legged canine. That's the denoted meaning. Connotation is perceived definition, representing social overtones, cultural implications, or emotional meanings. As an example, the word "dog" can have several different associations. In Indonesia, calling someone a dog is a grave insult. The Boston Consulting Group's Growth Share Matrix contains a quadrant devoted entirely to products with low market share or growth—also known as "dogs."

Hopefully the reader's inferred connotation is the same as the author's implied one. The less familiar the writer is with their audience, and the more diverse that audience, the more important connotations become. In certain contexts, words that appear benign to the writer may be considered offensive by the reader. This applies to descriptive terms and in the context of race and gender. In a business setting, there's a risk that phrases which are commonly understood in one language may have a different meaning to non-native English speakers. This requires the writer to proceed with care, utilizing empathy and conscious self-reflection to anticipate and understand reader perception.

ACTIVE READING

Just as active listening is part of oral communication, active reading is part of written communication. How so? Reading allows us to discover ideas, develop our opinions, and think new thoughts. It helps us to see familiar objects and situations in new ways.

Stephen King is one of the most successful authors on the planet, and he said, "If you don't have time to read, you don't have the time—or the tools—to write." The ability to read well is a foundational skill for anyone who wishes to write well, even in a business context. Reading provokes thinking and stimulates emotions, challenges our assumptions, surprises us, and helps us to make sense of our lives and the world. It also satisfies our intellectual curiosity. Unless you understand how it feels to be a reader, how can you understand the experience of *your* readers?

When we read, we focus not only on what is written, but on

how it's written. We seek out relationships between sentences, paragraphs, and ideas, moving from subjective reactions to more objective, analytic responses. When you read, engage with the text in front of you. Ask yourself what you like about it, and what you'd like to change. What works and what doesn't? When you do this, you become well-equipped to apply the same analytical eye to your own writing, and to serve your readers. You can write with a general reader in mind, but remember that your work will always be subject to the interpretation of individuals. When you read, ask yourself where there is potential for misinterpretation in the text you are reading. As you write, apply the same high standards. Where do you risk misinterpretation from your readers?

If you want to improve your writing, start examining how words are used. Let's take "loaded" as an example. It can mean "drunk." In a sports context, it can refer to a roster that's stacked with star players. A gun can be loaded. There are also other meanings. These distinctions may appear trivial, but they are important to write or read information accurately. You cannot analyze situations effectively unless you identify how language is used.

Look at the content and ask yourself what it is telling you. What is it asking you to do? Can you read it smoothly? If not, why not? What are the barriers to your understanding? Are there are a lot of long, complex words, or is the message expressed in the simplest possible terms? Does the writer use rhetorical techniques, such as logos, pathos, or ethos? Do they relate to you through stories or parables? Take the time to examine texts and ask yourself why they have been written in that way. Investigate how people use language as a tool, and use those insights to improve your own writing.

To borrow an old phrase, learn to read between the lines. How is the text constructed? In a business situation, text may be written in a disjointed structure. Was the author sloppy, did they not know better, or were they simply overstretched while trying to meet a deadline? How can you avoid this and make your writing flow and easy to understand, regardless of time pressure?

When reading, write as well—purposeful note-taking is a powerful tool. If you're reading a physical report, write your thoughts on it as you read. When reading a physical book—that you own, hopefully!—take notes. Capture ideas that stand out, eloquent phrases, and uses of specific techniques. Create an index for easy cross-referencing at a later point. This is a way to physically engage with the written word and helps when you write your own work.

Reading actively enables you to reflect on an author's ideas, while sharpening your awareness of the optimal structure for specific written documents. You will be able to see issues and flaws within texts that you read, and understand how they can be improved. Read iconic texts and investigate what makes them successful. Why is Dr. Martin Luther King, Jr.'s 1963 *Letter from Birmingham Jail* so powerful? Why does John F. Kennedy's inaugural address still resonate with us today? I use famous works with consultants and my college students, because they contain the classic elements of rhetoric, are written beautifully, and remind us of what's at stake when we communicate. Compare well-written texts with more familiar business writing, such as a company report or your own work. What techniques can you apply to make them more compelling?

When you look at writing from multiple angles, you gain additional insight on what it takes to construct text. Language is an essential foundational element. Legendary self-development instructor Earl Nightingale famously said that people should read extensively and learn in three areas: their primary language, profession, and passion—or favorite hobby. He valued one's language as the initial, most essential area of study.

Language is a rich and complex medium. At its best, it creates and expresses meaning, allowing others to infer valuable information from a specific combination of characters and numbers. Too often, language usage leads to misunderstanding and confusion. This is especially true in a global work environment, where we work not only across time zones but also across countries, often with people for whom English is a second language. In these situations, the use of metaphors and imagery may cause meaning and insight to be lost in translation.

I work with people around the world, and that diversity has been one of the most enjoyable aspects of my consulting career. Even in the United States, people come from many different cultures and backgrounds. It is our responsibility to be clear about the meaning of the words we use, so our diverse colleagues can understand our intended meaning. Even if I want to use flowery language, I'm aware that it may inhibit comprehension, defeating the purpose of communication in the first place. Even simple terms can create confusion. In the United States, saying "let's *table* that topic" means "let's postpone, put it on the table for later." In India, the reverse is true. When an Indian colleague wants to table something, it means they want to discuss it right away, to "put it on the table to discuss now." This same word has opposite meanings in different cultures.

Readers make inferences naturally, and this is a good thing. It means that they are paying attention, internalizing your words, and applying them to their situation. Consciously or unconsciously, they're asking themselves whether what you have written is believable and persuasive. When you understand this, you can present information in a way that makes it easier to understand and act upon. Think of your reports and other written documents as invitations to participate. Encourage the reader to ask questions and to reflect on your ideas and conclusions. Engage in a conversation with your reader. Yes, a conversation. If you can anticipate their likely questions, your text will naturally draw them through the document. If persuasion is your objective, your odds go way up if they enter into the pre-planned dialogue you've established for them.

One of the ways you can practice active reading is to record your observations in response to what you read. This keeps track of your thoughts and helps you understand why you think the way you do. Again, this will be helpful if you need to convert your thoughts to the written word at a later date. In a business context, the importance of reading is often given lip service, but the truth is that it's hard to make time to read for work. Why? Because we associate typing, talking, and other signs of outward activity with productivity, while reading is considered a leisure activity. If we sit and read, we feel that we are not doing anything.

Activity alone is not necessarily effectiveness. Looking busy is not the same thing as engaging productively. You may not look as though you are doing anything while reading, but it is a mental activity. View reading as exercise, as an invest-ment. Taking the time to read broadens your thinking and plays a role in making you more productive when you *do* sit down to deliver other aspects of your work. As a writer, it is a privilege for others to read your work, whether in a personal or professional context. Strive to help writers get as much as possible from the time and effort they invest, by being a good reader yourself.

Be aware of the medium in which your work will be read. Are you writing for print or digital, blog or ebook? All of the above? In a blog, you can link readers to other relevant articles and sources. Do you want to do that, or will it distract them from the thread of your article? Books have always had footnotes, but now footnotes in ebooks can transport the reader instantly through hyperlinks. Again, it is worth noting that footnotes and bibliographies can be considered the original World Wide Web, though they were certainly not instantaneous in the way the internet is today. It is important to give your readers options for further exploration, but not overwhelm them with too many alternative threads that may distract them while reading your document.

EMAIL AS BUSINESS COMMUNICATION

While the guidelines above apply to any type of business communication, each type of communication has unique strengths and limitations. Let's discuss the primary mode of business communication—email.

Email has become ubiquitous. These messages are so easy to create and send. What could be better? The only disadvantage, of course, is that everyone else can create and send emails too. We all have finite attention spans, and every email we send competes with dozens, perhaps hundreds, of others. Email overload has become one of the major productivity problems for businesses in the twenty-first century.

Do people read your emails? Do they respond? Where relevant, do they act on them? If you want your emails to make more impact, take steps to improve them. First, think about how your email will be seen. Probably, it will be one of at least twenty on a laptop screen or mobile device, followed by hundreds if not thousands in their inbox overall. That means you can only guarantee that the recipient will read the subject line and perhaps a couple lines of preview text. Make them count.

Choose a subject line that is specific enough to explain what you want, then get to the point in the first two lines of your message. On the other hand, be careful with techniques such as marking emails "urgent" and using ALL CAPITAL LETTERS. As you can see, when you do this too often, it has the opposite effect to the one you intend. Don't waste an entire line with a salutation, but you can still make your message personal by addressing the reader by name on the same line—"Susan, am following up on the request you made..."

The more recipients your message is distributed to, the more likely you will be to lose the attention of each one. Each person will see many names and assume that someone else has it covered. As a rule of thumb, it's better to ask one person at a time for help than send out a blanket email to several people. If you need to ask more than one person, connect with them individually. Nonetheless, company culture varies, and so do roles. Some roles, like managers, have a heavy communication element, while others—like software developers—who focus on creation have less. Also, there are times when it is valuable to include additional people in an email if all recipients benefit from knowing who has seen the message. Meeting minutes and congratulatory announcements are examples where people like to know the broad recipient group. Even then, it is best to use the blind copy function (BCC) and be sure to mention the recipient list in the first line of the email so all are aware. That way you communicate with all who receive the message, and also prevent an accidental "reply all" that fills others' inboxes. This approach to email may take a little more time, but will reduce the junk you create and people will know that when you send something, it is worth reading.

Emails are quickly created, consumed, and deleted, so you may think that normal writing rules do not apply. This would be a mistake. Emails are the memoranda of the twenty-first century, and they often become records of commitments made and actions taken. In short, emails last forever, or at least per corporate archival policy. Use proper spelling, full words, and accurate sentence structure. Keep your signature up to date, but think twice before inserting images and logos.

They may show up as attachments and clutter the message after multiple replies and forwards on a conversation thread.

Email has become the medium for most business letters. As with more formal written communication, keep the recipient in mind and ask yourself what they need to know. Give them concise headers, comprehensive summaries, and a readable flow. Add charts and graphs where necessary, but avoid turning your email into a slideshow. If you do use slides, remove the borders before adding them to larger documents, to look more professional and avoid unnecessary formatting.

WRITTEN COMMUNICATION AS A SOURCE OF FULFILLMENT

Written communication fulfills many roles in business, from keeping day-to-day operations running smoothly to facilitating major decisions. In large part, your professional effectiveness is driven by the quality of your written communication. The good news is that there are established and accessible principles and techniques, along with a library of communication templates to increase your productivity and impact. With effort and practice, you can develop the skills and habits you need to succeed. This also increases the fulfillment you receive from your work, knowing that your results represent the best you can offer and convey both important information and your personal style.

CHAPTER FIVE

FRAMEWORKS AND ESTIMATION

"You don't have to be a genius or a visionary or even a college graduate to be successful. You just need a framework and a dream."

—MICHAEL DELL

Like most consulting firms, we strive to hire smart, accomplished people from university campuses. Quite often those people arrive with an abundance of self-confidence. By the time we see them, they already have a track record of success. They have earned strong grades and received a lot of positive reinforcement. They graduate from their universities with the belief they can conquer the world. We recruit from universities who tend to prepare them well for the workforce.

However, nearly half of college students who graduate, do so without the complex reasoning skills to manage knowledge work, according to a prominent survey released in 2016 by the Council for Aid to Education, formerly part of think tank Rand Corp. This Competency Learning Assessment (CLA+) relates to base level reasoning competencies. On average, students do make progress in their ability to reason, but because so many start at a large deficit, many still graduate without the ability to read a scatterplot, construct a cohesive argument or identify a logical fallacy. That is the bad news. The good news is that these skills can be learned through awareness and practice. This chapter builds on the critical thinking and communication chapters, with a focus on skills that are core to business consulting.

Tony was a recent campus hire on our consulting team. He was an economics major, highly intelligent, and did well in interviews, but he struggled once assigned to client work. Although he was properly prepped for his initial engagement, he was ineffective compared to his colleagues on the project. As partner for the client, I saw that he was struggling and worked with him myself. Despite his background in statistics and econometric modeling, he had trouble applying analytical frameworks and estimation. This deficiency was holding him back, as many consulting assignments depend on the use of these tools to frame problems for deeper analysis.

We discussed the fundamentals of frameworks and how to apply them, and he realized that presenting his work effectively relied on more than just data and rote formulas. It required him to understand how a framework (model) that highlights an important but abstract concept can be applied to real world business situations to solve problems. For example, a simple operating model can be understood to have a service delivery layer, an operations layer, an applications layer, and an infrastructure layer. This framework organizes people, processes, data, and technologies into a set of capabilities that can be measured and then improved. As Tony understood this, he focused on learning business frameworks, then used them to structure his thoughts and actions.

This gave him the benefit of additional relevant experience, despite being new to the firm. The frameworks we used were based on the results of many earlier projects, and the best thinking available. They formed the mental scaffolding that allowed him to start with and build upon the thinking of others. In effect, he stood on the shoulders of giants, applying the previous insights of brilliant strategists and thinkers to his own project by using and interpreting their models. The work he was doing would normally have required several years of experience, but the frameworks we used enabled him to start with those tools and insights and create more value, sooner.

For anyone in an analytical role, especially highly talented people who simply lack experience, frameworks act as a force multiplier. Like Iron Man's suit, they provide the power to augment and amplify their brilliance. Framework usage is more than a consulting skill. It's a thinking skill. One of the themes of this book is that we live in an age where information is available to everyone. Almost everything you want to know is only a few keystrokes away. What's the differentiator? How we *use* that information. Frameworks and estimation are ways to analyze data in an accelerated manner with confidence.

WHAT ARE FRAMEWORKS?

Frameworks are a basic structure underlying a system or concept. They are systems of rules or ideas used to plan or decide something, or a supporting structure around which something can be built. In a consulting context, frameworks are a combination of both rules to simplify a complex task and a structure to aid in doing so. Used effectively, frameworks eliminate unnecessary components, aid decision-making by highlighting relevant criteria, and embed learning based on past experience. Many objects and phenomena in the business world are too complicated and abstract to be comprehensible in their entirety, at least in practical terms. For example, what exactly is an organization? There are complex answers, but an organizational chart is a simple way to quickly grasp one important dimension—reporting relationships. An organizational chart is an example of a framework. It's unnecessary for most people to understand all aspects of an organization in excruciating detail, but reporting relationships are very useful. Frameworks provide a method of quickly conveying the essential elements of a situation in a way that can be readily understood.

Frameworks should be as simple as possible, while representing a broader system with sufficient integrity. Models are good for physical objects and resemble the things they represent. As we move towards abstraction, frameworks take the place of models. This is especially useful in a business context, where charts, graphs, and maps allow for the consideration of complex problems without delving into all the details. Just as scaffolding helps builders bring some structure to their work and start the process of construction, so frameworks assist businesspeople to give problems shape and definition.

There are people who think that frameworks are difficult to comprehend, especially by those who lack a formal consulting background. This is not true. My daughter Katherine was a psychology major with great grades, but no consulting background or previous exposure to frameworks. She interviewed for an analyst position with a leading consulting firm and, prior to her interviews, I shared with her a primer on frameworks and a few examples. With only a couple weeks of review and practice, she grasped the concept, passed the case interview and secured the job, and became effective as a consulting analyst. Frameworks are accessible to everyone if they have the right content to review and a mindset to learn.

Here's a simple example of a framework in action. When I was in college, I learned about integral calculus and how to calculate the infinitesimal area under a curve. I returned home to visit and spoke with my younger brother, who was curious about the topic but struggling with the concept. I'm a tennis player, so I grabbed a tennis racket and used it to demonstrate the principle. The strings form rectangles, beneath the curve of the racket head. As they get closer together, they approach integration. In theory, the distance between strings could become infinitesimal. Those are the basic principles of integral calculus, explained with a tennis racquet.

My brother did not grasp all the details, but the physical model helped him understand the concept. It doubled as a framework, containing just enough relevant information to give him a broad understanding at the level he needed. The point is that even common objects can provide insight into something not easily observed or comprehended.

Analytical frameworks provide structure and support to solve a known class of problem, based on patterns from previous work in similar areas. Full analytical frameworks like software architecture are composed of six components: tools, solution patterns, model forms, research techniques, skills, and categorization of complex information. If this sounds intimidating, it should, as there is a lot behind full frameworks like this. While good for highly technical fields like software engineering, many so-called frameworks are actually lightweight and useful for quick analysis. These "practical" frameworks are more common in consulting, containing only as many tools—and as much rigor—as needed to address the level of analysis required.

A popular consulting framework is SWOT analysis: strengths, weaknesses, opportunities, threats. Simply taking stock of each of the four areas is helpful for an organization to plan its strategy and make decisions. Another prominent framework is Porter's Five Forces model, which we discuss later in this chapter. It organizes—you guessed it—the five strategic forces affecting a business.

Frameworks such as these guide and accelerate information gathering, ensure thorough analysis coverage, and provide practitioners standard result formats. This accelerates progress, especially in the early stages of analysis. By removing extraneous information, frameworks improve focus. They represent relationships between attributes or components, bringing further insight. Frameworks also lend themselves to visual representations, generating clarity and enabling reuse. Once applied to a specific scenario, they can be reapplied many times, whenever a similar class of problem is encountered.

Nonetheless, frameworks have limitations. Narrow, proprietary frameworks should be handled with care. They're useful in highly specific situations, for example in a specific industry, but may not be suitable for other purposes. Worse, improper use can lead to inaccurate results. Imagine using a retail consumer marketing model for a business-to-business distributor channel. Different assumptions, metrics, and cost structures. Frameworks aren't a silver bullet and need to be used intelligently. By their very definition, they simplify situations. The risk is that if misapplied they may oversimplify situations and mislead.

Frameworks are intended to be representations only of the area selected for analysis. Therefore, they arbitrarily highlight certain attributes and ignore others. This can lead to people overlooking relevant information. Think of frameworks as a tool. In the right scenario, they are highly useful, but if you need a flat-head screwdriver and you only have a Phillips, it won't do the job.

WHAT ARE THE HALLMARKS OF A GOOD FRAMEWORK?

There are several ways to tell whether a framework is valuable. One is to consider whether it is mutually exclusive, collectively exhaustive (MECE). Mutually exclusive categories require each piece of information to fit into only one category. This allows issues and supporting examples to be deconstructed and prevents double counting. When a framework is collectively exhaustive, all relevant information is considered. While there are some corner-case criticisms of

MECE (like some situations where redundancy is the desired attribute), it has stood the test of time as an effective means to organize information.

Another hallmark of a good framework is that it flows logically. For example, a dataset could be organized into small, medium, and large categories. It wouldn't make sense to organize it into small, medium, and orange. If a framework is to yield useful information, data should be organized into a manageable number of categories or items. This means three to five elements per grouping. This is enough to support hypotheses, even if one of the elements is later disproven or dismissed as an outlier, but not so many items that they become confusing. If more than five categories are identified, this is a clue that they should be regrouped or combined.

Good frameworks are flexible and reusable. In other words, a framework should be applicable to a class of problem, with the potential for tailoring to specific uses. Broadly speaking, frameworks can be divided into categories, hierarchies, and matrices. Ultimately, all frameworks contain categories or categories of categories. Hierarchies are a way of distinguishing between different category types, illustrating a parent-child relationship between informational elements. They allow for increasing levels of detail at lower levels. A hierarchy could be an issue tree or an organizational chart. Matrices can be complex, but the best business frameworks are usually an array of two or three rows by a similar number of columns. This allows a limited number of important variables—such as variations on marketing strategy—to be compared or contrasted for specific scenarios.

I have chosen some of the most popular and useful frameworks to cover in the rest of this chapter:

- Porter's Five Forces model
- Business model
- Operating model
- Value realization
- Decision making
- 2x2 Matrix

While these are common framework types, there are many more—in fact, hundreds. Some are works of genius, while others may be considered statements of the obvious. The good news is that many of them are available, free, to anyone with internet access.

PORTER'S FIVE FORCES MODEL

Dr. Michael Porter is recognized as the world's leading business strategy expert, with eighteen books, numerous articles, and long tenure at Harvard Business School. He was also on the board of my previous firm, and I learned a lot from his involvement with our leadership team. His Five Forces of Industry Competition model analyzes the nature of competition within an industry. It can be applied to any analysis of a company's competitive position. These five forces are:

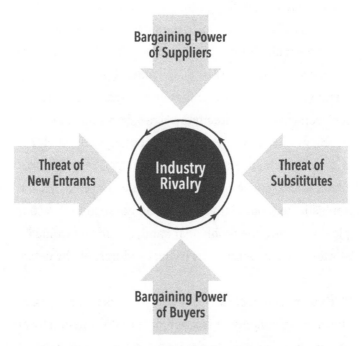

These forces work together to shape company performance. While company strategy and direction are important, Dr. Porter's model illustrates other relevant industry factors. Do customers have readily available substitutes? Are suppliers strong enough to demand high prices? Is competition strong? Note that the framework does not specify how to analyze each area or benchmarks for each industry. While his original work was based on actual examples, it was abstracted to a strategic level that provided a starting point to organize thinking and understand relationships of major entities.

BUSINESS AND OPERATING MODELS

A business model is the way an organization creates, delivers, and captures value, along with assumptions about what that business will and won't do. In the simplest terms, it is how a company makes money. For example, the complementary products—or "razor and blades"—model is based on selling an initial product below profitability and making money on replacements. Also, "freemium" is a subscription model for digital products, where a limited product is provided free to attract users, but customers are charged for additional features and services. Business models can be complex and sophisticated, but many analyses do not require this complexity to solve the problem at hand, and in fact would be slowed down or derailed by trying to address all the detail.

The business model canvas is a framework that addresses this need to simplify. It is a template to document new or existing business models, showing an organization's product value proposition, customers, and other important dimensions of its business environment. A business model canvas has nine categories.

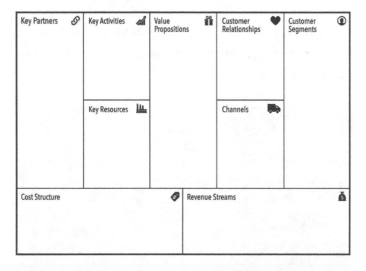

By understanding how a company creates value, serves customers, and incurs cost, a consultant or any professional is better equipped to relate their specific work to the bigger picture.

If a business model illustrates how a company makes money, an operating model reveals how it runs. It is the operational design that provides the capability to deliver the company strategy. There is no single model that can describe operations. At a strategic level, it can be the degree of integration among business units, from a tightly integrated company with a single profit and loss (P&L) statement to a distributed set of independent businesses. There are also operating models for industries, like eTOM (Enhanced Telecom Operations Map) for telecom companies, or functional areas like ITIL (Information Technology Infrastructure Library) for IT service management.

Although they vary widely, operating models have common elements and typically contain some combination of the following items:

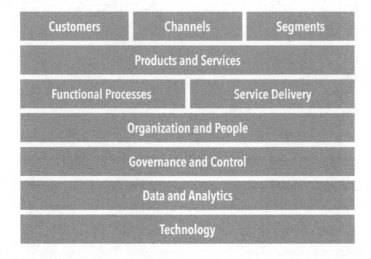

These layers in the stack each have different characteristics and capabilities required. For example, the organization layer includes the organization charter, roles, and responsibilities, while the functional process layer contains the processes, flow, and dependencies.

The point is that whatever the industry, whatever the functional area, an operating model of some kind exists. Even a highly complex entity like a global corporation can be viewed through a relatively simple framework. Use them well, and you can gain the vicarious benefit of years of experience from the outset.

VALUE REALIZATION

The objective of any company is to create and maintain a competitive advantage, and the measuring stick is value. Value realization itself can be used as a framework. How do we define value? Simply put, as benefits minus cost. However, value is a complex variable to measure. For example, how do we measure the value of customer sentiment? Frameworks can play an essential role in determining how value is created and measured.

In a consulting context, I have used my firm's Value Realization Method™ (VRM) many times, to assist clients to understand and then increase value generated by their operations through transformational programs. Every business ultimately competes based on the value they provide their customers, so maximizing value for each constituent component is important. To do this, it's necessary to understand what customers value, and how a company delivers it. This VRM framework starts with a strategic view, looking at shareholder benefits in the form of free cash flow and capabilities. It then looks at transformational elements in the form of change initiatives and the funding needed to deliver them. There are several tools used within VRM to make this happen, and the value diagram is the most visible. It links the components of free cash flow to operational levers, to business processes, and to specific initiatives that will drive the value. This establishes a clear line of sight from actual work delivered to the financial goals. VRM also adds an important metric to measure project success. Are projects not only on time and on budget, but also *on value*?

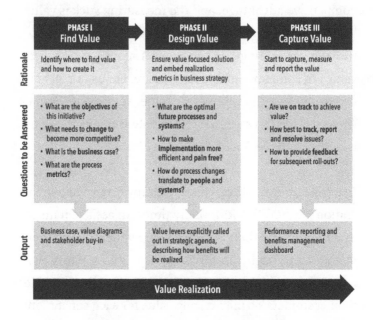

	PHASE I Find Value	PHASE II Design Value	PHASE III Capture Value
Rationale	Identify where to find value and how to create it	Ensure value focused solution and embed realization metrics in business strategy	Start to capture, measure and report the value
Questions to be Answered	• What are the **objectives** of this initiative? • What needs to **change** to become more competitive? • What is the **business case**? • What are the process **metrics**?	• What are the optimal future processes and systems? • How to make **implementation** more efficient and **pain free**? • How do process changes translate to **people** and **systems**?	• Are we **on track** to achieve value? • How best to **track, report** and **resolve** issues? • How to provide **feedback** for subsequent roll-outs?
Output	Business case, value diagrams and stakeholder buy-in	Value levers explicitly called out in strategic agenda, describing how benefits will be realized	Performance reporting and benefits management dashboard

Value Realization

This approach improves financial results, whether at a project level or for a large business transformation initiative. Just as important, it has a role to play to shift the mindset of professionals from self to service. When we focus on delivering value for customers, clients, and colleagues, it becomes apparent in the way we conduct ourselves and do business. This is not easy. It's hard to identify how your efforts will generate value, and to demonstrate that value. At the same time, this approach is highly effective and provides a competitive edge to those who truly practice it.

Historically, companies sold features and functions, and then evolved to solutions. However, value has become the staple of large initiatives, and certainly consulting work. In large, highly competitive proposals, it's standard to talk in terms of return on investment and value. As a day-to-day practice however, most people don't think in this way. It is easy to fall back into self-interest, instead of asking, "How can I improve the profits of my client, and increase my service?"

Mack Hanan pioneered this approach in the 1970s, and his books *Consultative Selling* and *Competing on Value* captured the essence via the phrase "norms." What does this mean? It means that true value is the *financial value* you can normally deliver, not just a consistent product or service. Most companies and people are not quite sure of the value they deliver, so they over- or under-estimate their worth in the eyes of customers, clients, employers, and others. The objective is to become so competent and confident about what you deliver that you can present someone with evidence, ideally in financial terms, describing the normal range of improvement you generate. When you can do this, it represents a huge competitive advantage and makes it easier to convince clients to place their confidence in you. This applies to internal projects also, as you may be competing with colleagues to fund your initiative. Or you may be competing for a promotion, and need to provide compelling evidence to make your case. This sounds difficult, and can be exceedingly so. It is at best a journey of discovery and requires regular reflection. Nonetheless, it is important to focus attention on value and service, and to see them objectively through the eyes of someone else.

In summary, value is an additional perspective and advantage you can bring to your work. The goal is to make the value you deliver *secure*, *substantial*, and *sequential*. In other words, clients should feel confident that you can deliver value, understand that the value you provide will be significant, and know that the value will be ongoing. How can you do this? Know your capabilities, understand what customers prioritize, and make sure your work addresses those needs.

DECISION-MAKING FRAMEWORKS

When conducting an analysis, it's tempting to jump in, crunch data and create reports. Good insights, however, originate from a thoughtful work plan. A work plan consists of two components: an activity map and a thinking map. When most people think of cases or projects, they think initially of activity maps, the Gantt chart that shows tasks to be performed. They neglect the importance of thinking maps.

Thinking maps identify major issues. They cover the development of an initial hypothesis, analysis, message, an understanding of what needs to be accomplished, and an assessment of the information and data that will be required. Many people skip this step because they feel that there's no time, or they think they already know everything they need. However, going down an unproductive path consumes precious resources, especially time. After weeks spent moving in the wrong direction, there may be no time to conduct a meaningful analysis. That's why a thinking map is important.

A thinking map can also prevent analysis paralysis by determining early the goals and the parameters which will be used to judge the value of the results. Modern software tools enable endless iteration, and it's tempting to conduct analysis after analysis, even when there's no further value to be gained.

There are three primary thinking maps that are useful for most situations you may enounter: the decision matrix, the issue tree, and the hypothesis approach. Tony Leopold is a friend and an executive at a leading fintech company. He spent many years at Bain Consulting and then led strategy for a major public corporation, and he swore by these three tools. The decision matrix is the easiest of the three to use, and it is used to choose the best available option. For example, perhaps you're choosing between two new jobs. The first is better paid, but it will require you to travel a lot, and the industry is high-risk. Another job offers lower compensation, but is local and more secure. How do you decide which one to choose? To use the decision matrix, simply establish a list of relevant criteria and assign a weight to each one. At first glance, it may appear difficult to compare the different options. Determine the relative value (weight) of each factor to you. Score each criterion, multiply by the weight, and add up the weighted criteria. If you have established the right criteria, weighting, and scoring, the highest weighted score will be the best choice.

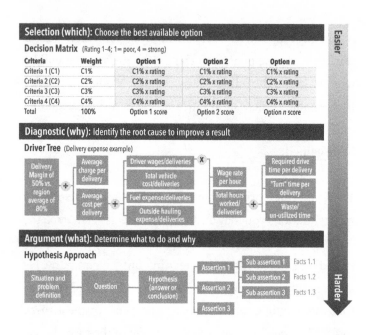

The issue tree is a diagnostic approach. It takes a question or problem and helps identify a root cause to direct improvement efforts. For example, you may be concerned that the profit margin on a product is too low. Since profit margin is cost subtracted from price, those can be initial branches on the issue tree. Then you can deconstruct each one further, into types of cost and price factors, showing the relationship between factors (sum, difference, multiplication, division)

at each step. Rather than taking a superficial view to assess whether the cost is too high or the price too low, you can compare sales volume in different regions, show discount amounts, and consider the impact of overhead allocations. This approach provides depth and clarity on where problems truly exist, and that allows you to address the root causes of these problems and take action in the areas that will make the most impact.

You can use issue trees to look back and improve a result, and you can use them to look forward, asking what *may* happen and how to optimize that future outcome. They are best used when the problem or objective is clear. They are not as effective in determining a new course of action.

A hypothesis is a proposed explanation made on the basis of limited evidence as a starting point for further analysis. The hypothesis approach can be used to determine what to do, and why. For example, perhaps you believe that a business model can't scale profitably because there are too many manual steps involved to acquire customers. Should you scale, or not? By testing the hypothesis, you determine whether to move forward or not.

Start by defining the question, and doing just enough research to understand the situation. Many an initiative has been delayed because someone wanted to read everything they could on a topic, just in case it would help or provide an easy answer. Easy answers don't exist, and you can waste a lot of time in the pursuit of complete understanding. Develop the hypothesis and its conditions ("what must be true"). As data is collected and analyzed, it may confirm the hypothesis, which is great. If not, refine the hypothesis and try again. This approach can work well because it doesn't require you to know everything about a problem before you start to resolve it. Instead, it asks you to take a stand, then quickly prove or disprove it. A hypothesis is a starting point for experimentation, not an endpoint, allowing people to get to the vicinity of an answer, regardless of where they started.

There are two challenges when using the hypothesis approach. First, to use it successfully, you must take a stand with incomplete data. This can be scary, but ironically, the earlier you can do this the better. Why? Because taking an early stand gives you permission to be wrong. If you are already deep into a process before you take a stand, you will be far more invested in it, as will your colleagues and clients. There will be far more pressure to be right. Which leads to the second challenge. Be willing to adjust your conclusion based on the facts. If the facts don't support your hypothesis, you have a bad hypothesis, and must let it go. Our biases blind us to the possibility of discovery, and we must be vigilant to evolve our thinking based on the data and what the facts tell us.

As with any approach, hypotheses carry risks. You may fail

to consider certain possibilities, because they do not occur to you. You may be tempted to justify your initial hypothesis, forcing the facts to fit the hypothesis, instead of the other way around. At the same time, the hypothesis approach allows freedom to tackle any issue, no matter how strategic or novel, and does not require much in the way of prerequisites. It also carries the side benefit of being a great learning tool. The more of these analyses you conduct, the better your judgment becomes.

THE 2X2 MATRIX

We've covered several types of frameworks. One that deserves special attention is the 2x2 matrix. It's perhaps the most famous—or infamous—framework in business. Why infamous? Because the 2x2 matrix can appear straightforward, some business leaders roll their eyes at the prospect of using them, claiming that they are too simple. Despite—or because of—this simplicity, however, well-designed 2x2 matrices are clever and powerful.

What makes them so useful? First, they are clear, easy to understand. A 2x2 matrix consists of only four quadrants. Compare this with a 2x2x2 matrix, which involves several more cells across three dimensions. It's more complex to create and harder to visualize on the two-dimensional surface of a piece of paper or screen. Even a 3x3 matrix contains more cells and unnecessary complexity than the simplicity of a 2x2 array. The best 2x2 matrices utilize this simplicity to create a contrast between the points in each quadrant. Consider this example: ease of implementation compared with amount of value.

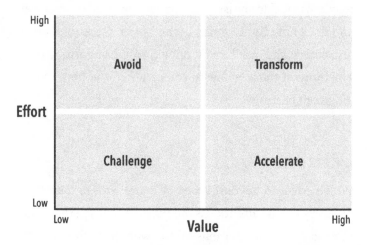

A course of action that is easy to implement and high value is a no-brainer. It's clear that it should be a high priority. The opposite is true of an option that is difficult to implement and low value. In life, however, most choices aren't that straightforward. How about choices that are easy to implement but low value, or difficult to implement but high value? How can you choose between them? Perhaps the easy/low-value options are a good way to create a sense of momentum and generate progress, even if the changes themselves are minor. On the other hand, perhaps the difficult/high-value ideas are so valuable that they are worth investing in over the long term. Also, what will it take to move an item from a less desirable quadrant to a better one?

An interesting element of 2x2 matrices is that they often unearth tensions between multiple options. These matrices allow us to learn about the problems we wish to resolve, and enable people to consider complex situations in simpler terms. The core variables are simply shown on the two axes. To enrich the analysis, we can include additional variables through the size or color of each data point. It's important to choose the right variables, not simply complicate the chart with non-essential data labels and formatting.

The 2x2 matrix is useful for solving dilemmas. A dilemma is defined as a choice between two alternatives, neither of which is desirable. In life, we are often faced with a choice between imperfect situations. The 2x2 matrix allows us to look at our dilemmas from multiple perspectives and make trade-offs. Dilemmas may be uncomfortable, but they force us to think and develop deeper understanding. It is not possible to attain all our objectives simultaneously, like high profits, high growth, and low risk, so we need a method to identify the best answer for our imperfect situation.

EIGHT ARCHETYPAL DILEMMAS

As with the Hero's Journey, there are several archetypal dilemmas that arise again and again, and understanding them helps us make difficult choices. In their insightful book, *The Power of the 2x2 Matrix*, Alex Lowy and Phil Hood identified eight of the most common archetypal dilemmas through a rigorous process of data gathering and synthesis. Many life—and business—dilemmas can be categorized into one of these eight archetypes. They are:

Head and heart. How can we choose between what we think and what we feel? The toughest choices are between what makes sense and what feels right. A classic example comes from the Bible, in which God asks Abraham to sacrifice his son, Isaac. His heart is obedient, but his head resists. Eventually, his heart prevails and he is rewarded for his faith.

Inside and outside. How do we align the internal and external demands placed on us? Systems are most effective when they are matched with the demands of their contexts. When they fall out of alignment, something needs to change. Under Lou Gerstner, for example, IBM took the decision to restructure from a hardware to a services company to meet the demands of a transformed marketplace.

Cost and benefit. What is the price of getting what we desire? All efforts to predict the future involve risk, choosing the course of least pain and most gain. Walmart promises "everyday low prices," whereas Whole Foods charges more and sells the brand on delivering other types of value. The trade-off may change again, following Amazon's purchase of Whole Foods.

Product and market. What are the options, based on our current situation? We can alter the products we offer, how we present them, or where we sell them. The market changes over time. The PalmPilot succeeded where the Apple Newton failed. Later, however, the iPhone redefined the market, and the PalmPilot faded away.

Change and stability. We want to grow, but we also want to be safe. How do we balance those desires, keeping our lives fresh without falling into chaos? Companies and people need change, but there is a limit to how much they can absorb at any given time.

The known and the unknown. How can we map our knowledge against other people's knowledge, what we don't know, what no one knows, and assess the relative importance of each?

Competing priorities. What's urgent and what's important? How can we determine what we should do first, and avoid the temptation to tackle immediate tasks and put off the truly transformational ones?

Content and process. The content is the *what*, the process is the *how*. How do we balance our focus between our products (what) and supporting processes (how)? How do we optimize our portfolio with the resources we invest?

The 2x2 matrix appears simple, but it can be used to address some of the deepest questions we encounter as human beings, giving us a framework with which to determine the relative importance of each dimension.

In this chapter, we have covered several frameworks and how to use them. The real power of frameworks becomes apparent when you create one to meet your own needs. This is especially true of the 2x2 matrix; you can create this yourself with a little practice. You should use existing ones where they fit your needs, but there is nothing more professionally empowering than being able to create something new when existing tools do not solve your problem. Here is a simple method to do so.

1. Identify the problem space. What is the general problem

to be solved? Don't get too narrow at this point, because you do not yet know where the real conflict lies.

2. Determine the objective. What will the 2x2 matrix help you do? Change your product portfolio? Choose a software product?

3. List the situational elements. Brainstorm all the features you can imagine and why they are desirable or a challenge.

4. Categorize the elements. Group the elements from step 3 into logical categories.

5. Prioritize the categories. Determine which categories are most important.

6. Select the axes and name the quadrants. The axes can be dimensions like temperature, with low and high at the end points. The quadrant names will take some effort, as they should embody the situation at each quadrant of a matrix. As an example, if profits are high but industry growth is low, that quadrant can be named "cash cow," not simply profit-high/industry-low.

7. Test the matrix on actual examples. Run some examples through your 2x2 matrix and see if it serves its purpose well. If not, make some refinements; perhaps change the name of a quadrant, or even choose a new axis.

Creating a 2x2 matrix is a thinking exercise, a way to use your brain to solve a problem where no tool existed before. In addition to helping you solve your immediate problem, it is a great to way to practice critical thinking and add intellectual capital to the world of analytical frameworks.

Frameworks are important because of the tremendous intellectual potential they provide, but it's just that—potential. To realize their full value, you also need to structure your thinking effectively. Critical thinking organizes concepts into compelling qualitative arguments, yet there is still something missing. An extra level of structured analytical reasoning is needed to address problems and convey recommendations in a clear and concise manner.

Conventional wisdom suggests that you should gather all the facts, think hard about the problem, and then show your complete thought process. However, in business, you only have a limited amount of time to convey your point. Fail to do this effectively and you will lose the attention of the people you want to reach. The Pyramid Principle is a highly effective framework to win—and keep—the attention of your audience, whether in presentations or written reports.

The Pyramid Principle is a way to organize ideas and insights into a logical framework that addresses an important question or topic. It was developed by Barbara Minto, McKinsey's head of training in the 1970s, and she codified the Pyramid Principle into a best-selling book of the same name. She was an expert in turning top business school recruits into highly skilled consultants at a rapid pace. This method was powerful, enabling highly intelligent but raw talent to quickly develop the analytical ability to consult executives of major corporations. How? By focusing consultants to share the "so what?" (what we think about a situation), not simply the activities (a summary of what we've done so far).

It is called a pyramid because there is a main message or answer, which is supported by major points. Together, these form your recommendations, further supported by the facts and data underlying each point. This principle is based on the premise that ideas in writing should always form a pyramid under a single thought.

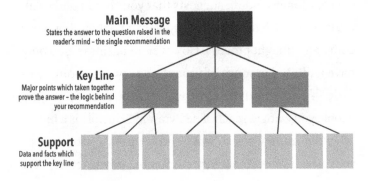

Main Message
States the answer to the question raised in the reader's mind – the single recommendation

Key Line
Major points which taken together prove the answer – the logic behind your recommendation

Support
Data and facts which support the key line

The Pyramid Principle follows the deductive and inductive logic covered in Chapter Two. In nearly every project, we conduct analyses and develop conclusions. The Pyramid Principle provides a method to communicate that thinking to others. When we use this structure, we deliver the answer first, and then support our conclusions with underlying points and data. For the audience, this is a very different experience from suffering through a series of sequential data and convoluted arguments before eventually seeing a conclusion and recommendation.

Building on Chapters Three and Four, effective communication balances your objective as a communicator with the goals of your audience. We want the audience to do something, so we put things in terms they can understand and make the message clear. A logical structure converts the information we collect, analyze, and synthesize into powerful, fact-based recommendations. The pyramid structure makes the message precise and helps us be clear about what we choose to communicate to the reader, preventing messages that are unintended or intellectually empty. It also reveals potential gaps in our thinking, enabling us to anticipate and respond to the reader's questions before the communication is delivered. Finally, the pyramid structure provides clarity to the reader, minimizing the effort they must expend to understand the message, and eliminating the possibility that our message is misunderstood or ignored entirely.

How does this work? Think about the arc of a story. Good stories don't start by dumping a lot of complex information on their audiences. They set the context, creating a mental picture in the minds of readers or listeners. Next, some form of complication emerges, a conflict in an otherwise peaceful situation. This leads to a question. How will the hero or heroine—in this case, your client or audience—respond? Finally, there is an answer or resolution, with major points and supporting detail provided in the pyramid structure.

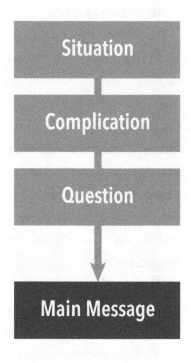

Let's work through this structure using a fictional shoe company as an example.

Situation: "The Nice Shoe company is a major player in the footwear industry. For years, the company has exhibited a steady increase in annual revenue and profitability." This simple line establishes context, familiarity with the company, and a baseline scenario.

Complication: "This quarter, for the first time, Nice Shoes' profitability unexpectedly dropped to negative net margin." The issue is immediately obvious to the audience. This creates a sense of urgency, compelling your audience to pay attention.

Question: "How can we reverse this decrease in margin and restore Nice Shoes to profitability?" This move opens a discussion, similar to ancient Socratic dialogues. The question follows logically from the complication, setting up the rest of the presentation. For the sake of this example, we are using a simple, obvious question. In practice, the question would likely be more complex and subtle.

Answer: This usually won't happen on the first try. Converging on the best answer is typically an iterative process. The answer or main message will be supported by the pyramid logic. The answer must address the audience's major concern or need. The first level below the answer is the key line, containing the major points. The supporting data and facts come below the key line.

A point needs to summarize or synthesize the items grouped below it. In any one group, the ideas must relate to each other logically, and they must be MECE (mutually exclusive and collectively exhaustive). This means that each group is complete, distinct, and includes all the points necessary to support the summary idea above it.

Strive to make your answers as simple as possible within these constraints. In his groundbreaking 1967 book, *The Psychology of Communication*, George Miller demonstrated that human beings can hold approximately seven separate items in short-term memory. In fact, he found that the variation was plus or minus two, meaning some people could remember only as few as five items. Therefore, aim to provide between three and five major points to support your main recommendation. This gives you leeway to get one or two points wrong, while also keeping the number manageable.

People tend not to listen to things they already know. They are more interested in learning new information, especially if that new information promises to deliver them benefits. Making a statement to your audience that tells them something they don't know will automatically raise a question in their minds. They will be focused and intent, keen to hear an answer to their question. A question-answer dialogue maintains the listener's attention. However, keep in mind the topic must be of interest to your listener. This question-answer cadence is a central part of the Pyramid Principle.

The Pyramid Principle is effective because it incorporates both natural storytelling attributes and sound logical reasoning, through a combination of vertical and horizontal logic. The vertical logic represents the storyline (question-answer dialogue), and the horizontal logic is about the kind of reasoning. For the vertical logic, in the same way we read a story top-down, we read one sentence after the other. We start with the main idea, then a question is raised, and then we answer the question. This is how the Situation-Complication-Question construct begins the pyramid, and it also explains the relationship of the answer to its major points and their supporting details. Vertical logic answers the questions "how" or "why." To support a "how" question, list the steps to show how to accomplish the point. For "why" questions, list the reasons why that point is valid. The steps or reasons become the "boxes" that support the main point in the key line.

Horizontal logic answers the question raised by the point above it in the pyramid. Each answer is based on a supporting set of data, either an inductive grouping or deductive argument. Building on the reasoning section in Chapter Two, an example of inductive logic is, "Athletes are strong because they train a lot, they live healthy lives, and they have to compete." That statement provides a list of reasons *why* the point ("Athletes are strong") is valid. A deductive reasoning example is, "Athletes are strong. I am an athlete. Therefore, I am strong." The initial premise, the second premise, and the conclusion are all linked interdependently. Much like the broader topic of critical thinking, there are guidelines to use when constructing inductive and deductive logic for the Pyramid Principle. Below are a few of the most important ones for each type.

Inductive groupings need to be logically parallel, independent, of equal hierarchical importance, and ordered (chronological, structural, degree, or importance). Inductive logic groups items by their plural nouns, such as steps, reasons, or problems. Scrutinize the groupings to make sure they are "tight" and relate to each other in a MECE way. A common mistake is to use labels instead of complete thoughts. While it is easier to think of a single word, complete sentences allow you to test your logic at each level and for each grouping.

Deductive logic presents an argument in successive steps and relies on the reasoning process to move from general premise to specific conclusion or recommendation.

Unfortunately, deductive arguments require a strictly ordered chain of ideas, reflecting a line of reasoning that leads to an inevitable conclusion. While the implied certainty sounds good, this means that any flaw in the reasoning, any break in the logical chain, can void the argument. To prevent this, pay careful attention to the premise and its following interdependent points.

Why is all this important? Because the Pyramid Principle enables you to communicate with greater impact and reach a more executive audience. It is easy to translate a well-structured pyramid into an effective presentation. The Situation-Complication-Question summary becomes your first page, and the answer or main message becomes your second page. Each main point becomes a section in the presentation, with a setup page and a page for each significant supporting data point. Storyboarding horizontal logic is the connective tissue leading the reader from one page to another. The header for each page—slide—is the main point, and the body of the page contains the inductive or deductive items that support that point in the story. Simply following the Pyramid Principle approach will increase the structure and quality of your presentations and reports.

The Pyramid Principle is a powerful tool and can certainly help create better presentations. However, its chief benefit may be that it helps us become better critical thinkers and increase our impact overall. To realize the benefits, you need to practice the Pyramid Principle and make using it a habit when you produce analyses, presentations, and reports. Let me repeat: this takes practice to master. Read this section a few times, check out other references, and practice in your own work. When they initially try it, the Pyramid Principle is not comfortable for most people, because it exercises their mental muscle in new ways. Also, many people are simply not exposed to it early in their careers, so they are not aware of it and lack practice. In spite of this—or perhaps because of it—the Pyramid Principle can be a secret weapon for anyone, especially junior professionals, to improve their thinking, amplify their impact, and accelerate their career growth.

ESTIMATION

Estimation is another essential skill for analysts. Initially it may not appear important. Why bother estimating when we can simply conduct an analysis with exact amounts? The reason is that estimation allows us to reach an approximate answer quickly, and determine which questions are worth pursuing further. Imagine that someone asks you to calculate 101 multiplied by 99. That's a difficult calculation, but you can easily estimate the answer. How? What's 100 multiplied by 100? In this example, you can get within 1 percent of the exact answer with a quick estimation (10,000 versus the exact answer of 9,999). Estimation helps us create reasonable hypotheses, faster.

Estimation is a proxy for perceived judgment. It's not meant to take the place of an exact answer when required, but to provide an approximate, directionally correct answer when that is sufficient. The capability to estimate allows you to quickly identify potential solutions or to refute those that are not feasible. It also shows you understand the most important elements of an analysis or case. Estimation is often used in consulting interviews, because they're a good way to assess how well candidates think on their feet.

How many cars cross the Golden Gate Bridge in a day? How many ping-pong balls can fit inside a semitrailer? How many people globally are flying in airplanes at this moment? These questions require an enormous amount of work to answer accurately with detail. With estimation, you can give approximate answers in minutes, without a calculator, based on reasonable suppositions.

How might you do that? First, consider the major components of the question. Deconstruct it. Using the ping-pong ball example above, ask yourself how large is a ping-pong ball? What are the rough internal dimensions of a standard semitrailer? You may be guessing, but your guesses can be educated. You have some idea of the diameter of a ping-pong ball and how large a semitrailer is, which you can use to find the trailer's interior volume, into which you can divide the volume of a ball. With that basic understanding, some rounding and basic arithmetic, you can reach an approximate answer in minutes with only pen and paper. Let's try this in real time.

Step	Calculation	Estimation Logic ("mental dialogue")	Estimation	Exact Calculation
1	Identify the problem components	Determine semi-trailer volume, then individual ping-pong ball size, then divide to get the number		
2	Estimate semi-trailer length	About 4 cars long, at about 10' per car, so let's say 40'	40	53
3	Estimate semi-trailer height	Pretty tall, let's say 10' (basketball goal height)	10	8.42
4	Estimate semi-trailer width	More than the size of a car, less than 10 feet, but 10 is a round number, so let's go with it	10	8.04
5	Estimate semi-trailer volume	Length x width x height (10 x 10 x 40') ft³	4,000	3,587
6	Estimate ping-pong ball radius	Ping pong balls seem larger than an inch, so let's say 1.5" diameter or .75" radius	.75	2.03
7	Estimate ping-pong ball volume	A circle is $\pi\,r^2$, and volume is a third dimension, so let's cube it. Then, π is close to 3. So, (.75 x .75 x .75) x 3, which seems like <1 x 3, so let's call it 2"	2	2.03
8	Convert units to be the same: ft³ to in³	1 ft³ = 1' x 1' x 1', or 12" x 12" x 12", or 144 in² x 12", which is 1,440 + 288 = 1,728 in³	1,728	1,728
9	Estimate semi-trailer volume in in³	4,000 ft³ x 1,728 in³/ft³; let's go with 2,000, which means 4,000 x 2,000 = 8,000,000 in³	8,000,000	6,198,774
10	Divide interior volume by volume of a single ping-pong ball	"8,000,000 divided by 2 (let's see, this is a tough one…)"	4,000,000	3,059,202
11	How close did we get?		31%	

Note that, even with inaccuracies, even getting the spherical volume formula wrong, the estimated answer in the example is still within 31 percent of the exact answer, which could have taken a lot more effort to find. The point is that a quick, directionally accurate estimate allows you to work with a hypothesis. Even if we know the answer is incorrect, as long as we are true to our assumptions and approach, we have met the objective—and once someone improves our assumptions, our answers will automatically improve.

Like any skill, estimation requires practice, but it's worth the effort. You can practice anytime, in any setting. You will soon find that you don't need a calculator or a computer to estimate effectively. You can do it on the fly in a meeting. Businesspeople, especially engineers and accountants, are uncomfortable with ambiguity and uncertainty. Business takes place in the real world, however, and it's often messy and uncertain. Embracing ambiguity is an essential skill, and becoming more so. We live in a dynamic world, and rapid change is the norm.

We watched superhero movies as children, and—admit it—maybe even as adults. Who doesn't want a superpower, such as being able to fly or run much faster than mere mortals? Estimation is like a superpower, because it lets us do things much faster, with reasonable accuracy.

FROM FRAMEWORKS TO PRODUCTIVITY

If you are reading this book from cover to cover, you've probably noticed that each chapter builds on the previous ones, adding more skills to the repertoire of a services professional. This chapter built on the previous ones, adding frameworks and analytical reasoning to thinking and communication skills. As we move into a discussion of productivity, this trend continues. We shift our focus to discuss personal effectiveness. Without an understanding of how to be productive, the other tools in this book are of limited value. How can we bring together the skills we've discussed so far and put them into practice for maximum effect?

CHAPTER SIX

PRODUCTIVITY

"To think is easy. To act is difficult. To act as one thinks is the most difficult."

—JOHANN WOLFGANG VON GOETHE

Pamela was a marketing director at a small but rapidly growing company in the telecommunications equipment industry. Companies in this industry typically compete on product features, but it would have been tough going up against larger incumbents with deeper pockets. This company had great products but took a different approach, deciding to compete on productivity as well. Their leadership chose to maximize productivity through technology and insights.

Through intelligent use of software tools like Salesforce and Tableau, they automated their marketing, drove their decisions through data-driven insights, and blurred the lines between business and IT. Pamela and her colleagues in marketing understood and got close to their customers, and used sales automation to connect with prospects at just the right moment in their buying cycles. Other companies had similar tools, but this rising star generated much more productivity from them. Through doing so, the company maximized effectiveness and amplified the impact of their products to out-compete larger companies that simply did not move as quickly or efficiently.

A very different example of high productivity is the work of one of my clients, Michel Langlois, a Silicon Valley engineering executive who drove productivity through relationships and delegation. His productivity was based on finding ways to get the results he needed that others couldn't, often in a fraction of the time. Impressively, he did this across multiple disciplines, from engineering to marketing to human resources. A large part of Michel's productivity was the way he hired people he could trust, communicated what he needed, then held people accountable for high-performance results. He also enrolled supporters to his cause, often after they were initially indifferent or opposed to his ideas. Due to a disarming mix of clarity, charm, and passion, he succeeded in getting more done through others and inspiring their best work.

He insisted on board-quality content, but did not spend all his time creating slides and reports. Instead, he relied on people he could trust on his team and at firms like mine, so he could focus on gathering input, making decisions, and then sharing and selling his ideas more effectively.

There's more than one way to define productivity. My neighbor George was a software developer at a large tech firm and was very family-oriented. He woke up at 4:30 a.m. each morning to work out, and he finished his work at 6:00 p.m. every night. He organized his entire working schedule with surgical precision to ensure that he had as much time as possible for his family. Productivity isn't just about how much we can do at once, how much output we can create, or how much money we make. For some, it is simply freeing up personal time through discipline and prioritization. For George, it was about making the most of being a father and husband. He was a good employee who never skimped on his work responsibilities, but also had no desire to advance his career faster at the potential expense of his family relationships.

Productivity and self-help books are seemingly everywhere. It seems impossible to throw a rock without hitting a book about how to achieve more, hack life, and become superhuman. With all that content available, why aren't we more productive?

Let's think about what personal productivity is. In its simplest form, productivity is defined by output created divided by units of input. This translates as measurable, meaningful outcomes divided by the time taken to attain those outcomes. Productivity is *not* a measure of how many hours a person puts in, or how much they sweat. By definition, the more hours it takes us to achieve a specified outcome, the less productive we are. Working smarter, not harder, is a cliché for a reason. It enables greater productivity.

To improve or even know our productivity, we need to define our goals, because achieving those outcomes is what matters. Do you define goals in terms of work tasks like clearing the email inbox or creating more reports? How about career goals, like to make more money or achieve a certain title? Closer to home, are your goals to spend more time with family, pursue a hobby, or volunteer for a favorite cause? It is important to get specific and not hold back, even if your initial list is long and lacks priorities.

The next question is how do we reach those goals? What's the minimum effective dose—the smallest amount of work required to achieve the desired result? This is not to suggest skimping at work. In fact, it's the opposite. It requires knowing our work very well, to determine exactly what we want to accomplish, then do what it takes to accomplish that goal. This realization often brings out personal beliefs and biases in people. First, it means you—not someone else or your email inbox—control your schedule. Even if your manager is telling you what needs to get done, you still have some leeway about how to do it, and to seek out ways of doing it better. When we realize that we can accomplish more, sometimes in a fraction of the time, the question becomes what do we do with the extra time? Is it acceptable to read, take a nap, or even go home?

I have helped several clients optimize their factories through advanced planning and scheduling. When we finished our projects, the clients typically experienced large productivity gains, removing the need for hours of daily production part expediting activities. Production planners sometimes did not know what to do with that extra time, and it was a change management exercise to translate the additional time to true productivity gains. People sometimes feel anxious when they become more productive, because they are faced with new dilemmas. If chasing down components is no longer a big part of my work day, do I have the skills for the more advanced work I should really be doing? If you no longer need to catch up on emails late at night, can you invest in learning, or even simply relax and enjoy the additional time?

Being busy can be a personal security blanket. We may believe that if we're working hard we are making progress, and eventually we will get where we need to go. Even if we become productive on a given task, we feel we need to fill the additional time with a substitute, equivalent activity. Some companies have moved away from a culture of conspicuous hard work, including a few that block email access for employees on paid time off. An example is German automaker Daimler (Mercedes-Benz), which implemented a "no mail on holiday" email policy that ensures its employees take full advantage of their time off, without fearing an overflowing inbox when they return. Through this policy, employees have the option to set their emails to *autodelete* while away from the office. Nonetheless, these remain exceptions. At the time of writing, the "stay busy" mentality is still a major workplace problem.

I struggle with these concepts too, and am definitely a work in progress. I tend to follow productivity increases by taking on more commitments, then back away for a while, reestablish my footing, and repeat the cycle. The important thing is to be self-aware, to make sure your approach is right for you, and take stock of where you are on a regular basis.

A big part of becoming more productive is simply to shine a spotlight on the activities that *don't* contribute to your productivity. Remove everything that doesn't belong and you'll be left with what matters most. This does not require any sophisticated tools, only a healthy, unbiased look at the activities and processes you're engaged in, and the self-awareness to eliminate those that are unnecessary. Productivity is not about utilizing every life hack and time-saving tool. It is knowing what you want in life and aligning your activities to those goals to have a better chance to achieve them.

When taken to excess, the idea of productivity becomes

almost satirical. From the outside, we start to resemble hamsters, running faster and faster on our wheels. There's no limit to how productive we can become, but we need to ask ourselves why. What goals are we seeking to attain? There are plenty of people listening to podcasts and audiobooks at 1.5x normal speed, using the "too many podcasts, too short a commute" rationale. I get it, and yet the cadence of speaking, replete with the pause for effect, gets lost in the double-time, SmartSpeed silence remover. At the extreme, people can become increasingly impatient. When the headphones come off, normal speech pace becomes maddeningly slow.

Podcasts and time-sensitive news aside, reading a book can and should be a pleasurable experience. Perhaps reading a book slowly is akin to eating a meal slowly. Is it more productive to consume your steak twice as fast, or is it important to enjoy it? On the subject of multitasking, it is tempting to keep an eye on the smartphone while with others, but there's also something to be said for unplugging and enjoying the moment. Personally, I enjoy tennis; it is physical, outdoors—for the most part—and social. There are cool tech tools that can measure swings, racquet head speed, and court movement. So far, I have resisted the urge to use them, because I want to avoid being tied to a smartphone while playing tennis. At least for now, I don't want to take away from the tennis experience by my own efforts to become more productive.

Productivity has become an industry in its own right. It

has much to offer, but it's not a panacea. My friend Charlie Hoehn was a productivity machine as he collaborated on highly successful book marketing campaigns for best-selling authors, including Tim Ferriss. He even found a way to turn off the part of his brain that needed sleep (think of the movie *Limitless*). Did it make him more productive? In the short-term, yes, but then it fried his circuits. That crash caused him to rethink everything and led him in the opposite direction, looking for ways to reduce his stress levels instead of endlessly amping-up his productivity. Charlie has spoken and written extensively on this topic, captured in his wonderful book *Play It Away*. Before trying to become hyper-productive, ask yourself what you truly want to achieve. Then, design your strategy so that it meets your true objectives, and keep in mind that more time does not always equal more productivity.

The ancient Greeks had the concept of *arête*, which translates roughly as "moral virtue." They believed in education as more than an intellectual pursuit. In their eyes, it involved the mind (*logos*), body or emotion (*pathos*), and the soul (*ethos*). Sound familiar? Yes, these also roughly form the basis of rhetorical, persuasive speech covered in Chapter Two. Intriguingly, these concepts are as relevant today as ever, despite being largely forgotten in the modern world. The balanced combination of all three areas made someone a "whole" person.

At the simplest level, think about people you know who

may work too hard, sleep too little, and not eat well—that's most of us, at some point. Overwork leaves us vulnerable to burnout. Lack of sleep robs us of the time we need to restore and rejuvenate. Poor diet means a dearth of the nutrients we require to focus and be creative. In the long term, pushing to do more and more work is less productive than working smart. We all have deadlines, and sometimes meeting them requires us to get out of balance for a time. However, it is easy to fall into a rut, and then it takes conscious effort to work through it and restore energy. The restorative powers of sleep and exercise are amazing. We know this, and yet seem to have to rediscover it periodically after pushing the envelope a bit too hard.

In summary, take care of your personal *logos, pathos,* and *ethos* to help you stay fresh and maintain a healthy perspective. This will also make you more interesting to be around and more empathetic, and make it easier for others to connect with you. In the quest for productivity, these qualities are often neglected in favor of more tactical, short-term, and superficial markers of success, but they're equally important. Sometimes even more so.

In an industrial society, there was a prevalent view that specialization—reducing one's role to a rigid set of specific responsibilities, then going deep—was the way to succeed. Even if that view was ever right, we are in the digital age and the norms of industrial society are being reexamined and evolved. The capacity to think critically and creatively, to develop insights and communicate effectively, is more important than ever.

This is a major challenge for the big winners of industrial society. For example, doctors, lawyers, and accountants study for years to perfect their professions. They invest a huge amount of time and money in specialization, on the assumption that the investment will set them up in a satisfying and lucrative career. The same holds true for anyone considering a college degree or trade that requires extensive training. In a world where the market need is changing faster than the time to acquire skills and experience, is a profession worth it? Ironically, the more fluid and rapidly evolving the market, the more valuable the profession, if the core capability is frequently refreshed with newly relevant skills.

This book is not a diet and exercise manual, but it's worth mentioning a few basics. If you have a passion for sports or going to the gym, great. Otherwise, at least get enough sleep, take vitamins, and drink plenty of water. Find a way of being active that you enjoy, even if that's walking the dog. Revisit your goals regularly to ensure that you do not drift too far from them.

However hard you work, you can't do *everything* you want to do. It is necessary to accept some limits. At the same time, the human body is very resilient. If you used to work out in college, you can soon regain enough strength and stamina to make an appreciable difference to your performance. Too often, people believe that if they have made poor choices in the past, it is too late to make changes. I disagree. We are each a work in progress. We may be the sum total of the choices we've made to date, but that also means we can change as we change our choices. Like exponential smoothing, recent changes carry the most significant impact, so don't let the past get you down.

AUTOMATED PRODUCTIVITY

Since the first Industrial Revolution, humans have been automating up and down the value chain. It is a process that continues today, to a degree that would amaze people who lived only a century ago. Imagine explaining the concept of a remote-controlled electric garage door opener to someone living in the early twentieth century.

In the United States, none of us live without automation. The only question is how far we want to automate. A natural place to start is with our email inboxes. Every email represents an ask, a piece of information, or a potential commitment. Imagine your email inbox as a stack of papers on your desk and you will have a better sense of how much work it requires to stay on top of your correspondence. If you have a thousand emails in your inbox, imagine a thousand pieces of paper stacked in an in-tray on your desk. Even worse, many of those emails have documents attached to them, adding to the stack. Seeing that inbox as a physical, verrrrrry high stack, what would you do if someone asked you to take on more work? You'd probably refuse, knowing that you have a lot to do before you can make any more commitments. Yet, many of us happily accept more work when we have a thousand emails waiting to process, because we don't really see them, or fully consider the time and effort to complete them.

For most of us, the transition from physical to digital is inevitable and empowering. However, it is also good to think in physical terms, for example by picturing how much effort a request will take, so we can visualize our existing commitments and respect the limits of our capacity. Humans have been relating to the physical world since the dawn of time, but we have only recently come to grips with the digital world. Our minds are still wired to think in tangible terms, so translating our electronic requests to physical terms can help us plan and respond more effectively.

SHORT-TERM AND LONG-TERM PRODUCTIVITY

You are no doubt familiar with the parable of the tortoise and the hare. The lesson it offers is that life is a marathon, not a sprint, and the way to be successful is to move slowly and steadily. I disagree with that premise. A career isn't a marathon. It is built on a series of sprints—periods of intense activity—followed by periods of rest.

The slow and steady approach implies that we are most productive when working at half capacity, but is that really the case? Think back to the key accomplishments in your life. Were they achieved through slow, steady progress, or through bursts of high-intensity activity? Persistent progress does pave the way, but there are moments of truth when we need to push through and do things that are difficult, knowing that we can rest when we reach the other side. If we don't get after it, we're not going to win. Someone else will outthink or outwork us, and the opportunity will pass us by.

This should be encouraging. You don't need to kill yourself with work to succeed. Instead, you need to be prepared to work intensely some of the time. Think about a light switch. It's either on or it's off. You can't turn it half-on and expect it to function—and dimmers are just that: dimmer. By the same token, it is better to focus on work, then rest, than to be constantly, somewhat focused on work.

Reread the fable of the tortoise and the hare and you'll notice that the hare's defeat stems not from his strategy, but from his poor decisions. He is complacent, assuming he can't possibly be beaten. He is overconfident to the point of hubris, gets distracted, and takes a nap. Even then, he loses only by moments. Had he simply sprinted, rested, then sprinted again, remaining humble and focused on his goal, he would have outrun the tortoise with ease.

For many people, this a significant mental shift. They measure themselves by the clock, not by what they accomplish. It can be frightening to make an honest assessment of what you are truly accomplishing and to think about how you can increase productive time. How does this change our approach? It is impossible to run a marathon as though it were a sprint. We'd crash, and never finish. On the other hand, there's no sense in pacing ourselves through a sprint. Everyone will quickly overtake us. The analogy is simple, but applies to small projects and careers alike. Sprint, then rest, sprint, then rest. It also manifests itself in Agile project work, covered in a later chapter, which even uses terms like "sprint" to define project intervals.

This approach also allows for our goals to change. Although we can say that family is most important in our lives, there are times when a project takes center stage. At other times, we may be focused on a degree program or other personal commitment. Even within work itself, at any given time we're faced with a swirl of goals and obligations. If we are already committed to the career equivalent of a marathon, it's a big deal to change course. If we see things as a series of sprints, we can more easily choose a new direction, or course correct after missteps.

To choose a new direction, people need to reflect on their experiences and then take action. Stoicism is an ancient yet still highly relevant philosophy that provides daily downtime to do just that. To bring this philosophy to the masses, Ryan Holiday and Stephen Hanselman created *The Daily Stoic Journal*. It blends the flexible practicality of the Stoic mindset with the incredibly useful tool of a structured journal for morning and evening reflection.

Some personal development philosophies encourage people to live as though they will die tomorrow. This sounds good, but what would you really do if you knew you only had twenty-four hours to live? You probably wouldn't go to work. This highlights the distinction between short-term and long-term goals. When you have long-term goals in mind, you're willing to delay gratification so that you can achieve them. When you only consider short-term objectives, your capacity to delay gratification diminishes greatly.

This isn't to say that you shouldn't enjoy life each day. It's simply to recognize that delayed gratification is an essential part of any plan to become more productive. Without the capacity to delay gratification, there would be no society or long-term progress. Nobody would ever do anything that didn't bring them immediate satisfaction. When I graduated college, I had a choice between going to work at LTV Steel in East Chicago and going to Texas Instruments in Dallas, which held the promise of high-tech and an industry on the rise. The steel job paid 20 percent more than the one at TI, but I thought working in a high-tech firm was the right move for a freshly minted electrical engineering graduate, who needed to venture out of the Midwest to see a bit more of the world. Less income initially, and less familiarity, but ultimately that decision shaped my entire career.

Sustaining a long-term focus is not easy. Amazon is a good example of a company that does this successfully, forgoing short-term profitability to focus on the goal of being the biggest and best e-commerce retailer, among other things. Of course, it's easier to take that stance from a position of a $500 billion market cap and stellar record of growth. It was much harder when the company was small and had investors waiting to recoup their investments. To boost your own productivity, think about your long-term goals, then organize your life so that you serve those goals. Hyrum Smith, founder of Franklin Quest and the ubiquitous Franklin Planner, famously said that "It is only when our daily actions are in concert with our long-term goals, we then have a credible claim to inner peace." That is worth more than any bank statement or corporate title.

RELATIONSHIPS AS A FORM OF PRODUCTIVITY

Productivity is about being effective, not just efficient. There are multiple ways to be effective in a people-centered business such as consulting, some of which may not be obvious at first glance.

For example, have you ever considered the value of friendliness? Many people see life as a zero-sum game, or quid pro quo, only doing things for others when expecting to get something in return. When we take that attitude, we set ourselves up for a highly conditional set of outcomes. That adds stress to our lives, because every interaction, every transaction carries with it uncertainty over whether the other party will be friendly or play fair. An alternative approach is that you can decide to be friendly, simply because it is part of your values and who you are. Others may or may not reciprocate, but you can still decide that being friendly is how you choose to live. In some respects, friendliness becomes your gift to others, and gifts carry no conditions. Without this conditional uncertainty, you may also experience lower stress in your interactions and your relationships.

When we go beyond conventionally defined terms and limitations, we can always set ourselves up to be successful. As an example, large sales proposals carry the implicit question: "What if we don't win?" If the loss does occur, you could see all that effort as wasted. Alternatively, you could see it as an opportunity to build relationships, to get to know your prospect better, and to learn more about the subject matter. If you've conducted yourself with the attitude that you choose to be of service and learn everything you can from the experience, you can succeed even if you don't attain the immediate outcome you desire.

It's true that outcomes matter. It is important that you win the deal, complete projects on time, get deliverables approved, and secure funding for your projects. However, the truth is that we don't always get everything we want. Some outcomes are out of our control, but we can control our attitude, our response to the stimuli that act upon us.

People appreciate being treated with respect, to feel important. That should be a supporting objective for all projects or proposals, for colleagues as well as clients. One way to demonstrate respect is to give credit where it is due. It can be tempting to reference a concept or an insight without giving credit to the people who deserve it, even if unintentionally. If you lead a project, acknowledge the junior members of the team, those who supported it remotely, and whoever contributed intellectual property to the initiative. Make it a point to share compliments and provide positive feedback.

It may appear safer to put up an emotional wall in the workplace, but do not be afraid to show your humanity. This is not to suggest that you should pour your heart out to work colleagues, but allow genuine human connections to emerge. This is especially important in a digital world, where so much communication is conducted online. Taking the time to remember people's names and relevant facts about their lives is an excellent way to show that you care.

It may seem productive to keep emails as short as possible. People who use email heavily tend to become very brief, even terse, in their written communications, conveying a blunt, all-about-me perception. This may not be their intention, but it may be the impression perceived by their recipients. Taking an extra few moments to personalize emails can pay real dividends and build relationships. Be honest and straightforward in your communications, prizing integrity above expediency. Give and receive feedback graciously, without succumbing to defensiveness and insecurity. It may seem more productive to give negative feedback quickly and be done with it, but invest a little more time and remember that you are speaking with a human being who may experience an emotional reaction to what you say. This takes more time, but is the right thing to do and yields benefits long-term, which ultimately is productive.

Where possible, be encouraging and enthusiastic. Make yourself available for people when they need you. This, too, may seem inefficient, because the times people need you are rarely convenient. However, investing in relationships ultimately pays dividends. Only commit to things that you can and will do. Many of us are people pleasers (guilty as charged). We try to say "yes" to everything and then deal with the consequences as best we can, forgetting that delayed or broken commitments are worse than saying no up front. Saying "no" is harder than saying "yes". Like strategy, deciding what you *won't* do is a courageous act, because it allows you to focus on what you *will* do. This approach may not win you friends initially, but it will increase respect from your colleagues and your ability to complete what you commit.

Another asset of the professional is a short memory, at least psychologically speaking. Avoid dwelling on mistakes, both your own and those of others. Learn from them and move on. Taken together, the ideas above may not improve your immediate efficiency, but they can undoubtedly improve your effectiveness. That in turn will ultimately make you more productive. In the professional world, we rely on one another. Building relationships is not only a good investment, it makes working with other people more enjoyable, and our work more fulfilling.

PROCRASTINATION

Procrastination gets a bad rap. Sometimes, procrastination is a window into useful information, and it can be an effective prioritization tool. It may not make sense to do the thing we're putting off. Perhaps it isn't important, and there may be so much uncertainty that it should be postponed until we can complete the task once, without fear of rework. On the other hand, sometimes procrastination is truly a way of delaying tasks that we need to complete. The key is learning to tell the difference. One way to do this is to be aware of your emotional response. Are you frightened of the task, while knowing that you need to face that fear? Or are you weighed down by other priorities?

PRODUCTIVITY PRINCIPLES

In this sidebar, we cover productivity principles I have found to be valuable. When followed, these nuggets have served me well, and when ignored, have come back to bite. They can help guide your thinking and behavior, and hopefully can play a role in making you more productive, not simply a more efficient hamster on the wheel of life.

Generate insight. As a professional, your job is to generate insight, not just output. Always be thinking how you can help your clients or colleagues learn something new.

Collaborate. Collaboration and teamwork are essential elements of the consultant role. No matter how good you are, no individual knows everything or can make a project successful on their own.

Have fun. Find aspects of your work that you enjoy, and that you would do even if you weren't getting paid. This could be conducting client research, managing budgets, or training new hires.

Communicate. Communication may feel like an unproductive use of time. Perhaps it feels like it helps others keep tabs on you, but has no personal value. However, communication updates are needed for governance and to request help. It is important to find a balance, communicating enough to keep people informed, but not spending so much time on updates that it takes away from your own work.

Live with integrity. When you leave work for the day, you should feel good about what you've accomplished. If what you did was splashed across the front page of the *Wall Street Journal* tomorrow, would you be proud? It doesn't need to be an Enron whistleblower situation, perhaps simply taking the high road in a contentious discussion and not resorting to gossip or slander. This is especially true when you're under pressure to make decisions.

Build your success on the success of your clients. Many of us think that our top priority is to make ourselves successful. While we need to act in enlightened self-interest, the best way to do this is to focus first on making our clients (customers) successful, then our colleagues, and finally ourselves. If our goals are aligned, this other-centric focus should set us up for success as well, bringing the added benefit of wider support from others.

Deliver honest feedback. When you visit a doctor, you don't want them to tell you that you are healthy if it's not true. By the same token, you have a responsibility as a professional to deliver candid feedback. There is no reason to be disagreeable, but it's important to be honest. This shows respect and allows both parties to move forward.

Keep commitments and deliver finished product. In consulting, we use the phrase "client-ready," and my favorite, "done-done." Completed, checked, proofed, and ready to turn in as a professional contract deliverable. Many professionals submit work that is good but still contains a few errors. The manager, partner, or even worse, the client, should not be the final editor. Work should be done-done. This is the most important differentiator between a good worker and a true professional.

Navigate organizational politics. Organizational dynamics play a significant, if largely unseen, role in decision-making. Within your own company and in client organizations, be aware of these dynamics without getting caught up in the drama.

Share information. You may imagine that hoarding information gives you power, but in a firm of knowledge workers, overall effectiveness depends on you sharing what you know with your colleagues, while you hope they do the same.

Bring solutions. As you advance in your career, you will find that people bring problems far more often than solutions. It is rare that someone brings an issue, along with a few recommendations, and provides a few prioritized recommendations. If you can do that, you will be noticed and appreciated.

Become known for something. Develop a personal brand, and find an area to excel. Do you know a process or industry sector? Even if you are at the beginning of your career, can you take an idea and turn it into an effective visual? Can you quickly analyze data and develop insights? Whatever your "superpower," it is vital that you find a way to stand out. Even if it takes some time, simply focusing on this makes a difference.

Carry a motivational card. Tom Hopkins's 1980 book, *How to Master the Art of Selling*, is considered the best sales book ever written. He lived by a phrase he referred to as the "golden dozen." Twelve words: "I must do the most productive thing possible at every given moment." I still have the card I wrote those words on in 1988. The insight I discovered using Hopkins's phrase is that the most productive thing possible isn't always the most obvious. Sometimes it is completing a task, while at other times it is recharging your personal batteries, or unplugging with family. You can find your own phrase, but choose something that stares you in the face and guides your priorities.

Remember that everything counts. Whether we like it or not, we only have a certain amount of time on this planet. When we remember that everything counts, we make more deliberate choices. It doesn't mean we should be wracked with guilt or avoid making choices; just know that each decision matters and look forward to the consequences of your actions.

Act like you belong. Consulting is a competitive field, and so is any other profession worth entering. When you initially step into the arena, you'll likely be burdened by doubts and insecurities. Don't be arrogant, but do trust your abilities and demonstrate what you can do. Others will admire the effort and authenticity.

Practice gratitude. Whatever is happening in your life, you do not need to look far to see people in far worse situations. It is not always easy to maintain a sense of gratitude, but it's a skill worth cultivating. At the time of this writing, I recently returned from a visit to Berlin, where I stood in front of the Reichstag and the site that was once the SS headquarters. Millions of people were tortured and killed by the Nazis, through no fault of their own. If you have food on the table, freedom of activity, and the opportunity to work in a field you enjoy, you have plenty of reason to be grateful.

Be good at what you do and difficult to replace. Want to improve your income? The amount you are paid will depend on your ability to do what you do, the difficulty of your role, and how difficult it is to replace you. If you want to change what you're paid, change these things.

Face your fears. When you do what you fear most, you control fear. We are afraid of the unknown but have the capability to get past these fears. How? A little at a time, venturing outside our comfort zone, or perhaps by doing something bold that is frightening but potentially exciting as well. I have gone through this cycle multiple times in my life, and all good things have ultimately come from facing my fears at some level. Whatever strategy you choose, chip away at your fears—the result is worth the effort.

Short-interval scheduling. The Pomodoro technique was invented by Italian Francesco Cirillo in the 1980s, as a method of breaking down tasks into smaller increments. He found that work shrunk or increased depending on how much time was allocated to it. By forcing himself to break his work into small chunks, he became very productive. The technique is named after Cirillo's tomato-shaped timer. What is the Italian word for tomato? Pomodoro, of course.

Journal. As mentioned in the chapter on learning, keep a record of your thoughts and ideas. This can be intimidating, because you may be tempted to compare yourself with great journalers like Leonardo da Vinci and Ernest Hemingway. Write for yourself, don't worry about posterity. If you want more structure to get started, try *The Five-Minute Journal*. It was started by my friend Alex Ikonn and provides a quick yet psychologically significant way to record morning and evening reflections. Journaling draws out inspiration that might otherwise never see the light of day, giving you a fresh perspective on challenges and

We all have an enormous number of requests competing for our time and energy. Instead of giving every item equal status, consider categorizing them in this way, as described by Stephen Covey in his famous book, *The Seven Habits of Highly Effective People*:

If you procrastinate on the tasks in quadrants I or II, you need to muster your willpower and do what you need to do. If you procrastinate on tasks in quadrant IV, congratulate yourself—they were a waste of your time anyway. Initially, we think all our tasks fall into category one or two, but unless we're careful, wastes of time find their way onto our schedule. Why? Because they may be important to someone else. However, someone else's priority is not necessarily your own.

I subscribe to the *Economist*, one of the best news publications on the planet, and recommend it to anyone who wishes to cultivate a thoughtful, content-rich viewpoint on world affairs. I believe everything in the magazine is worth reading, but I never read every article because it takes a serious amount of time. That used to bother me, until I realized that even a quick scan and a selective reading of the most interesting articles is still worth more to me than other news content options. Choose your battles, prioritize what's most important, and don't beat yourself up over everything else.

PRODUCTIVITY ON YOUR TERMS

The truth for most people is that you can do anything you want, but you can't do *everything* you want. You must prioritize. If you don't do this consciously, make no mistake: you are already doing so unconsciously. You can do one or two things very well, but not four or five. If you spread yourself too thinly, you will have a lot of variety in your life, but you won't master anything.

Over the span of your life, there may be times when you choose to focus most of your attention on your career. At other times, you may choose to pursue another degree, care for a loved one, go all in on sports, or volunteer in your community. At some stage, you will find that you can't sustain all your interests and you have to make some decisions. In my experience, focusing on up to two areas is possible. For example, prioritizing family and work is a realistic goal. However, the wheels start to come off when you try to sustain more than two major priorities at once, say pursue another college degree on top of everything else. You simply won't have enough time and energy to give them everything you have. For those special situations when you have to do this, it is important to be honest with yourself and communicate with others about the impact, so that you can set and meet expectations.

However hard you try, you will never make everyone happy. As an adult, you must decide who gets your time and attention, and who doesn't. Again, you can make a proactive choice about this, or you can evade the choice and allow others to make it for you. Proactivity is empowering, but it also carries the burden of responsibility. It requires you to consciously make decisions that de-prioritize certain people and certain areas of your life. Passiveness may seem an alluring way to avoid responsibility, but it can create more pain, for yourself and others, because it leaves you vulnerable to simply following the priorities of others. This is tempting as a people pleaser, but impossible to sustain and still live life on your terms.

True productivity is effectiveness based on prioritization, not merely efficiency. Choose what to do, and reevaluate as needed. Embrace efficiency, but not at the expense of your humanity.

CHAPTER SEVEN

LEADERSHIP

"Leadership is not about titles, positions, or flowcharts. It is about one life influencing another."

—JOHN MAXWELL, AUTHOR, SPEAKER, AND PASTOR

There are few topics in business covered as broadly and deeply as leadership. While all the traits, behaviors, and styles are interesting, some are more useful than others on a day-to-day basis. This chapter will cover four forms of leadership we typically experience as consultants and industry professionals: thought leadership, servant leadership, relationship and network leadership, and change leadership (with an emphasis on change management).

THOUGHT LEADERSHIP

A thought leader is an individual (or firm) recognized as an authority in a specialized field, and whose expertise is sought and ideally rewarded. Thought leadership is commonly discussed in the business world, and to the average person, it may sound like another corporate buzzword. Behind this jargon is the authentic and admirable ambition of being a credible expert in an area that matters to the market. This can be an industry, a process, technology, or even a method like project management.

For our purposes, thought leadership is a goal, a journey. You don't have to be on the cover of *Harvard Business Review* (HBR) to be competent at your job, any more than you have to be Warren Buffet to successfully manage your investment portfolio. At the same time, recognition for your expertise within your firm or in the market is legitimate currency. For consultants, it is table stakes to play the game, and potentially a source of distinction for the individual and revenue for the firm. Thought leadership is sometimes thought to be only for senior professionals, but it is important for professionals at all levels. Even campus hires are expected to contribute to intellectual capital development, not just execute tasks.

In practical terms, thought leadership can be viewed as what you create, what gets published, its reach, and its impact. At the pinnacle, it can be the industry expert who provides the keynote at a conference and pockets the large speaking fee. Or it is the person who lands an article in an esteemed journal like HBR or mainstream business news like the *Wall*

Street Journal. However, those examples also discourage people from even pursuing thought leadership, viewing the effort as a veritable Mount Everest before they have even completed their first climb.

Starting out, thought leadership can be defined in basic building blocks: white paper, group presentation, or blog post on a platform like LinkedIn or Medium. Each time you convert your knowledge into the written word, you take steps toward thought leadership.

One of the best ways to develop your thought leadership capability is to read, study, and practice applying existing ideas to a new context. You can research another industry and consider how their ideas and practices apply to your own. When you take proactive steps to learn about your area of expertise and develop a point of view about your field of interest, you improve your content and take steps toward thought leadership.

Another technique is to understand the true influencers in your industry and follow them. What do they publish, post, or share? Where do they discuss the subjects you want to understand? Look for papers presented at relevant conferences. Even better, attend a conference in person. If your company won't fund it, find a way to attend. If you're a student, find a student pass. Nothing compares to hearing a true expert share their insights, and to be in the presence of many others gathered for the same purpose. Purchase the most important and respected books on your topics of interest. Above all, use them to develop your own perspective and then share it.

On many occasions, I've met people who describe themselves as thought leaders, yet they've been unable to tell me what they have published or discuss the views of the true leaders in their field. They know little about relevant industry events and publications, and have not read much on the subject. You can take this as a criticism of shallow thought leaders, or you can see it as an opportunity to raise the bar through your efforts. In a world of easily accessible media platforms, anyone has a stage to publish intelligent, compelling content. The only constraints are your creativity and energy to see it through.

If you truly want to be a thought leader, you will find a way. You'll buy the books. You'll seek out experts who can help you. These steps are not easy to take, because they represent a change in your status quo, your effort to reach another level. We may say that we want to be unique or stand out, but most of us also long to fit in, to be accepted socially. The idea of doing things that others in your peer group aren't doing can be scary. However, it is also liberating and makes you feel alive, when you believe in where it will take you.

How to get started? If you're truly starting from scratch, identify the best thing you have ever written, give it another edit, post it on your LinkedIn or similar account, and let everyone know. There! You are now published, and can direct others to your work. Then, incorporate the ideas and activities above, identify achievable goals and pursue them, gradually increasing the quality of your content and reach of your work. Work proactively with your own organization—many professionals give lip service to thought leadership, but it takes time, requires real effort, and you may not see obvious results for some time. If you can handle the delayed gratification though, it is a secret weapon that will help you grow your competencies, be a beacon for others, and accelerate your career.

SERVANT LEADERSHIP

The term "servant leadership" was first coined by Robert Greenleaf. At its heart, all good leadership is rooted in service. A servant leader puts others before themselves, with the aim of achieving organizational results by keeping in mind the needs of their people.

Leadership has become less about obeying the commands of a domineering authority figure. Leaders increasingly take the role of coach and mentor, communicating that they are part of the team, and exist for the team to succeed. Perhaps there was a time when effective leadership meant taking charge and barking orders. In today's world, however, leadership has become more about giving control than taking control.

As an example, let's consider a nuclear submarine. It is a complex ecosystem in which an entire crew lives for months beneath the surface of the ocean. In addition, nuclear submarines possess the firepower to destroy entire cities, so the need to make good decisions is exceptionally acute.

It is hardly a given that a nuclear submarine will operate effectively. Captain David Marquet, in his book *Turn the Ship Around*, describes the experience of taking command of the *USS Santa Fe*, a nuclear submarine with a track record of crew and operational issues. When he first took over, he tried to lead by issuing orders, but he found that crew members attempted to follow those orders even when it was the wrong thing to do. Altering his initial approach, he instituted self-organizing teams, in which each member took full responsibility for their role within the team. He had his crew use the phrase, "I intend to..." instead of, "Request permission to..." This seemingly small change in terminology turned passive followers into active leaders.

Due to this shift, each member of the team became a leader and assumed responsibility for their behavior. They became fully engaged in everything from clerical tasks to crucial combat decisions. The *USS Santa Fe* went from a poorly performing vessel with low morale and a dreadful retention rate to setting records for performance, morale, and retention. Over the following decade, a disproportionately high number of officers who served on the *Santa Fe* went on to become submarine commanders. Captain Marquet is an example of servant leadership at its finest. Rarely are the stakes as high, or the results as clear, but that approach is applicable to all organizations.

Servant leaders tend to demonstrate the following traits: awareness; community-building, conceptualization; empathy; foresight; growth; humility; listening; persuasiveness; stewardship; trust, and the ability to remove obstacles.

As organizations become flatter, even those who prefer to lead autocratically will find it increasingly difficult to do so. Millennials have already demonstrated that they respond better to coaching and support than to being told what to do. The nature of work is changing, and so must the nature of leadership. As operational tasks are automated, the remaining work becomes more complex and nuanced. How can a leader tell employees what to do if the leader isn't close enough to the customer to understand the issue? What roles does a manager have when each employee is defining their own problems, analyzing, and solving them?

This doesn't mean that leadership will become unimportant. There will always be a need for leadership. What's changing is *how* that leadership is demonstrated. Leaders need to bring something unique to the table, such as deep domain expertise. Think of the neurosurgeon who leads residents and interns, or the senior law partner who leads other attorneys and paralegals. It's no longer enough to be a rainmaker or industry guru without caring about employees. Servant leaders are responsible to help employees grow their skills and realize their potential.

RELATIONSHIP AND NETWORK LEADERSHIP

The great Martin Luther King, Jr. once said, "We are caught in an inescapable network of mutuality, tied in a single garment of destiny. Whatever affects one directly, affects us all indirectly." Whether we realize it or not, our success in life, our destiny, is tied to the success of others.

Consider this: Where were you when you first heard about your current company? Where did you receive the tip that led to you hiring your best employee? How did you determine the root cause for a problem that plagued your last project? Maybe these events were the result of coincidence—a chance conversation with a friend or colleague, perhaps. What you may not have considered, however, is the extent to which these discussions are not coincidences, and they arise from the relationships and networks in your life. While a cliché, in today's flat world, national boundaries, time zones, and lines of authority have become blurred. It is imperative to build relationships in our personal and professional life, and often they overlap.

An online search for "relationship and network leadership"

yields literally millions of results, directing you to gurus who promise expertise and success based upon their relationship and network methods. Is it that simple? What does it take to become an authentic leader in the area of relationships and networking? At leading companies, the focus is on developing patience, understanding, and appreciation of people, and the impact we have on one another.

In organizational science, most definitions of the word "leadership" include the concept of influence over others. In contrast, relational leadership is a social act. It's not about the leader exerting influence alone. It's about a process of engagement that influences the direction of an organization. Relational leadership is about developing, maintaining, and using long-term internal and external relationships and networks. This is not simply for personal and tactical reasons, but with the intention of becoming recognized as an expert and trusted advisor to many stakeholders at multiple levels. Relationship and network leadership is about *mutually beneficial* relationships, for both short-term and long-term gain.

Leaders with the best networks are friends and acquaintances with many of the people with whom they work. They understand that their legacy will endure based on the social capital they build and grow. Arguably, social capital is as important to the success of an organization as financial capital and human capital. A company with strong social capital will be rich in relationships that enhance cooperation and resource exchange, and cashing in this mutual "social income" is the cornerstone of exercising ethical influence.

Authentic leaders and change agents do not seek to manipulate or trick others for one-sided gain, or to become what leadership expert Robert Cialdini termed "smugglers of influence." Instead, they build their reputations and their networks on trust and charisma, in ways that are satisfying for themselves and others. The most effective networkers have no agenda or vested interests. They simply enjoy making genuine connections with people.

THE SIX PRINCIPLES OF PERSUASION

Cialdini's 1984 book, *Influence: The Psychology of Persuasion*, sold over three million copies and is considered by *Forbes* as one of the seventy-five smartest business books of all time. His Six Principles of Persuasion model has become the most robust and well-accepted framework in this area. We can use these principles to improve our leadership skills:

Reciprocity. We give back to those who have given to us.

The principle of reciprocity is consistent across all cultures. It is made more powerful when gifts are meaningful, personal, and unexpected, and when they take place at an appropriate moment. Another important aspect of this principle is a willingness to make concessions, for example by retreating from a larger request to a smaller one, to demonstrate a willingness to sacrifice individual needs for the good of the relationship.

Some years ago, the creative vice president of Infosys created one of the first internal corporate video networks, delivering news from within the company to tens of thousands of employees globally. Before the network was launched, senior management were supportive but unable to provide funding. Undaunted, the executive made concessions to get his idea launched, using existing infrastructure and bandwidth to create a proof of concept that broadcast a CEO speech in almost real time. That initial concession enabled a successful proof of concept and led to the support needed to scale the network. Within twelve months of launch, this video network became an integral part of corporate culture.

Leading marketer and friend Porter Gale, in her book, *Your Network Is Your Net Worth*, uses the phrase "give, give, get." In other words, expect to give to others twice before asking for anything in return. It's a mindset that ensures that she always contributes at least as much as she receives in return, which keeps relationships running smoothly. Initiating the principle of reciprocity with no hidden agenda is an excellent way of "digging your well before you're thirsty." While it may sound like common sense, it's uncommonly done.

Liking. We are more easily influenced by people we like.

Similarity, praise, and cooperation are three ways to trigger liking, especially when we take the initiative to appreciate others proactively, instead of waiting for them to act first. Adopt the mindset to always give people a chance, and assume they are good until proven otherwise. At times, they will let you down, but life's too short to worry about occasional disappointments. When you see the best in people, most of the time they will rise to the occasion.

Liking should be genuine, not contrived. As leaders, we can emphasize what team members have in common, or the characteristics the organization shares with its clients and prospects. In cases where you lack sufficient knowledge about other parties to understand them, it pays to invest time and effort to find common ground. Regardless of whether you are selling something or simply seeking information, start by listening to the views of the other party and seeking areas of agreement.

This principle can be hard to put into practice when working with diverse groups, especially for large programs. In these situations, it is even more important to invest time to understand other viewpoints and philosophies. A high-tech executive client and friend of mine once told me, "When joining an organization as an executive, it's important to quickly develop the relationship strength that creates sufficient credibility to lead transformation initiatives. It's a delicate balance, because you must deliver real results within a short time, yet you must also allow time to develop relationships before asking people for disruptive changes."

Authority. We follow those who we trust to demonstrate unique expertise.

Experts who demonstrate credibility, expertise, or trustworthiness can lay claim to significant authority. Visual cues of authority can be enough to stimulate this response. On the other hand, the lack of visual cues of authority can also undermine an otherwise authoritative impression. You may be highly competent, but what happens if you are poorly dressed or you speak indecisively? How will people perceive you? Old-school notions of status and authority may have changed, but every company has standards and style for credibility and competence.

One person's confidence is another person's arrogance. One person's modesty is another's apathy. Therefore, it is essential to know your organization and your audience. It's also helpful to ensure that you are known to those around you. Prior to going into a meeting for the first time, especially if you have a speaking role, ask the person who invited you to provide a brief email introduction to the other participants, and establish your role and your expertise before attending. If this is not possible, ask someone, perhaps the meeting organizer, to introduce you. The important thing is to make your introduction relevant to the audience, while revealing something of your expertise.

Another way to create a sense of authority is to volunteer to contribute to events highlighting an area of expertise. You could moderate a panel of experts, helping them to shine, or provide support behind the scenes. I have followed this approach several times throughout my career, both for my company's events and industry forums, to become better known in a new industry sector or functional area. It can be done on the grandest of stages or a humble departmental all-hands meeting. Anything you can do to establish and enhance respect will increase the impact that you make. The moderator or support role can be a rewarding experience, and has the added bonus of developing relationships with company or industry leaders.

Social proof. We decide what to do by looking at what others have done.

Social proof is especially powerful in times of uncertainty and is sometimes referred to as consensus. Influencing others to adopt your recommendations comes more easily when you can point to evidence of others doing the same. Lawyers use social proof when they refer to legal precedent, and in business it strengthens a business case to reference examples of similar successful initiatives.

Conversely, you can use social proof to argue *against* a suggestion, based on the poor experiences of others, or to show what might happen if a company doesn't adopt an initiative. In the internet age, online reviews have become a powerful tool to show others why a product or service is desirable, or to be avoided. The Net Promoter Score is an example of social proof boiled down into a single number to measure customer satisfaction and loyalty—"how likely are you to recommend this service to others?"

Consistency. We have a strong urge to remain consistent with our prior beliefs and behaviors.

This is especially true in situations where previous commitments have taken place in the public realm. As leaders, we should practice what we teach. Those who do so command respect and influence more easily than those who simply demand it.

Consistency is also relevant in scenarios where we seek the agreement of others. When we win their backing for small commitments, they are more likely to agree to larger ones. This is common in consulting. It may take a long time for a client to develop the trust to allow a consulting firm to conduct a diagnostic. If the diagnostic project is delivered successfully, then trust is established and the client may be more likely to agree on larger, more complex implementation program work.

Scarcity. We want more of that which is less available.

There's an old proverb that people buy fear of loss as much, if not more than, hope of gain. This can be the ability to secure a commodity that is in short supply, as opportunities appear more attractive when they are less available. Most people say that they would love to increase revenue, but they are especially keen to reduce cost. Even more so, they are really motivated to act if they need to minimize the risk of a compliance violation that puts them at odds with a statutory requirement.

Scarcity is well-known as a principle for selling, but it is equally useful for advancing an argument or developing influence. Whatever you're asking for, you can emphasize—truthfully and with integrity—what the company could lose if your request is not granted, what the audience will not get if your work is not approved. It's a persuasive approach if the audience understands and accepts the argument.

The simplicity of these principles belies their depth and the amount of research that has gone into them. If you take the time to learn and use them, they can be highly valuable to you to develop your relationship and network leadership skills.

CHANGE MANAGEMENT

What do leaders really do? They don't make plans; they don't solve problems. They don't even organize people—that's the job of a manager. What *leaders* really do is prepare organizations for change and lead them through that change.

In 1977 Harvard Business School professor Abraham Zaleznik published an article entitled, "Managers and Leaders: Are They Different?" He concluded that management is about stability, operations, and executing on known processes, whereas leadership is about pressing for change and helping people through unstable situations. Only individuals—and, by extension, organizations—that embrace both sides of this duality can thrive in turbulent times. It's great to thrive on change, but we still need some level of stability. Successful managers inspire people to follow them through change with the courage to take risks when necessary.

Change management is not an esoteric concept. It's relevant to every professional, especially anyone who seeks to advance in their career. You may not lead a massive change initiative, but wherever you are in your career, the most exciting and transformative opportunities occur during times of change.

To practice your change management skills, volunteer to support change initiatives in your company. As fishermen say, go where the fish are. Think about what's happening in your organization to make change happen. Large change initiatives may not take place frequently, but they are the proving grounds for future leaders. As an analogy, military leaders make their names in war, not peacetime, and business leaders make their names in times of change. Growth, restructuring, acquisitions, new product launches, enterprise software programs—each of these is an example of major change.

Change causes stress and yet, by doing so, it also reveals character and potential. If you can deliver in these circumstances, you demonstrate your capabilities to executives. Most of the executives I've worked with over the years have been involved in at least one transformational initiative, and these programs were instrumental to advance their careers. In consulting, everything we do involves some form of change or transformation. Clients hire us because change is hard, and most people don't like it. They delay accepting it until they have to act, which is often too late unless a leader and their team step up, help the organization see a better future, and lead them through the change. This is good news for anyone with the courage to see opportunity in change. In these situations, you can shine by simply learning to welcome and embrace the change as early as possible.

The first step is simply to accept and commit to change. This involves awareness, compliance, intellectual commitment, and emotional commitment. You may think that intellectual commitment is enough. We are, after all, professionals. However, we are human beings, and we do not leave our emotions at the door. Allow your positive commitment to show through your involvement. Beyond a personal level, you can support change at a team level, through what you do as well as what you say. As famous US poet Ralph Waldo Emerson said, "What you do speaks so loudly, I can't hear what you say."

It's important to take care of the people involved in transformation. Initiatives fail when people are not ready for them or refuse to adopt them, and numerous studies reveal that most of the top problems experienced in large projects are people-related. According to a 2017 McKinsey Global Survey, less than half of transformational programs meet their targets. Other studies show that as many as 90 percent of failures are attributable to shortfalls in people engagement. While the exact number is open to debate, the point is that while technology is important, it's the people aspect of transformation that typically has the most issues.

Niccolo Machiavelli wrote *The Prince* in 1513. Since then, the term *Machiavellian* has become shorthand for behavior that is devious or manipulative. Machiavelli, however, was simply observing what he saw in society, what happens in the real world. How does this relate to change management? We need to understand how people really think, feel, and behave. For all the high-sounding platitudes about the good of the company and shareholder value, people care about their families, their job security, and their financial prospects.

Beyond making change feel real, we need to understand that people are not all the same. Executives may have a different perspective from middle managers, who come from a different place than new hires. People have unique perspectives based on their individual experiences. To achieve change, it is important to understand what truly motivates people, and this varies by level, geography, and personal situation.

Holly Benson is a top change management consulting partner, World Economic Forum contributor on the future of work, and a close colleague. According to Holly, there are three primary requirements of change: "People must know what's expected of them, have the skills and tools to meet those expectations, and be held accountable to meet them." Think about these requirements in your own work. Do you know what is expected of you? Do you have the skills to meet those expectations? Are you accountable to meet them? Three simple questions, yet they contain a world's worth of value to drive successful change on a personal or enterprise level.

As discussed at the beginning of this section, every professional is in the business of change management. You may not be a change management specialist, but you are absolutely involved in change management. The world has always been changing, but the pace of change is faster than ever. The human brain is pre-wired to prefer stability to rapid change, and the accelerating speed of change can be hard for us to absorb and comprehend. Nonetheless, it's unavoidable. We all manage change in our own lives, for our families, and to some extent within our companies and our industries.

Once you understand this, you can embrace change positively. Learn to anticipate change, not to fear it. In the twenty-first century, this is a critical aspect of leadership. Change is happening. The differentiating factor is how we manage that change, and a proactive approach can give you a feeling of control, or at least influence, over your own destiny.

WHAT ARE THE PREDICTORS OF SUCCESSFUL LEADERSHIP?

Throughout history, the question of what makes a good leader has been discussed and debated. As far back as the sixth century, Lao Tzu, the founder of Taoism, described the qualities of a wise leader as selfless, hard-working, honest, fair, and capable of empowering others. In fact, he spoke of the invisible leader: "A leader is best when people barely know he exists, when his work is done, his aim fulfilled, they will say: we did it ourselves."

In modern times, dozens of studies have been conducted to determine the characteristics of an effective leader. Six skills are mentioned again and again: inspire action, be optimistic, act with integrity, communicate clearly, be decisive, and have empathy. There's plenty of evidence to show that not only are authentic leaders respected by their followers, they also have a meaningful impact on the company bottom lines. According to a frequently cited 1988 paper by David Day and Robert Lord, as much as 45 percent of an organization's performance can be explained by its executive leadership.[5] This makes good leadership a vital lever to create competitive advantage. How to do this? The best leaders develop genuine, authentic connections with their employees, customers, partners, suppliers, and the market. Relationships become less transactional and more multidimensional, embodying long-term goals.

Michel Langlois, a high-tech executive client and friend, has a great way to describe the role of leaders and employees. He says that employees are like citizens of a country. Each "citizen" carries certain responsibilities, and leaders must communicate and reinforce those responsibilities. Today's matrix organizations require executives and managers to lead deeply. Leaders need to become like founders. They need to passionately embrace guiding principles and make them real for their colleagues. Teamwork is a useful lens through which to study how leaders connect with their peers and subordinates. Research suggests that when team members share mental models, teams make more successful decisions. This shared understanding, when transmitted throughout an organization, also strengthens company cul-

---

5   David V. Day and Robert G. Lord, "Executive Leadership and Organizational Performance: Suggestions for a New Theory and Methodology," *Journal of Management*, Vol. 14, Issue 3 (1988).

ture. Without it, employees may lose sight of what is expected of them and lack a shared corporate perspective.

An effective leader doesn't try to be the smartest person in the room. They develop a network of relationships to bring together the people who can address the company's needs and problems. They may be experts in a specific area, but overall their ability to form relationships will be more beneficial to their reputation and true impact than how much they can sell, code, or create journal entries. As people move from individual engineering roles to leadership positions, I have often seen these highly intelligent individuals struggle with the relational skills to lead others.

Ultimately, leadership is for everyone, not only for senior executives. Thought leadership generates positive influence at any career stage, while servant leadership is a way to quietly shape the culture of an organization through understanding and empowering the people who work there. Relationship and network leadership provides a model for connections based on respect and mutual interest. Change management brings leadership to life during times of corporate transition. Far from being a sign of weakness, people can be more authentic, and ultimately more effective, using a relational leadership approach than an autocratic one.

PART THREE

EVOLUTIONARY COMPETENCIES

CHAPTER EIGHT

BECOMING AGILE

DESIGN THINKING, PROJECT-BASED THINKING, AND THE AGILE APPROACH

"What is design? It's where you stand with a foot in two worlds— the world of technology and the world of people and human purposes—and you try to bring the two together."

—MITCHELL KAPOR, INVENTOR OF LOTUS 1-2-3 SPREADSHEET

My firm was looking to establish a flagship office in Silicon Valley. We had a new CEO and several other executives had just joined the company. A traditional approach would have been to prominently display monuments to the company— pictures of the headquarter's campus, large power offices to showcase executives—and create a formal intimidating presence. Instead, we took a design thinking approach.

Instead of looking to simply project the company's brand, we wanted to convey a different message, and to create a different experience for employees and guests. Our design team spoke to everyone who would use the office, from senior executives to technologists. They observed the way people worked, understood their behavior and routines, and designed the space for the people who worked there. To do this, they followed five design principles.

First, they made the office *functional*. As a place of work, they wanted everything in the space to have a functional purpose. This meant resisting the temptation to splurge on expensive hero pieces such as works of art, or impressive pieces of furniture with minimal utility. Instead, they focused on meeting basic requirements such as comfortable seating, adequate writing surfaces, high-bandwidth internet, shared project rooms, natural light, and a good-sized kitchen.

Next, they concentrated on making it *flexible*. This meant creating a setup that could be quickly altered depending on the day's needs. Furniture was lightweight and easy to move, everything was on wheels, strong Wi-Fi installed, electrical lines dropped from the ceiling, and whiteboards could be shifted to create false walls, dividing up the space in response to the activities taking place.

Third, the space was *fluid*. Individuals could set up their desks wherever they chose, and those who were present took priority over those who were absent. Desks were not reserved and the office layout altered depending on who was in the building.

By the same token, the space was *flat*. A casual observer would have been unable to guess the job titles of people in the office based on the spaces they were occupying. Space was allocated based on roles and needs, not hierarchies.

Finally, it was *familiar*. The designers wanted the office to feel like a second home, not a sterile environment that employees couldn't wait to leave. This meant creating a welcoming kitchen with an inviting shared space. The only permanent piece of furniture in the entire office was a large bar-height wooden table that people naturally gravitated toward, and which became a social hub.

It would have been easy for our company to look at a traditional CEO office and copy its formal look and feel. We chose instead to think carefully about what the space was for and who would use it. We could have issued a top-down edict, but we preferred to seek out feedback and then design the space based on the information we received. The office was quickly put into use, but the real work had just begun. Every week small changes were made as employees provided additional feedback to make the space more useful, and to enhance the experience for all who visited. The office became a living lab, an ongoing experiment to help workers be more productive and evolve rapidly with the needs of the business.

The office space design approach above is a microcosm of how the company sought to serve clients and solve problems. The design team sought first to understand and empathize with the users, frame the problem before attempting to solve it, quickly create working prototypes, then frequently test and update. This approach is known as design thinking.

WHAT IS DESIGN THINKING?

The story above is an example of what design thinking can achieve, but what exactly *is* design thinking? I define it as a human-centered, whole-brain approach to understanding and solving complex challenges. Design thinking integrates the needs of people, the possibilities of technology, and the requirements of business.

Design thinking is also a method of increasing the creative confidence of people operating in an environment of ambiguity. What does this mean? We live in a world of uncertainty, the problems worth solving are often not fully known, and we need tools that bring to life the elements of innovation. These innovation elements are knowledge, imagination, and conviction. Design thinking includes tools to unleash those qualities, providing knowledge, releasing imagination, and building conviction through understanding, experimentation, and iteration.

People with creative confidence can leverage their own

knowledge, yet also articulate a broader vision. They can engage rapidly with those around them, make fast decisions, and succeed in new opportunities, bouncing back quickly from unsuccessful iterations. Design thinking encourages people to understand deeply, test early, seek feedback, and quickly adapt. In those conditions, is there such a thing as failure, or simply useful early feedback?

Analytical people tend to look at problems as puzzles to be solved: the problem is well-defined, and the trick is to rearrange the pieces or calculate the equation until finding the right answer. This focus on solving known problems works for optimization scenarios, but not to create breakthroughs or solve so-called "wicked" problems. Conventional thinking solves *puzzles*, design thinking addresses *mysteries*.

What's a mystery? It's a situation in which not only is the answer unknown, the precise nature of the problem is also unknown. The frenetic pace of technological innovation has created an urgent need for problem *finding*, beyond simply problem *solving*. In addition, the frontier of competition has moved from product quality to customer experience, dramatically increasing the importance of empathy.

Customers expect products to work well, meaning that quality is a minimum requirement, not a source of delight. Consider your automobile: when it starts each time you want to go somewhere, are you excited? No, because that quality is a basic expectation, and you will be upset if the vehicle fails to start even 10 percent of the time. For novel features, the functionality itself may spark delight for a period of time. However, today's novel innovation becomes tomorrow's basic expectation. Companies differentiate successfully by providing customers with a unique experience. This is not an issue only for luxury brands. Every company must understand their customers and consider how they can connect with them more effectively. Those who ignore this reality become commoditized and enter a downward spiral. Design thinking provides a way to keep the customer experience top of mind as part of an integrated view, together with functional feasibility and economic value.

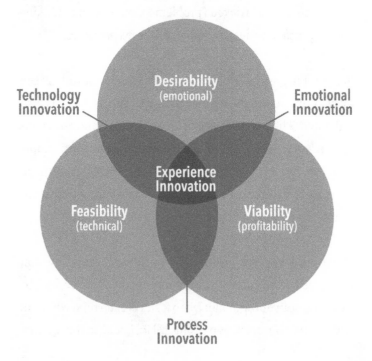

The concept of design as a way of thinking dates from the 1970s, when people like Herbert Simon and Robert McCann explored the design side of engineering. In the early 1990s, David Kelley and his colleagues at Stanford adapted design thinking for business purposes. For the following two decades, it was used to create better products. Gradually, design thinking became a way to develop vision, design organizations, and to rethink systems, processes, events, and even physical spaces.

Traditional creative approaches begin with brainstorming. We generate lots of ideas, then narrow the solution space through prioritization and testing, and work sequentially toward a solution. Design thinking begins with understanding the problem area through customer empathy and market research, then widens the problem space to understand the situation. The problem space is narrowed as the potential problems are framed and then specifically identified. Once design thinkers have a firm handle on the problem, they start to brainstorm and widen the solution space, to explore what is possible. At some point, the team prioritizes potential solutions and narrows the solution space, creating prototypes and testing frequently for experience, feasibility, and economic value. The best solutions can then be taken forward as proofs of concept, pilots, and possibly even implemented at scale.

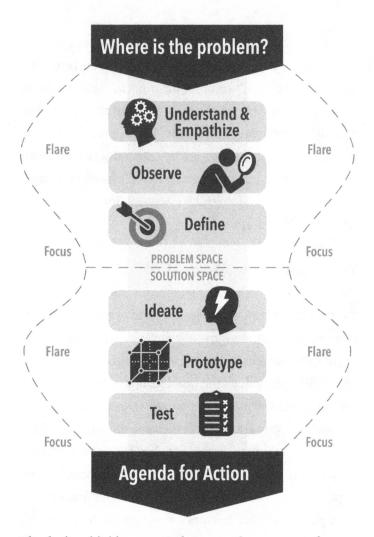

The design thinking approach may not be necessary for narrowly defined problems, such as routine analyses or process optimization in a mature area. The most interesting problems, the ones with greatest impact, are usually less defined. Finally, as automation and AI become pervasive, they will increasingly solve narrowly defined problems for us. The remaining work will be more creative and ambiguous, and design thinking is a good candidate for this.

Design thinking is a highly egalitarian approach. It encourages experimentation and respects the diversity of backgrounds and viewpoints represented by different people in a work team. A diverse team is an essential asset to make the most of a design thinking approach. Without a range of perspectives, the process will be less effective.

Design thinking has five major activities: empathize; define; ideate; prototype, and test. Let's discuss them in order.

Empathy. Empathy consists of understanding and observation. It is comprehending the customer or user. How do they behave? What influences their choices? Our firm worked with a major food retailer wanting to expand their activities in Mexico. Initially, they thought that they only needed to create a commerce platform to make it easier for people to order—they believed that the problem lay in the ordering process. Our firm advised them to wait, and a small team traveled to Mexico to interview a variety of stakeholders, including consumers they were trying to reach.

The interviewees said that, no, they didn't need a better way to order the product. What they needed was a sense of the brand being part of the community, and a connection with influencers within that community. This insight shifted the company's marketing. They moved toward loyalty programs and collaboration, instead of simply a tactical e-commerce platform.

To practice empathy, approach challenges with a beginner's mindset. Don't assume that you know the solution before you have fully understood the situation and defined the problem. What are people saying and doing? What can you infer about their thoughts and emotions from their behavior? What companies say about their customers may not be what those customers really want or need. Instead, speak with customers and observe their behavior.

Keep focus on the customer, the user, the major actor involved in the process. Identify each *persona*, the role played by an actor. Each persona is multidimensional, with demographics, wants and needs, and behaviors specific to them. Observe them in their element and think about who they are, what they do, and what they want to accomplish. When interviewing, don't simply accept the initial answer given. Dig deeper and find the motivations behind the responses. The "why" can be just as important as the "what."

Customers interact with a company in multiple ways throughout their life cycle, so map the different situations in which those interactions take place. This provides you with multiple data points for the customer at different phases in their journey, not merely a static view of their identity. There will be several different profiles of people who connect with the company, so identify and characterize each persona. How are the personas similar? How do they differ? While knowing the personas is important, it is only a starting point. It is also necessary to understand how a persona interacts with a company to order a product, to get their question answered, or whatever their goal happens to be. A *customer journey map* shows the story of the customer's experience. It not only identifies significant interactions that the customer has with the organization, it also brings out user feelings, motivations, and questions for each of the touch points.

These maps provide frameworks to improve customer experience. For example, a product might score highly in functionality, but if the ordering experience is painful they may go elsewhere. An online purchasing process may be easy, but returning items may be complex and time-consuming, or customers may simply *fear* that it will be. How does this affect the customer journey?

Amazon has invested massively to create a straightforward returns process and convinces customers that returning an Amazon purchase is simple and painless. As the world's largest online retailer, returns are an important part of their business and part of the overall customer journey. Relating the returns activity to the overall Amazon customer journey can put the returns process into the larger customer context, and identify areas with the highest potential for improvement.

Once you have created a journey map at a process level, you can assess the emotional state of customers at each step. As a customer persona progresses in their journey, their emotions may vary widely, happy at the point of purchase and perhaps disappointed with customer support. You can determine the "moments of truth," the most essential points in the customer journey. Not all interactions are created equal. Some weigh more heavily in the mind of a customer than others. If a company gets these moments of truth right, customers may tolerate minor irritations at other steps. If a company gets moments of truth wrong, the entire transaction, and perhaps the customer relationship, may be lost.

Define. Once you've identified personas, documented the customer journey, and understood the customer, you probably have enough information to define the problem at hand. If empathy is a process of opening up to understand the possibilities, definition is a process of converging on a problem statement. It's a time to identify the moments that matter and develop a point of view.

At this point, it's still too soon to leap to conclusions. Instead, the goal is to ask, "how might we?" How might we create a better experience? How might we accomplish X faster? Keep your thinking free of bias, personal preference, and assumptions. This is a time for problem definition, not solution brainstorming. If you have assumptions about what is and isn't possible, now is the time to question them. You may think, "we have to assume that customers won't do X," or "we have to assume that company Y won't change their operating model." Why do you think that? Examine your assumptions.

Also, guard against opinions disguised as facts. Stakeholders may *believe* that their views are objective and accurate, but the facts may not support them. A person's experiences often influence their perceptions in ways they are not aware. To unearth biases, ask people why they believe as they do. Are their responses based on data, or are they simply opinions?

Ideate. When the problem is sufficiently defined, it's time to ideate. This step is all about idea generation. Generate ideas from both inside-out and outside-in. What does this mean? *Inside-out* are ideas that come from inside the organization, with a strong view of the company context. *Outside-in* ideation comes from external trends, from experts in the field, benchmarks, or other external sources. When working with large companies, we often bring in the founders of startup companies relevant to the workshop theme. Executives from large companies enjoy talking to these entrepreneurs because they provide a fresh perspective and exposure to new ideas, and an attitude of experimentation. Large organizations seek to emulate small company agility and speed—and their willingness to embrace failure and quickly move on.

An often-overlooked way to generate ideas is to make the

process physical, engaging multiple senses. On one occasion, I facilitated a workshop for one of the world's largest computer manufacturers. The participants worked in middleware (integration software), far removed from the ultimate customer. The workshop venue was an interior conference room with no windows. The tables and chairs were decades old and were difficult to move. Even worse, the participants had a system going live that day and didn't want to be there. They were forced to attend by their boss. From a facilitator's standpoint, it was a design thinking nightmare.

As the workshop commenced, there was a predictable lack of excitement. The attendees went through the motions, but they lacked energy and enthusiasm. Noticing this, I got everyone physically moving and turned the ideation activity into a physical exercise. New ideas quickly emerged from standing up, moving around, writing on wall posters, and engaging in other physical activities. Susan was a technical director in the group who later commented, "Initially, I could barely think of a single idea, then after moving around and engaging physically, I could not stop creating them!" And she was beaming as she said it. While this was gratifying to hear, we simply created a context in which Susan and the other participants could better access and express their ideas.

Prototype. With several ideas to explore, it is time to create prototypes. For most of us, the word "prototype" has come to signify an incomplete but working version of a product, such as a computer or a car. In a design thinking context, a prototype is a model that simulates or demonstrates some aspect of what you hope to deliver. An early stage prototype is also called a low-fidelity prototype. It is early, and it is rough, but it conveys one or more relevant aspects of the solution in process.

High-fidelity prototypes are risky. If you invest a lot of time and energy to create a prototype, what happens if it doesn't work, and it is too late in the process to make significant changes? What happens if you ask people for feedback and they are unwilling to be honest with you because they know you've spent a lot of time, energy, and money on your model? They may say, "that's nice" and move on, not wanting to hurt your feelings. There is not much value in that feedback.

Low-fidelity prototypes, on the other hand, carry far less risk. You can show them early and request feedback without worrying that people will sugarcoat their responses. Most professionals understand on some level that rapid iteration can lead to better answers, but they do not try it on a day-to-day basis. Why? I think it is because many of us are still too anxious about presenting things that are not perfect. There are times, as discussed in Chapter Six, when only "done-done" is good enough. However, design thinking is different—it is for solving mysteries, and that is not a linear process. Creating low-fidelity prototypes is an excellent way to understand elements of a potential solution as early as possible, when changes are acceptable and more affordable.

Test. Finally, we move to testing. This is closely connected with the prototyping process, and it involves collecting more formal feedback. This means trying out prototypes early to see how they perform, instead of waiting until we have completed solutions before soliciting feedback or running formal tests. Early testing can improve decision making effectiveness.

Graham Passey was a rockstar consulting leader and a colleague who employed prototyping and testing to inform a personal buying decision. He was an avid smartphone user, and when smartphones increased in size, he was unsure how he felt about carrying something that large in his front pants pocket. He cut a thick piece of cardboard to the same shape and size as the new smartphone and walked around with it for a day or two. By simulating one aspect of the solution, he accurately tested the experience of carrying around a large smartphone, prior to the "high-fidelity" prototype of an actual purchased product.

He liked the experience, his test was successful, and he bought a new smartphone confident in his purchase decision. Note that his formal test only addressed one aspect of the user experience. Far from being inadequate, this was a highly effective test, as he was testing the only parameter that was unknown and mattered to him. After all, he had been using a smartphone for years and knew about the other functionality.

The traditional way to test has been to build something, then see if it works once complete. This can be an expensive and time-consuming approach. What if the testing breaks your product, or reveals a fundamental design flaw? In design thinking, our intention is to test certain aspects of a solution as early as possible, and to test smaller components of a larger solution. We want to glean as much useful information as possible, as quickly and inexpensively as we can.

The design thinking process is not linear. Although the steps do follow each other in a natural order, there may be times when it's necessary to pause during ideation and return to empathy, or to stop testing and generate more prototypes. Done well, design thinking creates a series of feedback loops, leading to more customer-centric and effective solutions.

DESIGN THINKING PRINCIPLES

You can apply design thinking to many initiatives. They don't all have to be "wicked problems" or mysteries to benefit. Even the "puzzles" mentioned earlier (where the problem is well-defined) can benefit from certain design thinking steps. If you're willing to practice, you can find value in these principles and become a design thinker yourself.

Learn by doing. When we train people in design thinking, we encourage them to jump in. We don't spend a lot of time on introductory documentation. The activities are interactive and experiential and can be applied to almost any scenario. The most effective way to learn is to practice. You can access a free version of the design thinking Virtual Crash Course from the Stanford University d.school (https://dschool.stanford.edu).

Develop champions. If you want to see design thinking take root in your organization, you need support, in the form of people who have bought in to the idea. This could be a project team, a department, or a member of senior management—ideally, all of the above. You may not be in a position to hire or train others, but you can seek out like-minded souls in your company, school, or even external groups like startup hangouts.

Collaborate. When you work with others, you'll develop a common repository of information and refine the innovation process. Share! Show others a growth mindset, and they will more than likely respond in kind.

Seek out mysteries. As discussed, design thinking is most effective in loosely defined scenarios, where there is uncertainty not only about the solution, but also about the problem itself. Look for these types of problems and use them as opportunities to grow your design thinking skills. Don't go for the easy answer. Dive into the problem space and seek the best mix of experience, feasibility, and value.

Design for the extreme user. It is tempting to try to please the average user of a product, service, or process. However, extreme users are far more interesting. The extreme user is invested in your success. They love the product! They use it in ways you never thought of. Design for them. At the other end of the spectrum, the extreme non-user has never used your product. You want to know what it is about the product that offends them, or that causes them to see it as irrelevant. Designing for the extreme users on both ends of the spectrum yields insights that designing for the average user will not.

Work within constraints. Earlier in this chapter, we discussed the need to free ourselves from limiting assumptions. Constraints, however, can also spur creativity. For many years, Apple laptops didn't include a DVD player. Steve Jobs hated the design of contemporary players, with their clunky trays and moving parts; they simply did not match his elegant aesthetic. Before he consented to add a DVD player to Apple laptops, he insisted on a stringent design constraint. He drew a single line on a whiteboard and insisted that was how it would look. No light, no button. Only a slot. He was met with enormous resistance from the product team, but he insisted. When Apple laptops finally featured DVD players, that was how they looked. Their DVD player was a thing of beauty, contained few parts, and worked flawlessly—design thinking at its best.

DESIGN SPRINTS

Many companies have experimented with group brainstorming as a way of generating ideas and direction, with varying success. Brainstorming sessions are brief and tend to be high-energy and inspiring, but often they fade away without leading to concrete change. And yet, ideas are still generated and products still get launched. If traditional brainstorming doesn't work, the question is: where are the ideas coming from? What methods succeed where classic brainstorming sessions do not?

It turns out that the best source of ideas is people meeting in coffee shops, offsite, and wherever else they feel comfortable talking freely, generating ideas, and experimenting to see if they work. Formal "in-company" brainstorming sessions end too soon, and they are not consummated by creating something and quickly discovering whether it works. How long is long enough for these cycles, and not too long?

Google recognized the need to generate more results, sooner, and formalized the process into what is popularly called a design sprint. While design sprints are new, I have implemented several components of this technique with clients over the course of my career. However, a tip of the hat to the folks at Google Ventures for formalizing this and executing at scale, and of course for their incredible financial success that serves as emphatic and convincing evidence. The 2016 book *Sprint: How to Solve Big Problems and Test New Ideas in Just Five Days*, by Jake Knapp of Google Ventures, is a good read on the topic, and a valuable addition to your design library. Here is a design sprint schedule summary:

Week -1. To conduct a design sprint, it's important to be organized in advance. The week before the event, know what you want to accomplish and make sure that you have a team in place. Reserve a space that will be conducive to good thinking and book a facilitator with relevant domain expertise and the capacity to guide a team. Choose a meeting room that minimizes distractions, yet is convenient enough for outside experts to come in as needed.

Monday. Start with the end in mind. Agree on a long-term goal, even if there are limitations on how precise you can be at this stage. Map out the problems and decide what you want to accomplish during the week. Create maps of the flow, a simple diagram to show the story and how it fits together. Interview teammates and experts to hone the focus of the sprint.

Tuesday. Go through the ideas and refine them. Look for old ideas and new inspiration. Generate lots of ideas. Remix and improve the ones that are already there. Sketch them out so you have references to draw upon.

Wednesday. Start to narrow down the ideas into solutions. As far as possible, do this in a way that reflects the combined intelligence of the group. As you progress, produce a storyboard that represents the flow of the discussion. Plan the prototype you want to build. Recruit your testers for the Friday session.

Thursday. Build elements of the product—not the entire product, just aspects of it. Create low-fidelity prototypes. If they are physical, find a way to construct them, even if you need to make several iterations.

Friday. Test what you have built. Find a few people to try out what you've created and provide feedback. Keep your sample sets small, perhaps three to five people. Look for patterns and plan your next steps.

Week +1. Congratulations! You made it through an intense week of empathy, problem definition, and prototyping, and received valuable feedback on your product. Maintain momentum by publicizing the activities and the output, and move the product to the next level of formality, ideally close to production. Thank everyone involved, including those who did not attend in person, and those who provided people or funding to make it happen. Last, but not least, rest. Sprints in the running world are tiring, and so are design sprints. Recharge your batteries, and then look for your next opportunity to lace up your innovation shoes and conduct another design sprint.

Don't limit yourself to the duration above. You can conduct one-day workshops, and even one-hour focused activities. The important thing is to practice, practice, practice. Diana Liu is an experience design consulting leader. In my firm, she has been one-part ambassador and one-part cheerleader for design sprints. She has provided a good example of scaling design sprints to meet the need, budget, and availability of the stakeholders involved. And she is just crazy enough to get people excited and engaged in the process. If you're looking for a way to put design thinking into practice, design sprints are a practical and achievable way to make it happen.

They engage several people simultaneously, in service of a worthy goal, in a manageable timeframe. This makes them easier to commit to and participate in, while the constraints draw out creativity.

PROJECT-BASED THINKING

In 2005, my team was hired by a leading transportation client to improve their customer onboarding process. This company was a leader along the trade routes between China and the United States, where they were experiencing an explosion of growth. It was a huge opportunity, but also an equally large risk if they didn't get it right. They were dealing with manufacturers and suppliers in China, along with consumer goods companies in the United States. It was a complex network, featuring numerous systems, global coordination, security concerns, and the need to comply with multiple regulatory bodies.

The client was keen not to miss the opportunities presented by the rapid growth of trade between the two superpowers, while simultaneously aware of the complexity of their supply relationship requirements. They asked us to redesign and update the customer engagement processes within their old-school shipping company.

We arrived ready to perform a typical assessment and road-map over the course of six weeks. In the middle of our kickoff presentation, however, some of the clients present became agitated, insisting that they needed to go faster. They told us that they had been trying to solve the problems in-house for more than a year, they were feeling the pressure from customers, and they needed an answer immediately.

To an extent, this was a failure of communication. These clients had not participated in the initial expectation-setting phase of the process, meaning that they did not understand our original planned timeline, and we never received that valuable expectation-setting input. Nonetheless, they made valid points about the urgency to reach a solution. I succeeded in buying our team one additional week, and we met to revise our approach.

Clearly, we had no chance of compressing six full weeks of work into a single week, but could we develop part of the answer? Over the course of the next five days, could we give the client a glimpse into what was possible? My team was resistant, but we had little choice. If we wished to meet client expectations and make them successful, we had only one week to provide them some answers.

We started by deciding which aspects mattered the most. What questions needed to be answered? What known information could we start with? With time so short, we gathered the right people in a room and asked them to clear their calendars for a few days. Our common commitment was to immediately get to the point, so that we could identify the essential facts and make quick decisions. In five days, we gathered valuable input, defined a workable approach, answered the most pressing initial questions and set in motion the process of testing our ideas.

This won us the trust of our clients and gave us time to refine our answers, back them up with data, and create a more detailed implementation structure. They didn't have to wait six weeks before they started to communicate changes to their customers, and this was a visible step forward for their business. We then created a customer engagement operating model and related frameworks, enabling them to implement, scale, and even market the new approach.

This example was a visible reminder of the power of very short-term, focused projects, which we now call design sprints. Tight deadlines can drive innovation and produce better results and improved focus. With no time to waste, there is additional clarity and urgency. When a team understands what's at stake, they make more effective decisions. This is one reason why it is important to focus on outcomes and workable products, not merely better PowerPoint slide decks.

Early in my career, I noticed that many employees viewed their work in terms of tasks to be completed. If they completed their activities, they considered it success. However, they did not focus on delivering specific outcomes, especially measured in financial terms. This approach never made sense to me. Perhaps growing up on a farm, I had an early taste of project work and focus on outcomes. The tractor had to work, the barn needed painting, and so on. The ultimate outcome was harvest, whether in our garden or the farm overall. Regardless of effort expended, until the crops were picked and safely sold or stored, it was not complete, not "done-done." This is an ownership mindset, and everyone can cultivate it. Whether or not you own the business where you work or the school where you study, you can and should be the owner of "You, Inc." By taking responsibility for the outcomes of your work, as well as its long-term implications, your decision-making improves, your output takes on greater significance, and your work becomes more meaningful. It is also empowering, as you make decisions as an owner of your career (your business), not simply putting in time to earn a paycheck. You work *at* a company, not *for* it.

What does this have to do with project-based thinking? By taking an ownership mindset, project objectives become about value, not activities. You become a vested leader, not a facilitative manager. Executives tend to have an ownership mentality, and often they have some stake in the company, through options if not outright significant equity. They crave others in the organization to have that same mindset, and because it is so rare, they notice when employees do. An added benefit for consulting—project ownership means you are taking responsibility for delivering value. Clients notice that and see you as a true advocate for their business, and for them.

My internships and my first job out of college were all project-based. It was only when I received my first promotion at Texas Instruments that I was moved into operational work, as part of an extended job rotation program. After a focused month learning to manage the team and delivering product, I became bored, so I started experimenting with the design of the assembly line, ultimately improving productivity significantly. I created mini-projects that I could do before my day job started, and I used activity chunks of a week or less. This approach allowed flexibility and reprioritization to make sure newly important areas were quickly addressed. Looking back, this was a form of Agile delivery, with my own project backlog. The point is not that operations are unimportant. It is that even operational roles carry the potential for project-based work, and that you typically have flexibility to enrich your role by solving problems important to the company. Whether or not you are given a gold star (or pay raise) for your efforts, it is a learning opportunity, and keeps you growing, and enjoying your work.

Over the course of my career, I've seen project-based thinking move from the product development function to permeate all areas of business. However, application of project-based thinking remains uneven. As a result, those who are truly project-focused have an advantage over those who merely give lip service to the idea.

Project-based thinking is important in professional services, but even if you're in a functional or operational role, you can set yourself apart by adopting these principles. Over time, senior management at your company will appreciate the outcomes you generate and the energy and focus you bring to your work due to project-based thinking. Regardless of your work environment, you can arrange your working life in a project-based approach.

How can you do this? The first step is to take an ownership attitude. Take responsibility for the quality of the result, not just completion of the task. The second is to be client-centric. Who is receiving your output, and what are their expectations? The third is to frame your work in terms of project parameters like time, budget, quality, and requirements. Think like an owner, construct your working life around the needs of your clients, and distribute the work into projects with clear, achievable outcomes.

You can apply project-based thinking to your career as well. The portfolio career has become an increasingly common concept. The job for life no longer exists, which means you will need to prove yourself to a new manager or employer on a regular basis over the course of your career. You will even change careers at least a few times along the way. You will be hired based on what you have achieved recently, not an impressive but dusty resume with accomplishments in the distant past. A portfolio approach will improve your working life and give you more leverage with your clients, your managers, and even your company. There's an old saying that runs, "good firms can fire their clients." This simply means that not all business is good business, and sometimes the client fit is not aligned to the strengths and values of the firm. In practical terms, a project or any situation should be beneficial for each party involved. Far from being a negative, this means better results and a more positive environment for all concerned. Think about the people you work with and the projects you take on, and prioritize those that generate enthusiasm and learning. Does it mean that all projects and work will be your dream job? No, but this approach will empower you to think about your clients and your work, and to create more impact and fulfillment.

Pursue the projects you *do* take on with passion. Your work is an opportunity to express yourself. For some people, this is an uncomfortable idea, but caring about the outcomes you achieve is a differentiating factor between the average employee and the true professional. When you complete a project, take time to reflect on it. What did you learn? What would you do differently next time?

In a professional services firm, the clock is always ticking. Fees are based on billable hours. However, instead of thinking about how many billable hours you can charge to a client, think about how much value you can deliver in those hours. If you adopt this mindset, you may find that low value tasks are avoided, or at least are given less time. Think more content, less administration.

At its best, a professional services firm is a meritocracy for talented people. Partners are happy to work with junior consultants, because it allows them to achieve more. Junior employees, eager to learn, are happy to work with senior practitioners because they can learn at an accelerated pace. This mutually self-reinforcing structure can apply to any professional environment where knowledge and learning are valued, clients are prized, and project-based thinking is applied.

AGILE THINKING

In September 2001, the 9/11 Commission Report asserted that the FBI's lack of technological sophistication was a key reason why the bureau failed to connect the dots prior to the fateful attacks of 9/11. In 2006, the largest software program in history, Sentinel, was created to address this weakness, with $450 million approved to fund improvements and a planned deployment date of 2009. In March 2010, the program was shut down, with only half the project complete, and more than $405 million already spent. Independent analysis estimated that at the same pace, it would take another six to eight years to complete, at a further cost of $350 million.

The FBI decided instead to bring development in-house and switch to an Agile approach. By November 2011, the project was complete. In twenty months, using only 5 percent of the remaining budget, the Agile approach achieved what a traditional approach had failed to do in more than four years. The number of outside contractors was reduced from 220 to forty. Direct employees were reduced from thirty to twelve. What did they do, and what is this "Agile" that had such a dramatic impact?

Agile is a project-based approach that is often misunderstood, with many people wondering exactly what Agile is. Is it a fad? A methodology? Is it barely restrained chaos? I define Agile as a project delivery mindset, based on values, guided by principles, and manifested through practices. Using Agile, requirements and solutions evolve through the collaborative efforts of self-organizing, cross-functional teams. Design thinking determines *the right thing to build*. Agile is the process of *building the thing right*. Together, they work symbiotically to create products that customers genuinely want, with more value sooner, with less risk.

At the core of Agile is a mindset. As legendary technologist and venture capitalist Marc Andreessen famously stated, "software is eating the world." Yes, software has become part of every product. This also means that the values which drive software creation are inescapable across every business function. The role of the traditional middle manager is becoming marginalized, as the winners in this new world are hands-on leaders who are deeply immersed in their craft and who lead through direct impact. The Agile approach is hands-on, less administrative, and continuous. It is more about collaboration and velocity and less about command and control. The days of being the messenger between senior management and the rank and file are gone. Email, video technology, and other collaborative tools enable and accelerate this trend.

For those who prefer a hierarchical approach to work, this is frightening. For true professionals, it is liberating. Like William Gibson's famous quote about the future, disruption is not evenly distributed, and there will undoubtedly be a new set of winners and losers as the Agile mindset becomes the norm. By reading this book, you have already shown an interest in understanding these trends and making the most of them.

An Agile mindset assumes that change is inevitable and constant. Therefore, it makes sense to embrace and expect change, focus on rapidly delivering value, and learn from each iteration. This means identifying the most important task and getting it done first. When in doubt, it means deferring decisions to the last possible moment, because circumstances may change, and cause rework anyway. When projects are due to begin, it means getting started as quickly as possible and learning as they proceed. Agile practitioners do what is needed based on a prioritized backlog. They focus on the simplest things, organizing work so that it delivers product to customers as quickly as possible.

Agile is both a set of practices and a way of living. It is possible to "do" Agile and not "be" Agile, but if there is not a match between Agile and how your organization actually operates, it will not be sustainable. You can understand the principles of the discipline, but to truly "be" Agile, it's necessary to embrace the Agile mindset and adopt core Agile values and principles.

THE AGILE MANIFESTO

The Agile Manifesto consists of four core values and twelve principles. Seventeen leading independent-minded developers met together in Aspen, Colorado in 2001 and formulated what they considered the most important aspects of software development. In accounting, law, and other mature professions, there are overarching frameworks that guide the practice. Software had plenty of practices for specific tasks, but the Agile Manifesto provided a statement of values, a guiding light to think about these tasks in a new way. These are the four values in the Agile Manifesto:

- Individuals and interactions over processes and tools
- Working software over comprehensive documentation
- Customer collaboration over contract negotiation
- Responding to change over following a plan

These four values are further supported by the twelve principles of Agile:

- Our highest priority is to satisfy the customer through early and continuous delivery of valuable product.
- Welcome changing requirements, even late in development. Agile processes harness change for the customer's competitive advantage.
- Deliver working software frequently, from a couple of weeks to a couple of months, with a preference to the shorter timescale.
- Business people and developers must work together daily throughout the project.
- Build projects around motivated individuals. Give them the environment and support they need, and trust them to get the job done.
- The most efficient and effective method of conveying information to and within a development team is face-to-face conversation.
- Working software is the primary measure of progress.
- Agile processes promote sustainable development. The sponsors, developers, and users should be able to maintain a constant pace indefinitely.
- Continuous attention to technical excellence and good design enhances agility.
- Simplicity—the art of maximizing the amount of work not done—is essential.

- The best architectures, requirements, and designs emerge from self-organizing teams.
- At regular intervals, the team reflects on how to become more effective, then tunes and adjusts its behavior accordingly.

These four values and twelve principles form the backbone of Agile thinking. It may be clear that Agile makes sense for small, in-person teams, like startups, but some might argue that it doesn't work when applied to large projects or multibillion-dollar global enterprises. However, large companies like Exxon, Capital One, Charles Schwab, and Google have been early adopters, and I have helped large clients apply Agile principles as well.

Another common belief is that Agile isn't suitable for distributed teams. Again, this is not true. Agile does require distributed teams to adopt the same principles as co-located teams, with additional practices to accommodate time and location considerations. If this threshold is met, Agile can function effectively across distributed teams. Finally, some people believe that, because Agile stresses the importance of adaptation, it requires no planning. This isn't the case. The cost of planning can exceed the cost of experimentation, and Agile attempts to find the right level of planning while moving quickly to execution through short cycles known as sprints.

Agile invites us to work in a way that makes sense. We create backlogs, execute sprints, and receive feedback. Agile is built around narratives such as the user story, which captures how a user will interact with a product. Taken together, these stories build into features, then epics, which essentially are very large user stories. Epics also provide meaningful touch points to determine the overall purpose for the work and its customer.

Both Agile and Scrum—the lightweight Agile framework that allows software development to be completed in sprints—have inspired a substantial and growing body of knowledge, complete with roles, ceremonies (activities), and artifacts that provide details about executing the Agile framework, though these details are beyond the scope of this book. There are plenty of free or low-cost ways to learn more about Agile, and I recommend agilealliance.org as a good starting point.

Over the course of my career, I've seen design thinking, project-based thinking, and Agile emerge and become popular. They've manifested in different ways at different times, and have even been called different names. Yet, they have moved inexorably toward the mainstream. As the clock speed of business has increased and technology has permeated more deeply into all aspects of work, these principles have moved from the fringe to the new normal. No longer can they be considered an interesting side topic. They are fundamental to working life in the twenty-first century.

Not all industries have adopted them enthusiastically, at least not at the time of this writing. Activities that depend on physical resources, such as mining and farming, may seem to have less need for design thinking and Agile, and their "software eating the world" implications. However, even these industries heavily use analytics and artificial intelligence, and are rapidly innovating to reimagine their purpose and potential in exciting new ways. In the next chapter, we cover these and related areas of data visualization and automation, which are driving transformational change across all industries.

CHAPTER NINE

ANALYTICS, DATA VISUALIZATION, AUTOMATION, AND AI

"The greatest value of a picture is when it forces us to notice what we never expected to see."

—JOHN TUKEY, AMERICAN MATHEMATICIAN

The world is connected, and the exponential pace of change is driving evolution faster than at any time in history. Much of this book focused on timeless skills that are as valuable today as they ever were. This chapter is a glimpse into the future—the new world of work. Technology has already made a huge impact on our personal and professional lives, and that impact will only continue to grow. As a current or aspiring professional, this shift will profoundly affect your career and your life.

We focus here on four aspects of this technology megatrend: analytics, data visualization, automation, and artificial intelligence (AI). My intention is not to strike fear into the hearts of readers, but to reassure you that you can look forward to these changes. They can and will represent exponential improvements, if you accept and engage proactively with them.

As you read this final chapter, ask yourself the question: What do companies do? What is their product, their purpose? There was a time when it was a simple task to define them. No longer. Is Tesla's purpose to build cars, or as their corporate site states, "accelerate the world's transition to sustainable energy?" Is GE Aviation an aerospace manufacturer, or a machine-learning analytics firm? Even Mark Fields, former CEO of Ford Motor Company, said, "We have to be a software company."

Software is changing the very definition of a company's core business. Every element of their activities is affected by the digital revolution. Not everyone will become a data scientist or a software developer, but everyone should have a perspective on these areas and be able to relate to them in personal terms.

ANALYTICS AND DATA VISUALIZATION

We humans have been conducting analyses for centuries, if

not millennia. The tools available to us have only improved over time, and cloud computing power has enabled us to take another big leap forward. I began my career analyzing specific problems in factories to improve product flow, reduce defects, and ensure that customers got what they ordered on time. In the 1990s, I jumped on the Lean Six Sigma bandwagon, all the way to attaining Master Black Belt status. Six Sigma techniques aim to reduce variation, to error rates of fewer than three defects per million opportunities. Lean is about reducing waste, which sounds seductively simple but is complex in the real world.

Over time, however, even these robust disciplines became necessary but not sufficient. The proliferation of data and the need to respond quickly at lower cost means that minimizing variation and waste also require process modeling and optimization. In the late 1990s and early 2000s, manufacturing optimization tools transformed the plant floor and planner's role. During my early years in manufacturing, every day started with a part expediting meeting, followed by a race to chase down the missing parts and avoid starving the production line. There was a lot at stake, there was always a part shortage somewhere, and people were seldom calm.

As advanced planning became widely adopted, we were able to plan weeks in advance, always looking ahead to see what would be needed. Those early morning expediting meetings were no longer needed, nor were the roles to solve the expediting problems. They now had other problems to solve, problems that involved more thinking than chasing, and many workers could not adapt. Increasingly, people working in manufacturing are judged on their ability to plan, model, and think. For some, this means liberation and growth as they are freed from the drudgery of low-level tasks and inadequate job tools. For others, it means uncertainty and anxiety as they struggle to adapt to the new skills required. This scenario has also played out across other functions and other industries.

This illustrates a principle for any kind of change. When a new capability comes online, it removes the burden of an entire set of rote activities and requires more analysis and problem-solving skills. On the one hand, many people rejoice because they no longer need to do something boring and frustrating. On the other hand, those who derive most of their value by performing the redundant tasks are faced with a stark choice between adaptation and redundancy. They may need to retrain and redefine their roles.

Digital technology has accelerated and magnified these disruptions. Although computers have been around for decades, the digital age only really began in the early 2000s, along with the concept of so-called "big data," so large or complex that traditional processing is inadequate to handle it. Data has exploded in volume and variety, and according to IBM, 2.5 quintillion bytes are created each *day* (that's one followed by eighteen zeros). Ninety percent of the world's data was created in the two last years. It's hard to get your head around these numbers, but the point is that access to data at this scale has profoundly changed business and people's careers.

While it's possible to do amazing things with data, analytics is only as good as our ability to interpret the results. This is no longer the exclusive domain of data scientists. Every professional is a communicator, and data is a vital part of business communication. Visualization is essential to develop insights and communicate in a compelling manner. The good news is that there are some basic principles and guidelines that anyone can learn to establish competence in this area.

First, start with a goal. What insight do you want to deliver? Conduct exploratory data analysis to understand the big picture. For example, you might use cluster analysis to identify common groups in a large data set. You could also use visualization to create a dashboard to communicate multiple performance aspects in a single view. Visualizations can also be used to tell a story. For example, you may want to explore demographic shifts in the United States over a period of several years. You can use data to tell that story.

To create a data visualization, three major components to consider are:

- **Persona**. Who are you trying to reach? Are there multiple personas?
- **Value Decomposition**. What are you analyzing, and how will it benefit the user?
- **Design framework**. How will you create the model, get the data, and present it?

Data visualization skills are based on these three fundamental areas. As with design thinking, a persona represents a proxy for a larger user group and a way of relating to a larger audience. Persona analysis is about taking a user-centric approach. Gather requirements, observe people, conduct interviews, and synthesize the input.

Once you have identified your persona, develop scenarios, so that your analytics are scenario-driven. Look for the value. What improvement is needed? Link the data to value, so you can measure relevance and impact. This connects your financial goals to customer-facing goals, then deconstructs them into their constituent parts. Ideally, you want to create direct line of sight between your source data and your business objective.

When you are ready, produce models that represent what you want to display. Keep your goal in mind, and remember who you're serving. This will enable you to stay focused and resist the temptation to create pretty visualizations that have no value.

WIRED FOR VISUALS

The human brain is wired for visuals. Thirty percent of the cortex is devoted to neurons that process visuals, and it takes us a mere 150 milliseconds to begin processing a complex natural image. We visualize a hundred times faster than we can read. When a picture is added to text, people remember 65 percent of information even seventy-two hours after exposure. Images add impact.

There are limits to memory, however, and it's important to respect these constraints when designing visuals. By following perception-based rules, we can present data in a way that highlights important information and patterns. Perception is achieved through short-term memory, which can only hold three to seven chunks of data at one time. When telephones came into popular use, it was determined that the longest numbers people could easily remember were seven digits long. Add a three-digit area code, and voilà, nearly a billion possible number combinations, each memorable to its owner.

Imagine reading from a table: your brain may see every number as a separate "chunk." With the same information presented as a bar graph, however, you can see the entire graph as a single chunk, enabling you to take in far more information at once. Have you ever read through a list that's not in sequential order? If so, you'll know that it's painful to read. Each entry appears as something distinct to identify and process. Read the same list organized in a way you find natural, say alphabetically, and your brain will move rapidly and smoothly from one piece of data to the next.

Another aspect of visual perception is pre-attentive processing. Although an entire object may require some conscious effort to identify, the basic visual attributes that make up an object can be perceived instantaneously, without conscious effort. In a long series of numbers, it's hard for the brain to pick out patterns. However, if the desired data is highlighted in another color, it is easy for the brain to identify them. There are other pre-attentive attributes besides color. Orientation, line length, line width, size, and shape are the most common ones. Well-designed visuals make use of these qualities to quickly draw the reader's eye to the most significant data.

Pre-Attentive Attributes

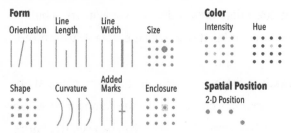

The third aspect of data visualization is called Gestalt Principles. Gestalt means "pattern" in German: as the chart shows, these principles are ways in which we can use patterns to quickly and easily perceive data.

Gestalt Principles

Proximity	Similarity	Enclosure	Symmetry	Closure	Continuity	Connection	Figure & Ground

When you follow these simple principles, each chart you create will begin to resemble a professionally designed visual. You don't need to be a data scientist or a graphic designer to produce high-quality data visualizations.

COMMON DATA VISUALIZATION MISTAKES

What are some pitfalls you want to avoid when displaying data? One is to not exceed the boundaries of a single screen. Have you ever looked at a page of data and been unable to see everything you needed to see? Vertical scrolling is sometimes necessary, but avoid horizontal scrolling. It distracts the reader and creates unnecessary additional effort.

Another trap is to provide insufficient detail or context for data, like poor titles or lack of annotation. At the other end of the spectrum, don't provide too *much* precision either. Nothing is gained from calculating values to four decimal places unless that level of detail is relevant to the task at hand. A common mistake is to scale axes disproportionately or only show the portion where differences occur. For a percentage scale of 1 to 100, it may save space to start the scale at the lowest value, but this can lead to a misleading perception of change,

EDWARD TUFTE'S TEN RULES
OF DATA VISUALIZATION

Edward Tufte is arguably the world's foremost expert on modern information design. I participated in his workshops and read his books during my career, and they have greatly influenced my approach to information design and visualization. His works should grace the bookshelves of anyone interested in this field. Tufte synthesized his philosophy into a set of ten data visualization rules. They are as follows:

Show your data. Imagine seeing an image and wanting to get a sense of scale. Use a ruler, or similar embedded method to indicate size.

Use graphics. Graphics contain a lot of information. A landing signal officer on an aircraft carrier uses clearly identifiable signs with images, not words. Similarly, road signs use shapes, colors, and other visual attributes to convey messages.

Avoid chart junk. What's chart junk? All visual elements in charts and graphs that are not necessary to comprehend the information represented on the graph, or that distract the viewer from this information.

Maximize the data-ink ratio. The portion of a graphic's ink devoted to the non-redundant display of data information—in other words, the true content. Every pixel on the page should support the story you want to tell. Do you need a border? Probably not, but if so, use the least noticeable difference (grays, not blacks) in your formatting.

Use labels. Mark each axis and data point as relevant, and in close proximity to the actual data. Make references as clear as possible for your reader.

Utilize the macro and the micro. For visuals with widely varying scale, show the big picture and details simultaneously by expanding (exploding) where you need to illustrate specific points from a different scale.

Use separate layers. Show multiple levels through distinct layers. For example, in music, there are separate staffs—lines with musical notes—for the alto and the treble clef. This concept is useful for building schematics and business concepts like architecture.

Use small multiples. Small, thumbnail-sized representations of multiple images or graphs displayed all at once. Allow the reader to immediately and in parallel compare differences, which are highlighted for easy understanding.

Use light and color. While tempting, it can be difficult to correctly use color to enhance graphics. First, do no harm. Maps are a good example of a context where color does add insight to graphics.

Understand the narrative. Make sure that the story you want to tell is sequential and laid out in a way the reader can understand.

inflating and sensationalizing perceptions of otherwise small changes to data.

Think carefully about how you display data, to eliminate the risk of displaying it in a distracting manner. Visualization tools are powerful and create eye-catching output. However, highlighting aspects that aren't important just to spice up a graphic makes an analyst look unprofessional or as though they are trying to divert attention from another, potentially negative point.

In summary, keep the reader's experience at the forefront of your mind. Your aim is to deliver a message to them, as clearly, accurately, and compellingly as possible, with the content guiding the way. Anything that detracts from those objectives diminishes the result.

CHOOSING CHARTS

What's the best way to display your data? This chart shows the most common data relationships.

Nominal Comparison

Simple comparison of the quantitative values of subcategories. Example: number of visitors to various websites.

Time Series

Tracks changes in values of a consistent metric over time. Example: monthly sales.

Ranking

Shows how two or more values compare to each other in relative magnitude. Example: historic weather patterns, ranking from the hottest months to coldest.

Correlation

Data with two or more variables that may demonstrate a positive or negative correlation to each other. Example: salaries according to education level.

Part-to-Whole Relationships

Shows a subset of data compared to the larger whole. Example: pecentage of customers purchasing specific products.

Distribution

Shows data distribution, often around a central value. Example: heights of players on a basketball team.

Deviation

Examines how data points relate to each other, particularly how far any given data point differs from the mean. Example: amusement park tickets sold on a rainy day versus a regular day.

The chart below shows the most common chart types and appropriate situations for their use.

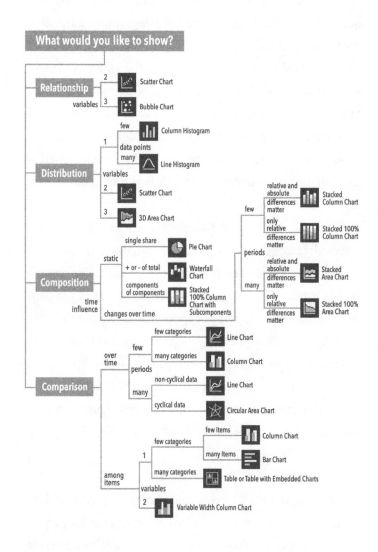

Sankey diagrams are a specific type of flow diagram, in which the width of the arrows is shown proportionally to the flow quantity. The most famous Sankey Diagram, and arguably the greatest statistical graphic design ever created, is Charles Joseph Minard's 1869 depiction of Napoleon's march to Russia, the campaign of 1812. Minard was a pioneer of the use of graphics in engineering and statistics, and was a leading engineer in France. He created the graphic to highlight the horrors of war and the impact on its soldiers. With it, he succeeded in capturing six types of data on a single two-dimensional page.

It shows: the number of Napoleon's troops; the distance traveled; temperature; latitude and longitude; direction of travel; and location relative to specific dates. The army's course is traced in gold and black, with the size of the path representing the number of men remaining in the army. Starting at a robust 422,000, troop strength dwindles to only ten thousand as the mission completes. Along the bottom of the map is a depiction of the dates of the march, along with the temperature on the return trip, made during winter and dropping to as low as a bone-chilling thirty-six degrees below zero Fahrenheit.

The graphic is a masterpiece that shows the power of data visualization, while also conveying an important story about the human impact of war. It is worthy of every professional's attention, and a full-size print hangs in my library.

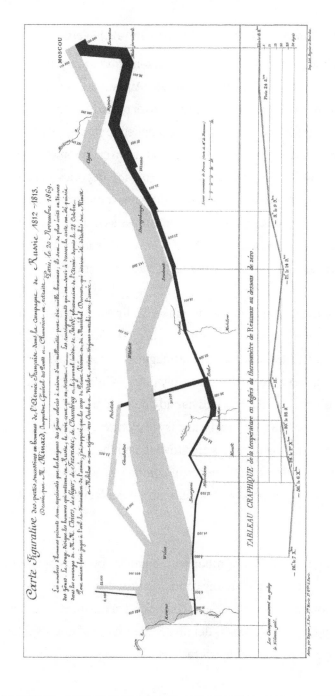

AUTOMATION AND ARTIFICIAL INTELLIGENCE

Though often bundled together, automation and artificial intelligence (AI) are distinctly different. Automation is essentially technology through which a process or procedure is performed without human assistance. It is applied to stable, rule-based processes, such as in repetitive production or customer service. AI—which can be divided into two broad categories: machine learning and deep learning—addresses more complex questions and challenges. Don't view these as independent, but as complementary capabilities on a spectrum of efficiency, insight, and action. Let's look first at automation.

When we think of robots, we typically think of humanoid mechanical objects, such as in the *Terminator* movie franchise. Alternatively, we may imagine a legion of articulating arms on automotive assembly lines. While these types of robots do exist, robotics has advanced to include software robots. They may not be as easy to picture, but they are very real, and the numbers are growing rapidly. Software robots are well-structured pieces of computer code that emulate what a human would do, essentially replacing keystrokes with software code.

You're probably familiar with business process outsourcing (BPO), which many companies use to reduce outlay by moving work to lower-cost countries. For the most part, BPO applies to work that is detailed, repetitive, and not essential to a company's core operations.

Robots take the logic of BPO to the next phase, taking outsourcing from low-cost labor to no human labor at all. Software robots—or "bots"—don't take breaks, go home for the night, or need vacations. In addition, they record keystrokes and transactions, adding to an ever-growing enterprise knowledge base. Robot process automation (RPA) is the rapidly expanding next frontier of BPO, representing the full digitization of manual processes. If work can be quantified as a process and has a policy, it can be automated.

This type of automation works well with processes that are deterministic, rules-based, and repetitive, where the goal is to increase efficiency. Usually it is a cost play, but automated processes can also improve a customer experience through consistent, fast completion of customer-support activities. It isn't as effective for processes with high uncertainty or ambiguity. At its core, RPA is a modern-day Six Sigma project, reducing variability while it improves speed and takes out cost.

The next level of sophistication is predictive computing and analytics. We can't travel to the future, capture data, then return to the present and analyze it, but we can do the next best thing. We can predict the future using historical data and other relevant factors. Sales forecasts and supply chain planning are forms of predictive analytics. It is a trend that continues to grow in importance, improving forecast accuracy and limiting future process disruptions.

As professionals, everyone needs at least a basic competency in this area. Using analytics to drive operations and anticipate failures, we can develop predictive models for anomalies and failures. We can then look for predictive indicators, create intervention models, and ultimately automate recommendations for how to address them.

Here's an example of how this can work. My firm worked with a client in the automated teller machine (ATM) business. ATMs were an early example of customer service automation as wonderful money-dispensing robots, but with the growth of digital banking there is a risk that they will drift into irrelevance. It's more important than ever to sustain service levels, in this case ATM uptime, while managing service costs. We were asked how to better predict when machines would fail. Our team pulled operational logs from a sample of machines and analyzed them. We applied the design thinking principles above, understood the customer and environment, then defined the problem statement.

We looked at all the fault codes and determined the most common ones. We found the top three fault codes and were able to predict several days in advance, with up to 90 percent accuracy, when an ATM would fail. This enabled the client's service technicians to plan their routes accordingly, visiting locations where they were most likely to be needed, with the right parts in their truck.

Beyond predictive analytics lies cognitive computing, which is a combination of machine learning and deep learning. Machine learning is a technique that helps computers learn from existing data, such as past behaviors, outcomes, and trends. The term "machine learning" may sound new, but some of the ideas and algorithms have been around for decades. Alan Turing proposed his famous "learning machine" in 1950, and Arthur Samuel coined the term "machine learning" in 1959. In the twenty-first century, computing power has finally become powerful enough to extend these ideas beyond the lab and into business in a meaningful way.

Machine learning allows computers to build a knowledge base that facilitates intelligent decision-making. It moves from process discovery to process mining to develop insights. Machines can select pieces of information that will have an influence on future behavior, and use those pieces of information to learn. This can lead to more sophisticated, proactive bots, which can learn enough to ask questions and make recommendations, although the potential is even far greater.

The other primary component of AI is deep learning. Deep learning imitates neural networks, locating connections between nodes of which we may not be aware. At the time of writing, deep learning is already taking shape, with a limited number of engaging use cases. AI programs can perform unstructured text analytics, in which they look at text and infer knowledge. This will transform customer service, sales, marketing, and operations. Current examples include object detection for visual quality defects and automatic machine translation—useful for selling products across languages.

Automation and AI are taking on greater and greater significance, a trend that will only continue and even accelerate. The good news is that, like previous business transformations, automation and AI implementations will need to be driven by business value. Technology, including automation and AI, needs to create results and amplify existing capabilities to be of value.

THE DIGITAL REVOLUTION

Will robots create a utopia of wealth and leisure? Alternatively, will they take our jobs and leave us impoverished? It's not important which side of the debate you take. What's important is the realization that automation and AI will bring profound change to our professional lives. They will radically shift the way we live and work, and most of us are unprepared for this shift. Let me repeat: most of us are not prepared for this change. Let's not fear the future, however. When we understand these concepts and their principle levers of change, we can jump in with both feet and learn the skills we need to succeed. Anticipation or fear, the choice is ours, and in this case, fortune favors the bold.

The four topics described in this chapter are prominent components of the so-called digital revolution. Data visualization is important for communication and to generate insights. Analytics are the horsepower that drives effective decision-making. Automation is the digitization of business, and AI is the intelligent next layer of that digitization, leading to increasingly intelligent decisions and corrective or preventive actions.

CONCLUSION

A NEW WORLD OF WORK

"Everyone must leave something behind when he dies. A child or a book or a painting or a house or a wall built or a pair of shoes made. Something your hand touched some way so your soul has somewhere to go when you die, and when people look at that tree or that flower you planted, you're there.

It doesn't matter what you do, so long as you change something from the way it was before you touched it into something that's like you after you take your hands away. The difference between the man who just cuts lawns and a real gardener is in the touching. The lawn-cutter might just as well not have been there at all; the gardener will be there a lifetime."

—RAY BRADBURY, FAHRENHEIT 451

My purpose in writing this book has been to share a perspective on the most important skills in business life and in some respects, life itself. Ultimately, any skill can be learned. Everything described in this book is based on my curiosity and a lifelong love of learning, and often from getting it wrong the first time. If I can leave you with a single message, it is to encourage you to pursue your curiosity, with persistence, framed in service.

For many years, art and business were considered separate entities. Creativity wasn't considered a suitable topic for the workplace. Times are changing, however. As businesspeople, we now express our creativity in a business context. We respect not only art or science, but a combination of both, which also helps us become more whole, integrated human beings. Our works of art are analyses, presentations, and products. The more we can express ourselves through our work, the more meaning we will find in our lives and the more effective we'll be. In addition, those around us will surely appreciate our contributions more fully.

All we have left when we leave this world is what we have created and given to others. This book is a way for me to give you a tool kit that I hope will help you create your own works of art, while achieving your personal goals. Each chapter stands alone, but is also part of an integrated guide for your journey of discovery. This book started off as a primer on essential consulting skills. It has become a guide for any professional, and an invitation to explore further and deeper, and eventually to create your own legacy.

CONSULTING THE INFOSYS WAY

As professionals, we view our work as a *profession*, with intrinsic quality. We hold ourselves to a higher standard than simply trying to complete tasks and avoid the ire of clients. Professions such as accounting, law, and medicine have crafted codes of ethics to ensure that practitioners keep a sense of higher purpose in mind while they work. Some aspects of these codes are admittedly driven by regulatory compliance. Others are uplifting and inspirational.

Consider the Hippocratic Oath that defines the work of medical practitioners: "First, do no harm." Over the years, consulting has developed norms and tenets, but historically it has not been guided by a similar set of principles. In 2004, consulting industry leader Steve Pratt became the CEO of the newly formed Infosys Consulting, Inc. and decided that consulting as a profession needed a formally articulated set of guiding values and practices. To meet this need, he wrote *Consulting the Infosys Way*, which integrated the best work of industry pioneers such as Edward Booz and Marvin Bower with the world-class corporate ethics of Infosys Technologies.

Consulting the Infosys Way is as relevant today as it was when Steve Pratt penned the original words in 2004. At the time of this writing, Steve is the CEO of Noodle.ai, a leading enterprise artificial intelligence applications provider. He is also a colleague and friend, and I have been fortunate to work with him and play a role in bringing his words to life. Over the years I have periodically refined and added to the document, and I offer it here as a gift to all consultants—and professionals in any industry—who aspire to do better work.

HOW WE TREAT CLIENTS, OUR FIRM, AND EACH OTHER

Consulting the Infosys Way describes who we aspire to be. On good days, we meet our aspirations. We understand that no one is perfect—and we all do our personal best to improve every day. We understand that great firms and great cultures are created one interaction at a time.

OUR VALUES

At our core, we are a values-driven organization. When we make tough calls, we go back to our values for guidance.

Client Value: First and foremost, we are dedicated to making each client a stronger competitor. Only through superior client value will we thrive.

Leadership by Example: We have the courage to act first and set an example—both as individuals and as a firm. As leaders, we are active in client service. We share our lessons.

Integrity and Transparency: We treat clients and each other with respect and are open and honest in our dialogue. When in doubt, we disclose.

Fairness: We create agreements where we would be willing to take either side.

Excellence: We pursue excellence always. We have the humility to recognize that learning is a continuous process.

We remember our values through the acronym C-LIFE.

OUR MISSION

Our mission is to become the most respected consulting firm in the world. Specifically, we will become the number one firm as measured by the business value we deliver to clients per dollar spent on fees. We will become the number one firm judged by the attraction, retention, development, and excitement of top consulting talent. And we will become number one in terms of growth and net margin per professional, so we may invest further in innovations, in our people, and in returns to our investors.

HOW WE TREAT CLIENTS

Priorities

Client service is the most important job in our firm. It is the most recognized and the most rewarded. Our innovation and market development functions will be focused on clients. We always look out for the client's interest before the firm's or our own. We focus on making clients more valuable through strategic and operational improvements.

We focus on *business value* created for clients rather than client satisfaction. A focus on satisfaction may inhibit candor. A focus on value aligns us with the client's long-term interests. We roll up our sleeves and do the work. No one is a pure manager. All consultants serve clients.

Every professional in our firm should be able to explain how the role they are playing on any engagement links back to the value created for that client. When asked what we are doing, we answer in these terms.

Tough Issues

We tell it as we see it—even if the client doesn't want to hear it. We are candid when presenting our view of client performance. We are well-intentioned. We are obligated to disagree with our clients when the facts and our beliefs warrant it. We praise clients for what they do well.

When we debate with clients, we are respectful and fact based. We put ourselves into the clients' shoes and see their perspective. We ask for help in tough situations and understand that this is a sign of strength and maturity. When we are unsure of the answer to tough questions, we look to our values to guide us.

Who We Are

We are leaders. Leaders help those around them become successful and raise their team's aspirations. We are professionals. Our motivation to do well comes from within. We are creative and strive to break new ground. We understand that our firm has a heritage and reputation as a pioneer in the business community and clients expect us to bring new perspectives and ideas to each engagement.

We are fact based in our analyses. Facts trump opinions and anecdotes. We are positive and optimistic. Great accomplishments come from tenacity and perseverance.

Our Value Proposition to Clients

Our fundamental proposition is that when a client hires our firm as their partner to make complex changes to operations, the client will end up as a more competitive company than if they hired any other firm. We do this by forcing a tighter connection between operational changes and business value, as measured by free cash flow or the creation of shareholder value. We align changes across technology, finance, performance metrics, process design, and information flows.

How We Approach Client Service

We work *with* clients rather than *for* clients. We act as peers at all levels in the client organization. We are neither above nor below clients. We only work for clients where we believe we will have an impact and where the client treats our people with proper respect. We refuse to serve bad clients.

We compete aggressively in the market to help our clients win. We believe modern global business leaders must focus on a blend of strategy and technology to get ahead. What makes us different is our intelligent combination of these two disciplines. Teamwork is key.

We use specific metrics to link all activities to the business value they create. Specifically, we use the Value Realization Method and process improvement metrics as the link between shareholder value creation and technology, process, people, and data changes.

We use the scientific method rather than the engineering method to solve problems whenever possible. Typically, we start with a hypothesis and then collect data to prove or disprove the hypothesis. However, we also use design thinking to understand the context, define the problem, and rapidly prototype to develop solutions.

We believe diversity of all types fuels better thinking and better consulting. Looking at a problem from different perspectives allows us to see more dimensions and more solutions. Specifically, we combine financial, process, people, information, and technology perspectives. We take on new engagements where we believe we can help the client become more competitive, where we can develop our people, and where we are able to strike a fair agreement.

When we start an engagement, we follow a process to get our team in alignment and to ensure each team member optimizes their learning and contribution. We make realistic commitments to the client and then we do what it takes to meet or exceed them.

When estimating how much effort it will take for an engagement to succeed, we use all our experience and tell the client our honest estimate, regardless of what the competition does. We never purposely over-estimate or under-estimate.

We act as one team in front of the client. Any internal issues are kept within our firm. The program leader is the decision maker for all program-related issues. The account relationship leader is the decision maker for all account issues beyond the program.

We keep clients' confidential information in strict confidence. We refer to clients by name only after receiving their permission. When in doubt about the sensitivity of information, we protect our client's confidentiality.

The goal of each client meeting is to help the client in some way. We are helpful in every situation. We conduct each engagement as cost effectively as possible. We charge clients only as we would invest our own money and time.

HOW WE TREAT THE FIRM
Our Brand

We understand that the reputation of our firm is formed each day by our behaviors. We continue to improve the positioning of our firm as a globally respected company.

We adhere to brand guidelines by using standard deck formats, email formats and others. We inject creativity into these templates through our ideas and insights rather than by flashy formatting.

Our client site dress code is in keeping with the executives of the client organization. Ideas and actions should be the centers of attention rather than our dress. We build our brand one client at a time and one person at a time. Word of mouth and client testimonials are our main brand-building mechanism.

Our Heritage

We are respectful of our firm and our heritage. We are proud members of our firm and look for ways to help all of our colleagues succeed. We are creating the leading fifth generation consulting firm. Tomorrow's heritage.

First Generation: Booz, Allen. Hire retired executives for time and motion studies.

Second Generation: McKinsey & Co. Professionalize the business. Train MBAs like a law firm.

Third Generation: Big Eight Accounting Firms. Focus on technology to transform operations.

Fourth Generation: Infosys, then others. Optimized global engagement teams. Link strategy and technology.

Fifth Generation: Infosys. Leading the human-centric digital revolution. Combine intelligent automation with customer- and user-centricity. Renew current operations and define new businesses, all in a culture of continuous learning and innovation.

Improving the Firm

We contribute intellectual property that may benefit others in their engagements or careers. We look to use the best combination of global resources to operate our firm when possible. We are realistic about what works and what does not. We seek to push the boundaries of what is possible— automation, elimination, and relocation. We stay within the bounds of what works.

We hire professionals who are in the top 10 percent of their peer group at their previous firms or in other accomplishments relevant to their role at our firm. We promote people to leadership positions only if they raise the average talent level of the leadership team.

We raise our standards each year. Each consultant is evaluated relative to their peer group.

If we see internal changes that could improve the way our firm serves clients, we let our leaders know.

HOW WE TREAT EACH OTHER

Each leader has the responsibility to teach others. Each of us also realizes that we must learn constantly to stay relevant and improve. We are confident but not arrogant. Arrogance closes one's mind. Only open minds can learn. And we must learn so that we get better each day.

We can disagree with each other, but we must not be disagreeable. We let each other finish their thoughts before speaking. We do not interrupt. We are concise. We give feedback to each other in a timely and constructive way. We are not offended when we are told we have spinach in our teeth. Our feedback is intended to help each other improve.

We make personal connections with colleagues. We hire interesting people. We get to know each other. We give back to our communities and do our part in times of crisis.

Our objective is to develop our consultants into outstanding executives capable of leading complex global businesses. We are proud when our leaders take senior client positions or become university professors.

We reward intellectual creativity. We expect our people to constantly ask, "Is there a better way?" We encourage our people to make smart mistakes and build new ideas. Everyone is responsible for the generation of new ideas.

We share information openly with one another. We use the following guidelines for our email communications:

Responsiveness: We respond to urgent emails as quickly as possible, and no later than the middle of the next business day.

Format: We follow our standard email formats. Branding starts with consistency.

Copying people: We copy as few people as possible on our emails. We rarely use "reply to all."

Flame mails: If we are angry, we pick up the phone. Flame mails don't work and often come back to haunt us.

Length: We keep emails brief. If we must write longer emails, we format them so they scan well.

BCC: We avoid using BCC except for group-wide messages, noting distribution in the email body. This helps us to avoid using "reply to all" (see above).

Return receipt request: We rarely use return receipt request as it implies that the recipient will not read our message.

Subject line: We use a meaningful subject line that represents the content of the message. In this way, we can more quickly triage messages that require action.

We set boundaries between work and home life and we respect each other's boundaries as often as possible. We also understand that sometimes we must sacrifice these boundaries to ensure excellence in client service.

When we must counsel a member of the firm for performance reasons, we do so in a manner designed to help them be successful and advance in their career. We are respectful and compassionate.

We value our alumni and treat them as we would like to be treated. We understand that all consultants go through times in their lives when they must put more intense focus on a personal situation. We will be flexible in helping consultants through these times.

Consultants who are malicious, mean, or manipulative will fail in this firm. Our people have good character.

Meetings

We are on time to meetings. We give each other full attention during meetings and contribute our ideas. Each meeting has a stated objective and actions.

We have an obligation to dissent. It is unacceptable to criticize after meetings if we did not speak up during the meeting.

We listen to each other's dissent and understand that it is intended to be constructive.

We are appropriately formal for each circumstance. Most internal meetings are business casual.

We are a compassionate meritocracy. We judge people on contributions to clients, the firm, and each other. We treat clients, competitors, and our colleagues with respect.

Our interpersonal style is positive, optimistic, and friendly. We understand that candor, strength, and toughness can be consistent with using good manners and mutual respect.

Twenty Keys to Interpersonal Effectiveness with Clients and Colleagues

- Be friendly
- Smile
- Show people you think they are important
- Share the credit
- Acknowledge when people do well
- Be interested in people
- Open up to others—let people know you as a person
- Remember people's names
- Remember the facts of people's lives
- Do the right thing even if it is not convenient
- Be honest and straightforward
- Give and receive feedback graciously

- Be constructive
- Listen well and write things down to help you remember them
- Let people save face
- If you are wrong, admit it
- Be encouraging and enthusiastic
- Be there for people when they need you
- Only commit to things you can and will do
- Be positive—refrain from giving constant reminders of what is wrong

HOW WE COMMUNICATE

WRITTEN DOCUMENTS

We understand that documents presented on a screen must be different from documents to be read. When presenting on a screen, the smallest font should be 18-point, or slightly smaller for secondary points. When presenting from a screen, we eliminate most text and memorize supporting details.

Charts and graphs are preferable to text. We highlight insights and support them with data. Data alone should not be regarded as insight. We reference the sources of all data.

We name our files in a consistent manner:

- Client Ticker Symbol
- File Name

- YearMonthDay
- Version
- Author

For example:
INFY_Consulting the Infosys Way_20120301_v3_kavanaugh

We present our conclusions first, then our supporting arguments. We do not make the client wait until the end of the presentation to learn about our recommendations.

LANGUAGE

Our communication style is direct and professional. We are not afraid to show personality. We use jargon free language. We understand that consulting-ese is often used to hide ignorance. Good ideas stand best when presented clearly.

We are provocative speakers, and we use storytelling to better relate to our audience and make our points effectively. Our written communication has impeccable spelling, grammar, format, and overall visual appeal. Our words are the packaging that clients experience, and that packaging must support the impact we deliver—this is essential to cementing the reputation of our firm as a high-value brand.

We use the active voice whenever possible. We use forms of the verb "to be" rather than passive verbs. For example, we use, "This is how we solve problems," rather than, "our approach for solving problems."

The language we use to describe what we do and who we are is very important. We use the following vocabulary:

Consulting is a *profession* not a business or an industry. We have a professional responsibility to do what is right for our clients, much like doctors and attorneys. Like other professionals, we have *clients*, not customers. We are a *global consulting and IT services firm*, not an offshore outsourcing firm.

We have *colleagues*, not employees. Our colleagues are *consultants*, not staff. When speaking with clients we refer to ourselves as *our firm*, rather than by our internal affiliation. On engagements, we rarely refer to our internal titles. Instead, we focus on our role on the engagement.

Our consultants are *on-site* and *off-site*, not onshore and offshore. Our off-site consultants work around the world. We call this the *Global Delivery Model*.

As we continue to build our common culture, these are the words we use to describe ourselves.

P.S.: If your kids, nephews, or nieces ask, "What do you do?" one answer is, "I help companies run better."

HOW WE RUN OUR BUSINESS

We run our firm with financial discipline. We believe this is a key skill that our consultants must develop to be great executives. We believe this is a deficiency in the training of consultants in most other firms.

Our discipline applies to submitting reports, engagement management, and expense management. We understand that our revenue is generated by client service. We understand the linkage of client billings to our financial results and the funding of the bonus pool. We understand there is no money tree to provide other funding.

We also understand that our personal time and expense reports are our only mechanism to recognize this revenue. We understand time and expense reports are a pain and seem mundane. We do them anyway.

We spend the firm's money as if it were our own. We are intelligently frugal. We understand that operational excellence creates strategic possibilities. We spend money to build a great firm.

Our mental model for running our business is as follows:

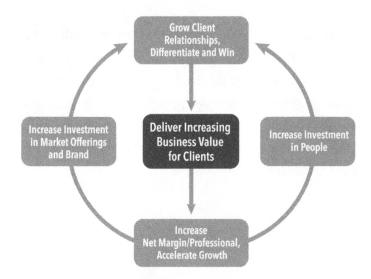

We avoid the following cycle:

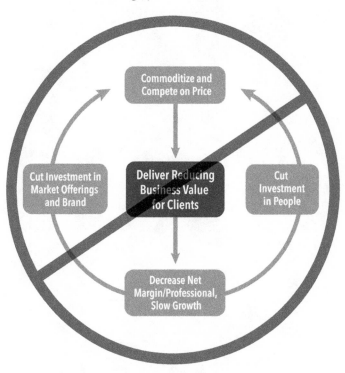

Consulting the Infosys Way is a set of behaviors to which we aspire, a virtuous cycle. They are guidelines rather than a rigid set of rules to be followed without thought. We hire smart people and expect everyone to apply judgment. We are not a big dumb firm. We try to avoid the vicious cycle. Instead, we rely on each other, our good intentions, and our good judgment.

HOW TO ACE AN INTERVIEW

Here's a scenario I see all too often when interviewing aspiring young consultants: A candidate spends hours researching in preparation for the interview, gaining more and more confidence each day as the interview approaches. However, on the morning of the interview, they wake up and realize that for all the information they have, they still don't know how to perform under pressure in the interview.

Don't get me wrong. Preparation is critical. But performing in an interview is a whole different ballgame. During preparation, candidates have lots of time to research and consume information about the company. In an interview, they have mere seconds to take in new information, decide what's important, and construct coherent responses that make the case they are a strong candidate.

Succeeding in interviews, therefore, requires a unique skill set. To aid you, I've written this guide to acing your interview, covering everything you need to do on the day of your interview to raise the odds of receiving an offer. For a broader, longer resource, check out my Complete Guide to Getting the Job at jeffkavanaugh.net. It includes the information below, along with a section on the research phase, the follow-up, and a whole lot more.

THREE CRITICAL PRE-INTERVIEW STRATEGIES

Your interview starts the second you wake up on the day of your interview. Showing up at the right time, with the right mindset and materials, is key to success. Here are some essential strategies to pursue.

1) BE AT LEAST FIFTEEN MINUTES EARLY

Arriving on time can be interpreted as being late, and arriving early perceived as arriving on time. Get to your interview venue at least fifteen minutes early. Account for the possibility of traffic, a metro that is running late, scarce parking, or a labyrinthine building masquerading as a college career center or corporate office.

By arriving early, you mitigate a lot of unnecessary stress. When you remove this superficial layer of distraction, you allow yourself the opportunity to remain calm and focused, unlocking your true potential. Give yourself time to enter a high-performance "zone."

2) BE A SPONGE FOR NONVERBAL INFORMATION

As you walk into your interview, be alert and aware of your surroundings. Take them in and analyze them. Doing this can help you fill in data points that may help you. For example, make a connection with the receptionist or assistant, if there is one, and ask about anything new or exciting. You never know when a reorganization, merger, or some other significant event has been announced, or even better, occurred but not yet become public information.

When you are ushered into the interview room, take account of the decor. If it is the personal office of the manager, ask yourself what you can glean about his or her personality. Is he a family man, with pictures of his children? Does she have sports memorabilia of a team that she loves? Are there awards or degrees adorning the walls?

Use this mental exercise to piece together subtle clues about this person which may aid you during the interview. Unconsciously, it will help you contextualize your story to the interviewer, to make it more relevant for them.

3) BRING PHYSICAL COPIES OF YOUR RESUME

Bring a letter-sized portfolio and writing pad, containing several copies of your resume. Yes, your interviewers already have your resume, but that does not matter. Bring it anyway.

You should not assume that your interviewer is intimately familiar with your resume, or even that they have read it. Perhaps your interviewer will spontaneously pull in a colleague to participate in the interview. Pull out a second copy of your resume for that colleague to use. Maybe your original interviewer experiences an emergency which prevents them from being present, and someone else is called in to cover for them. That person may not know anything about you, nor have access to your application. Pull out your resume and give it to them. You will already have made a good impression.

There are some candidates who seem to do everything right, and you can join them by doing the little things that make a difference. One of those little things is to bring a physical copy of your resume to the interview.

HOW TO COMMUNICATE DURING AN INTERVIEW

When your interview conversation starts, there are several approaches you can use to make a positive impression. Beyond the obvious avoidance of unprofessional language, there are several lesser-known ways to enhance your impact, and they are listed below.

1) USE SILENCE TO CONTROL THE CONVERSATION

You're in an interview, so you will be asked a lot of questions. Many people feel pressured to respond immediately. They may believe that hesitation shows weakness. I believe the opposite.

There is no urgency to answer questions before taking some time to think. Consider Don Corleone in *The Godfather*. He was the main character, not because he had the most lines, but because of his impact. He had very few lines, yet his status was inversely proportional to the number of words he spoke. Why? Because all else being equal, fewer words with the same content equate to more impact and presence.

This tactic also buys you time if you are having difficulty answering a question. Instead of launching into a blubbering, half-baked response, use silence to convey that you are thinking in a relaxed and confident way. These pauses provide you with a moment to review your thoughts, synthesize your answer, and communicate it confidently.

This is especially important when there are multiple people interviewing you at once, which happens in a panel interview. Trying to respond to more than one person at a time can be confusing and may project an inability to focus, or insecurity. Pause, contemplate one question at a time, organize your thoughts, then proceed. Do not try to answer multiple questions at once. Sort them out, even write them down if needed, so you can address each question or sub-question concisely and with insight.

2) MAINTAIN THE RIGHT TONE

It is important to walk the fine line between firmness and aggression. You want to convey confidence, but it is important that you don't try to take over, jump in, or interrupt. Notice how professional interviewers converse: they don't look for an opportunity to interrupt you, nor do they sit passively waiting for you to drive the discussion. They're active, engaged, and solid in their words and gestures.

Here are two tips that make it easier to strike the right tone. First, use the Socratic method. Conclude your answers with a question. For example: "Does that answer your question?" Or, "Is there more detail you would like to hear?"

Another tip is to practice being concise. The fewer words you use, the more you will be perceived as confident and competent, if those words are specific and the story well-structured. This also gives you less opportunity to say something reckless, which usually happens when a candidate keeps talking in the hopes of finding a good response. Keep in mind your goal, which is to make an impact and get through to the next interview or—if this is the final interview—secure the job. The fewer words you can use to accomplish this, while still communicating your intended message, the lower your chances of saying the wrong thing. Like the Hippocratic Oath for doctors, a good rule is, "First, do no harm."

3) OPEN BY CONNECTING WITH YOUR INTERVIEWER

During the first few minutes of the interview, it is important to connect with your interviewer(s). If you've done your research on the company and the interviewer, you'll be well placed to ask them about themselves.

Don't think that they won't care or that your curiosity won't mean anything to them. We are all human beings, who like to make a personal connection. If you've done your research, be proud of your knowledge gained and show your interviewer that you've done your homework.

You can do this in a way that comes across as natural and relevant. For example, you can say something like, "I see your company revenues have been increasing, but the market size is actually flat. How have you accomplished that?" Sharing an insight early in the conversation makes a great first impression. Here is a suggestion for an approach to demonstrate your knowledge and share an insight with your interviewer:

- "When I was researching your company, I noticed that (give some facts)."
- "It's interesting, because (contrast a fact with another, related fact)."

- "Which got me thinking about X in this role (connect the earlier thought with the position you are seeking)."

This is a three-step process. First, collect facts. Then apply them to other facts to draw a comparison or contrast. Lastly, make a connection and articulate an insight relevant to your desired role.

4) MAKE YOUR ANSWERS VISUAL

You want your discussion to transcend the usual, to become memorable. To achieve this, look for ways to engage your interviewer visually. If they ask you how it was to work on a specific project, don't restrict your answer to a standard, boring verbal project recap. Go further. If there is a whiteboard in the room, get up and draw a table or graphic that describes what you did. Even something as simple as a Venn diagram or a list will make your answer more memorable. Perhaps something like, "There were three parts of the project and each brought its own challenges. Here is how they related to each other, and how I delivered the project successfully." Then expand on your insights.

Congratulations, you have converted a potentially generic, boring project summary into a multi-sensory and stimulating dialogue.

Of course, there isn't always a whiteboard in your interview room, but you always have a small, portable whiteboard at hand—a blank piece of paper. Pull out a piece of paper and use it to sketch your thoughts. This demonstrates creativity, confidence, and the ability to engage visually as well as verbally.

5) KEEP YOUR EYE ON THE CLOCK

You should always be aware of how much time you have left in your interview, so that you communicate all the points you want to convey. This is essential, because the interviewer may not manage their time wisely. Sometimes an interviewer will go off on a tangent based on an item on your resume and consume your limited, precious time.

I recommend going into any interview with three to five points that illustrate your experiences and strengths, points that differentiate you and that the interviewer must remember after you leave the room. These five points can be anything relevant to the job and your competition to fill the role. These depend on the person, because we all have different strengths. If you have outstanding grades but lack experience, then your points will be different than if you have mediocre academic credentials but relevant internship or full-time work experience.

Another effective technique is to bring up a crucial point by saying, "That reminds me of the time when..." Don't wait to be asked about these points. Work actively to bring them up. They are your trump cards and you will do yourself a disservice if you neglect to play them. This is what makes some executives—and politicians—so good at press conferences or interviews. Whatever question they are asked, they are skilled at relating it to the point they want to make. Practice this skill with a friend, and see how you can use their questions to weave your strengths into the discussion. Remember, that is the whole point of the interview, to make sure the interviewer leaves with the three to five points that clearly demonstrate why you are unquestionably the best person for the job.

Even if you are new to the workforce, you likely have more than sufficient experiences to demonstrate success to the interviewer. How you organize these experiences and communicate them will make all the difference.

6) SHOWCASE YOUR VALUE WITHOUT BRAGGING

This brings us to the topic of self-praise, or bragging. Again, it's important to walk a fine line here. This time, it's a line between respectful self-confidence and hyperbole. One way to convey this is through using examples. Rather than say, "I'm wonderful because I have already led five projects," say instead, "On the last five projects that I led, I typically encountered..." This establishes your credibility implicitly yet effectively, and without resorting to bragging.

The important thing is to highlight yourself and your accomplishments *in context*. If you want the interviewer to know that you have had experience in skill X, say something like, "The last time I used skill X..." If you want to talk about specific numbers in your accomplishments, say, "Of the fifteen people I managed, the one who stood out for me the most was John Smith." This showcases how many people you managed, matter-of-factly, not arrogantly.

HOW TO APPROACH DIFFERENT TYPES OF INTERVIEWS

It is important to understand the type of interview that you are about to face. For college campus recruiting, interviews are likely to be either behavioral or case interviews. What follows is a guide to acing both types.

VULNERABILITY IS KEY TO THE BEHAVIORAL INTERVIEW

In a behavioral interview, the interviewer evaluates your capabilities by asking about your past experiences. There are basically three types of questions in a behavioral interview: behavioral, leading, and theoretical. Behavioral questions relate to job-related past behavior (open ended, verifying, "why" questions); leading questions require "yes" or "no" responses; and theoretical questions are situation-oriented to test your ability to answer questions.

Behavioral interview questions follow these themes:

- "Tell me about a time..."
- "When have you...?"
- "Give me an example when..."

The tough one is, "Tell me about your biggest failure," or its equally sinister cousin, "What is your biggest weakness?" These can be traps, and the odds are that your interviewer has heard cookie-cutter responses way too many times. You need to stand out, but how do you answer? Be authentic, be yourself, be smart.

Tell your interviewer something real about yourself, on a minor but relevant matter. Reveal a vulnerability without caveats, and then be sure to follow it up with an explanation of what happened next. Either explain how you overcame it, or own it and simply say something along the lines of, "You know what? Despite the many things I've done well in my career, that was an issue. I learned from it, and it has made me a better person."

By speaking the plain truth, you have instantly enhanced your credibility, because you've owned up to a vulnerability. For example, "The first time I managed a team was difficult for a while because I projected my managerial style and didn't consider what members of my team wanted or what worked best for them. I learned that I needed to be more aware of how other people are motivated, and since then I have been more empathetic to colleagues on my team."

THE CASE INTERVIEW IS ABOUT PROVING YOU CAN THINK UNDER PRESSURE

Elite business schools and strategy firms typically use the case interview, and a veritable sub-culture has developed around case interviews and case thinking. A case interview is a hypothetical business situation, in which you are asked to complete an entire analytical exercise in a single setting.

A case interview tests both problem finding and problem solving. In its initial ambiguity, it is similar to design thinking. By the time people have graduated from college, they are usually good at problem solving. They memorize facts and use rote formulas to help them solve known problems, a skill set sometimes referred to as "plug and chug." But less time is spent learning how to identify and diagnose problems. Also, people tend to communicate their answers by explaining how they developed them. This is tedious for the listener, who needs a story with a quicker punch line. The case interview is designed to test for both these potential weaknesses. When you adequately prepare with this in mind, you can blow it away.

In a case interview, you typically either know your stuff and succeed, or don't and struggle. If you get a case interview and are not prepared, it is like hitting an invisible but very tangible wall. I lived the nightmare in my first case interview, and subsequently vowed to learn the relevant techniques and share them with others to help them avoid that situation themselves.

How do you go about this? First, be respectful and pleasant. You should ask if it is okay to take notes. I can almost guarantee that the interviewer is going to smile, even if only to themselves. This is what informed case interviewees are taught to do, and every case interviewer secretly hopes that you will do this and at least pass the first gate in their case interview evaluation.

Listen to the case background information and write down all relevant facts. Listen intently and understand the questions asked by the interviewer, clarifying where needed. Take a minute to think and to quietly identify which framework(s) make sense for the case you have been given.

Use mental models or frameworks to organize your approach to the case. Go into an interview with two or three frameworks that you understand and outline them in your notes, for reference during the interview. Use a framework relevant to the situation, such as an income model for financial contribution questions. Chapter Five provides a good source of information about frameworks and strategic thinking, especially the three decision-making frameworks: decision matrix, issue tree, and hypothesis approach. The important point is to have a few frameworks handy for commonly asked case questions.

The interviewer's case questions will likely build on each other, so address each one fully before moving on to the next. Determine what you need to answer each question, and see if you have all the data needed to do so. If not, ask additional questions to get what you need. If the interviewer does not know or is holding back, make reasonable assumptions and let the interviewer know what they are.

Ask questions, but remember that time will be limited, so determine which ones to ask and in what sequence. For example, if the case involves customer decisions, it may make sense to use the 3C model, which focuses on *customer*, *competitor*, and *company* issues. Start strategically and then get tactical, asking questions that help you understand market structure and company performance. For example:

- What customer segments does the company serve? What channels are used to go to market? What are product trends?
- What are competitors doing? Are they introducing new products? Are those products profitable, and are acquisitions an industry trend?
- Is the company making money overall? What are the revenue and cost trends? What units are doing well? Are there organizational issues?

Basically, ask questions to quickly develop a view of the company with a summary financial statement. Do not be afraid to get quantitative. In fact, ask for specific numbers and data points. People tend to ask general questions, but if you want to impress, get quantitative. Ask, "What was the revenue for major products or services? The costs? What is the margin trend year over year? Are there extraordinary events that influenced any changes?"

The person interviewing you may not have all the answers, but they will appreciate that you asked. They should have the information required to make a decision. When you gather enough data, use some simple math and round each number to streamline calculations—nothing fancy, unless you are allowed to use a calculator. You will be able to tell the interviewer where areas increased, where they decreased, where they diverged, and so on. The numbers themselves are a means to an end. The objective is to use the analysis to develop insights and to see what is not obvious. The interviewer wants you to uncover this accurately through critical thinking, accelerated through the use of frameworks and estimation.

Once you have enough information to answer the brief, stop—no more questions. If you're uncertain, you can ask, "Is there anything else you think I should know to answer the question?" This provides closure to the discovery stage and can generate valuable information from the interviewer. Then take a couple of minutes to complete your analysis and organize your answer. State your conclusion and support each point through examples, no less than three and no more than five. If there is a single overarching question, this will be a formal step. If there are several smaller questions, this will be a mini-cycle of question-analysis-recommendation repeated for each major question.

Your written frameworks don't have to be wordy or elaborate. You only need a few boxes or bullets that contain the main points. Remember, this isn't a four-week project, it is a twenty-minute portion of your interview to showcase your thinking.

Once you have completed these steps, you will have demonstrated a great deal about your capabilities. You will have shown that you can understand context, organize your data into a framework, analyze information, develop recommendations, and articulate them concisely to the interviewer. Remember, the objective of the case interview is ultimately to share insightful recommendations, so do it with some style.

If you can do all this, you will score well on the case portion of your interview cycle. For further study on case interviews, check out the book, *Case Interview Secrets* by Victor Cheng, former McKinsey consultant and friend. Victor has shared his perspective with millions of aspiring business consultants and is the global leader in self-directed case interview preparation.

HOW TO END THE INTERVIEW

Ending the interview can be a tricky proposition. This is your last chance to make an impression—good or bad. It is also the time to close the sale and end on a strong positive note. There are a few things to keep in mind.

1) MAKE SURE YOUR QUALITIES ARE CLEAR

At this stage of the interview, you've reached a stopping point. It's important to make a quick assessment of whether you've successfully communicated each of your major points. If not, do not panic. There is a way to still come out on top. Simply say, "There is something else that I wanted to make sure that we talked about. I want you to be aware of it because it is relevant to this job, and I'm proud of it."

If you have an advanced degree or certification—for example, if you're a certified public accountant (CPA)—bring it up. If you have had a unique experience such as an internship or special project, share it. If you have already discussed it, bring it up again for emphasis. Humans need to hear information multiple times before an impression is sufficiently ingrained. Think about what you're doing as informal self-advertising, to reinforce the most important points you want to make.

2) CLOSE WITH A QUESTION

After you have said all you want to say, close with a question.

A good standby is, "Is there anything else you haven't asked that you would like to?" If the interview is for an entry level job, you can ask "How did I do?" or "Is there anything I could have done better?" Asking frank questions like this will cause your interviewers to stop and think—and remember you. As long as you ask them sincerely, it is ok to use questions that put interviewers on the spot somewhat. After all, you have prepared for the interview, invested time to come to them, and you have earned the right to request honest initial feedback from the interviewer about your performance and chances to move forward.

Sometimes, this will allow your interviewer to drop their guard and ask something more revealing. For example, "Are you comfortable traveling a lot? This role may entail a lot of travel." Also, your question provides them with an opportunity to think outside of the box. Maybe you have impressed them so much that they have begun to consider you for another, more senior role. Alternatively, if you aren't the strongest fit for the current role, perhaps they can envision you in a different position. They may be willing to connect you with the relevant hiring manager.

3) SPEED UP THE COMMUNICATION TIMELINE

Most interviews end with the interviewer saying something like, "We'll get back to you." That's fine for the average candidate, but you don't want to be an average candidate.

Create a mild sense of urgency. You can mention that you are interviewing at other companies—which you probably are—and those interview processes are reaching a point of decision. Partner with the interviewer, helping them find a way to hire you on a timetable that is mutually beneficial. Remember, they are taking the time to interview you because they have a job opening that needs to be filled. They hope you will be that person. Help them make the right decision to recommend and then hire you.

To do this, you can say, "I have a few other opportunities that are progressing, and it would be good if we can stay in close contact so we can make the most of this one." This reminds the interviewer that you taking a job should be advantageous for both parties. It also levels the playing field somewhat by establishing a risk of loss for them, potentially increasing the likelihood that they will move more quickly with their most attractive offer. This approach is specific enough to reinforce your credentials, yet general enough that it provides flexibility, even if you are not quite at the offer stage with other companies.

Ask for their business card. If someone gives you their business card, they are giving you implicit permission to contact them directly. This will be handy when you come to write a follow-up thank you note.

4) DON'T BE COY, ASK FOR THE JOB

Most importantly, before you leave, ask for the sale. It amazes me how many people do not do this. Look the interviewer in the eye and say, "I'm excited about this opportunity. I want to work here. I would love this position."

Be authentic. If you want to be more aggressive, say something like, "Is there anything else you need to know before you can hire me?" If the interviewer says, "no," you're nearly there. Realistically, few interviewers can commit on the spot, due to feedback sharing, final partner approval, and HR background checks. Asking a question like this, however, will often elicit an honest—and uncensored—response, giving you an insight into what your interviewer really thinks of your candidacy. At minimum, it will demonstrate self-confidence and leadership on your part—which is a great way to end an interview.

5) FINISH EARLY AND LET YOUR INTERVIEWERS REFLECT

When you conclude your interview, get up, thank your interviewer for their time, and leave. Ideally, you will have managed the time so that you can end a few minutes early. Give the interviewer a few minutes of their day back. This allows them time to write up their evaluation of you. They will appreciate the opportunity to complete their evaluation on the spot, not later that evening or over the weekend.

The impression you make will be fresh in your interviewer's mind directly after the interview, and you want everything good they remember about you to find its way onto that evaluation sheet. If you are one candidate of up to eight consecutive interviews that day, this is especially crucial. You want them to remember you, not the candidates that came before or after you. Do not underestimate this point. It may provide the edge that gets you through to the next interview, or even secures you an offer.

ACKNOWLEDGMENTS

This book exists because of the teachers and coaches in my life, starting with Mom and Dad, whose teachings in the classroom, the ball field, and the farm, have carried me and provided footing and direction in the world at large. Apologies to anyone I have missed below; borrowing from Sir Isaac Newton, "If I have seen further, it is by standing on the shoulders of giants." Thanks much to all.

Coach Joe Todrank, who pushed so hard in high school basketball and introduced me to *Psycho-Cybernetics*. John Makuta, my first boss at TI, and still the role model for what a corporate manager should be. Tom Carey, the crazy Marine who taught me that it was okay to show passion in consulting. Stephen Chipman, the personification of poise and leadership at Grant Thornton. Jim Anderson, epitome of a software services leader. Dave Sutton, digital marketing genius before the term was even coined.

Steve Pratt, Romil Bahl, Ming Tsai, and Raj Joshi, whose original vision of a fourth-generation consulting firm still rings true. Eric Rich and Brandon Bichler, great on the guitar and even better as consulting colleagues and friends. Holly Benson, change management leader, in the consulting trenches together in the early days. Michel Langlois, client and friend, for showing how relationship savvy together with tech skills can accomplish anything. Dave O'Callaghan, for your trust on strategic projects and your advice on contributing in academia. Tony Leopold, for friendship and frameworks, one of the most strategic thinkers around.

To all my clients over the years, for placing your trust in me and my firm and allowing me to serve you. And my colleagues at Grant Thornton and Infosys Consulting, you have taught me more than I can ever hope to teach others. Graham Passey, Steve Seo, Mike Mazur, Gaurav Palta, Razab Chowdhury: the original band of brothers in IC MFG.

Special thanks to Tim Ferriss, who held an event where I serendipitously met many emerging authors and new masters of the digital age. Tucker Max, Shaa Wasmund, Porter Gale, Charlie Hoehn, Didi Tonev, Stephen Hanselman, Billy Myers, Victor Cheng, and all the other Kimonos: you have provided encouragement and so many examples of turning vision into reality—and having a ton of fun in the process.

To my publisher Zach Obront, appreciate the patience and tough love. Rob Wolf Petersen, whose editing prowess is matched only by his stamina on those marathon late night calls in Bali. And to the Infosys marketing team for your help in getting the word out over the years: Claire Hockin, Chiku Soimaya, Maureen McCann, Cristin Balog, Paul de Lara, Chris Fiorillo, and Erin Clarke.

To Tony Gerth, Alex Edsel, Vijay Khatri, David Strutton, and the rest of my friends in the academic community. You have shown me what consultative teaching can be, and allowed me to share my experiences with your universities and students. I have learned so much from them.

Again, to all my teachers and coaches over the years—you may never fully realize the impact you have on your students and players, and the essential role you play in shaping the next generation of talent.

Last but not least, to my wife and daughters Melanie, Katherine, and Terri Lynn. You let me do what I do, try crazy things, and pursue this enriching but 'all in,' time-consuming profession of consulting. It has been my passion and my gift to others, and I deeply appreciate you for letting me do it.

ABOUT THE AUTHOR

 **JEFF KAVANAUGH** is a senior partner at Infosys, one of the world's largest consulting firms with over $10bn a year in revenue and a market cap in the 11-figures. He also serves as an adjunct professor at the University of Texas at Dallas and writes at JeffKavanaugh.net.

INDEX

Bradbury, Ray, 363
BrainServe, 126
brand, 171, 304, 308, 311
business process outsourcing (BPO), 356-357, *see also* evolutionary competencies, artificial intelligence
buzzwords, *see* communication, jargon and buzzwords

C

calculate, 50, 77, 78
Campbell, Joseph, 15, 191
capital
    financial, 285
    human, 285
    social, 285
Carr, Nicholas, 156
CBS, 152
CE mark, 151
Chipman, Stephen, 160
chronemics, *see* communication, channels, chronemics
Churchill, Winston, 144-145, 173
Cialdini, Robert, 286
classic apprenticeship model, 31
cognitive bottleneck theory, 156
Colonel Sanders, 79-80
comma effect, 99
Commission Report, 9/11, 332
communication, 37, 52, 78, 84
    and "communication pyramid," 188
    as a learnable skill, 134-135, 177
    blog, 34, 202, 276
    defined, 134
    gerands, 182
    jargon and buzzwords, 140-145, 175, 182, 183, 278
    language as foundational element, 199-200
    risk, 88
    tools and pitfalls, 139-146
    video, 34, 43, 44
communication channels, 135-139
    chronemics, 135, 136-137
    haptics, 135, 138
    kinesics, 135, 137
    proxemics, 135, 137-138
    verbal, 135, 136
    vocalics, 135, 136
Competency Learning Assessment (CLA+), 208
Competing on Value (Hannan), 223

F

verbal, *see* communication, channels, verbal
vocalics, *see* communication, channels, vocalics
Vogler, Christopher, 191
Voltaire, 169
Volvo Cars, 70, 97
von Goethe, Johann Wolfgang, 249

W

Wall Street, 127
Wall Street Journal, 269
Welch, Jack, 103
Welford, Alan, 156
Who-What-Why approach, *see* approach, Who-What-Why
work smarter, 28
work-life balance, 27, 70, 257, 261, 324
World Bank, 33
World Development Indicators, 33
World Economic Forum (WEF), 54, 296

Y

Your Network Is Your Net Worth (Gale), 287

Z

Zaleznik, Abraham, 293

CPSIA information can be obtained
at www.ICGtesting.com
Printed in the USA
LVHW051733210120
644287LV00004B/786